LANDMARK COLLECTOR'S LIBRARY

OAKAMOOR
REMEMBERED

Peter L. Wilson

Published by

Landmark Publishing Ltd
Ashbourne Hall, Cokayne Ave, Ashbourne, Derbyshire DE6 1EJ England
Tel: (01335) 347349 Fax: (01335) 347303
e-mail: landmark@clara.net
website: www.landmarkpublishing.co.uk

ISBN 1 84306 146 5

© Peter L. Wilson 2004

Dedicated to my two Granddaughters,
Maria Florence and Cecilia Rose.
It is their heritage.

Print: Cromwell Press Ltd, Trowbridge
Design: Mark Titterton
Cover: James Allsopp

Front cover: Oakamoor Works, 1861

Title page: The glorious season of 1912 when Oakamoor won the Sentinel Challenge Cup outright in the same season that they were Champions of the Churnet Valley League. Standing; Jack Alkins, Club secretary, Joe Awty, John Robert Goodwin, George Swinson, Will Collier, Charlie Nichols, Will James. Seated; Sam Walker, George Bennett, Michael Bolton, captain, Tom Smith, Jimmy Alcock. On ground; Jack Johnson, Frank Walker.

Back cover top: Oakamoor Boy Scouts Football team, c.1915.

Back middle: School, 1974.

Back cover bottom: Oakamoor Rhythm Boys, c.1930.

OAKAMOOR
REMEMBERED

Peter L. Wilson

Landmark Publishing

Contents

Introduction

About three miles east of Cheadle in the Staffordshire Moorlands is the village of Oakamoor. It can be approached along the B5417, formerly part of the Blythe Marsh to Thorpe Turnpike Road of 1762.

Oakamoor has been an industrial site for over 800 years. The circumstances of geography and geology provided the natural conditions for heavy industry. There was ironstone at Consall, copper at Ecton, coal outcropping in the woods to the west, limestone on the hills to the east and a forest of oak and birch all around. In its heart was the power of the River Churnet which for centuries has been harnessed for driving all manner of heavy machinery. From soon after the Conquest, the iron industry concentrated in Oakamoor which had a substantial hammer forge, with furnaces at East Wall and the Old Furnace at Greendale originally smelting Consall ironstone by the bloomery process. Cox's *History of Staffordshire*, 1730, reveals the continuing importance of Churnet Valley ironstone when, around that time, 150,000 tons was produced each year. Oakamoor's connection with the iron industry came to an end in 1790, after a life of around 700 years.

At that time Oakamoor Works was bought by Thomas Patten, owner of the Cheadle Copper and Brass Works. The 'Copper Era' had begun. Copper ore was carried by mules from several sources, particularly the Ecton mines in the Manifold Valley, for smelting at Whiston and with some processing at Oakamoor. Patten built the Brass Wire mill in 1792, followed by other buildings, culminating with the 'Alton' Wire Mill of 1827. Activities continued for another 25 years when, in 1852, the Bolton Family acquired the works. Thomas Bolton and his sons Alfred Sohier and Francis Seddon could see the potential of Oakamoor in the burgeoning electrical telegraphy industry. Copper wire was needed for establishing a network of communications cables all over the earth. A few years earlier Samuel Morse had invented the Morse Code, that of transmitting dots and dashes by electricity, and by the same year of 1852, over 23,000 miles of copper wire linked cities in America. The 'Victorian Internet' came next, followed shortly by many submarine cables which were to link many countries all over the world. Oakamoor copper wire was in great demand for these projects, with the ultimate challenge of the day being that of laying a cable between Europe and America. The Oakamoor works of Thomas Bolton and Sons went into action, and in the first six months of 1857, 60 tons of copper wire was drawn for use in the first Atlantic telegraph cable. My great-great-grandfather, Richard Wilson, was the foreman wire drawer for this project and I still have his gauges and a record book for this and subsequent Atlantic cables.

With the increasing demand for copper wire in late Victorian times, Oakamoor grew as many homes were built to house the families of an increasing work force. Two schools and a Free Church were built, echoing the practice at that time of a number of enlightened industrialists throughout the land. The social side, too, was developed, with the formation of many societies and sports clubs in the village.

A.S.Bolton died in 1901. The demand for copper products fluctuated in Edwardian days, with dramatic increases of activity in the works during the two World Wars, when copper products were essential for the war effort. By 1960, the Oakamoor Factory was falling into disuse as activities were transferred further upstream to Froghall. The industrial story of Oakamoor came to an end on September 11th 1963, with the explosion that felled the big mill chimney. Old timers wept as their heritage faded with the blast. Gone, too, was the 'Knotty', Bottoms' Brick Works, many associated trades and services in this close knit industrial village

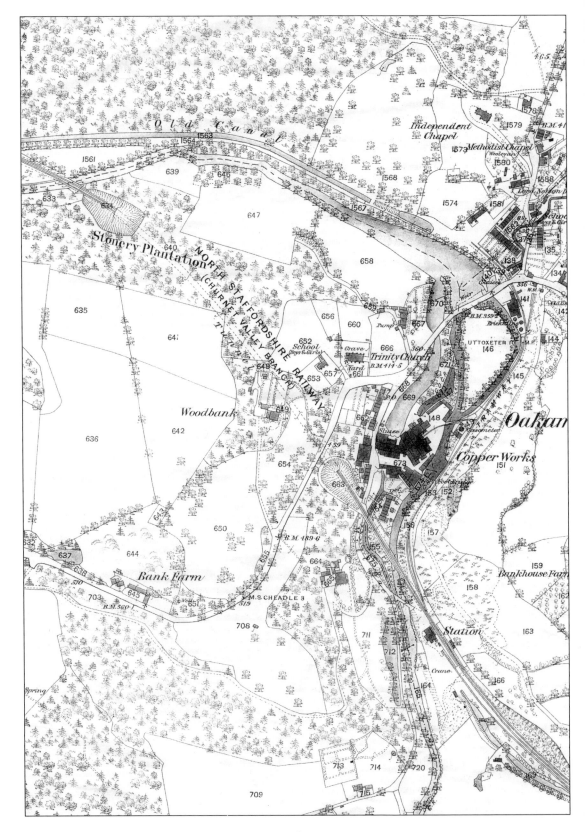

and, from former years, lime burning in the kilns which still stand near to the bed of the Uttoxeter Canal.

Perhaps one of the most graceful structures still standing in Oakamoor is the Churnet Bridge. Built of local stone in 1710, it was widened upstream in 1778 to comply with turnpike requirements. Almost 300 years on it is carrying more traffic than it has ever known since its beginnings as a cart bridge, as seasonal traffic streams across on the way to the 'honey pot' of Alton Towers. The nearby factory site, used by heavy industry for over 800 years, has now been landscaped as a recreational park. A heritage trail for this most interesting village has recently been opened so that visitors can become aware of its glorious past. Oakamoor is now a delightful residential village which still has a flourishing village school.

Much of the story of the copper industry of Thomas Bolton and Sons Ltd. has been told in the excellent book by John Morton, published in 1983. It is my intention, however, to concentrate on the social history of the people of Oakamoor, to describe how their lives were entwined with those of the Bolton family, village benefactors, how they were employed in the Works, where they went to school, where they worshipped, how tragedies and fatalities were counterbalanced by the support of a close village family, how they were uplifted by a plethora of clubs and societies. Was there any scandal? Who were the characters? We shall see!

Peter L. Wilson

Opposite: The 1879 Ordnance Survey, Printed and Published in 1881. This map is a 'watershed' map of Oakamoor, surveyed before a major expansion of the factory and the village. The river divides at the bridge, with the eastern course passing the three kilns of Bottoms' Brick Works, close by the lime kilns. The western course, the present course, rejoins the flow near to the Oakamoor Gas Works. The land between is the 'Middle Meadow' where many of Oakamoor's Horticultural and Flower Shows were held. This meadow was not built upon until the 1890s, when a major extension of the factory took place. Land was so short in those days that departments were built over the river! The Mill Pool stretched from Sunnyside, under the Oakamoor Bridge, to the dam near to the Admiral Jervis. The Coffee Tavern had not been built. The water wheels were within the old part of the factory, on the site that had been used by the iron industry for centuries. The mill race emerged directly opposite the canal workers' cottages, south of the 'Alton' Wire Mill, exactly where the present car park entrance is situated. Heavy vehicles are not permitted on this car park as the mill tunnel directly beneath might not take the strain! The water now emerges from a tunnel in front of The Island, before flowing under the railway bridge to rejoin the Churnet by Oakamoor Station. The station opened in 1849, with the track passing the Gate House on its way to Oakamoor tunnel. The 'Wing Line' was built in the bed of the old canal on its way to the factory and village. The points were controlled from the original signal box by the station. Oakamoor Lodge is shown nearby. Sections of the canal can be seen south of the station. A major section can be seen ending near to the Canal Cottage and stables in Jimmy's Yard. The old National School is shown near to Holy Trinity Church, with the newly built Mills School by the brook near to Starwood Terrace. Two Methodist chapels and the newly built 'Independent Chapel' are shown. There was no 'New Schools', no Churnet View and beyond, no East View, no Butcher's Shop and no 'many things'. What other observations can you make?

One of the earliest known photographs of Oakamoor Works taken by A.S.Bolton on May 2nd 1861. This shows the works at the time that the wire for the Atlantic cables was being produced. The big mill chimney dwarfs all the others. Directly behind the works can be seen Mill Road with the Admiral Jervis the central building. Standing high is the Oakamoor National School with a Chapel of Ease above, which was to become the Parish Church when Oakamoor became an ecclesiastical parish in 1864. In the trees is the second National School of 1856.

The Mills School and Star Wood Terrace, c.1895. A corner of the Wesleyan Methodist Chapel of 1860 can be seen behind the Mills School, but by this time the Chapel was used as the Infants' Department for the School.

Oakamoor Post Office, c.1905. The postmistress was Mrs Eliza Tipper. Letters came through Stoke-on-Trent, arriving at 7.15am. They were dispatched at 6.25pm and 11.30am on Sundays. Quite often letters would reach London the next day, with a return the day after. What of today?

Oakamoor, as seen from the stone outcrop of Lion's Rock above Stonydale, c.1948. German bombers never found the Works which was involved in the war effort for World War II.

Oakamoor, 1902, as seen from the top of the lime kiln. To the left is the end of The Square, with the Lord Nelson and the Memorial Free Church above. Directly in front is the end of Starwood Terrace, with the roof of the Mills School beyond. To the right is the Oakamoor Orphanage, above which can be seen the end of the Primitive Methodist Chapel. In the background, between the trees, is the house used as the Manse to the Memorial Church since 1920.

1 The Iron Story

"Any old iron, any old iron, any, any, any old iron?" Indeed there was. Eight centuries worth, with the valley sides of the Churnet around Consall and Froghall riddled with workings so profuse and extensive that as century followed century, a point was reached where many subsequent prospectors fell upon 'old men's workings' in their desperation to find further seams of iron ore. North Staffordshire iron ore was worked from soon after the Conquest; prospectors were still sinking shafts right up to the early years of the twentieth century. This valuable ore of iron, haematite, was brought to various places in the valley, particularly to the Oakamoor area with names such as East Wall, Mather's Wood and the Old Furnace being prominent. If a great area and depth of slag can be a guide as to size and importance, East Wall was the largest. It is practically impossible to dig down at East Wall Farm without hitting the slag of the past. Why was the iron ore brought to these remote places? At Domesday, this land was apportioned to the lesser Chedle Manor, an area named 'Hounds Chedle' that was so wild that it was only fit for hunting, so wild in fact that it earned the derisive nickname 'Dog Chedle' as it was unfit for habitation. This lesser Chedle Manor, owned by the Santcheverel family since Domesday, 1087, was declared 'waste.'

It had other attributes, however, such as dense woodland which provided charcoal, coal outcropping nearby, and limestone a little further away to the east, all ingredients for the smelting of iron ore. Powerful tributary streams and the Churnet itself were to provide water power for working bellows, hammer forges, slitting and rolling mills and the like. It was soon to reveal its natural treasures, however, as by c.1290, when the Santcheverels transferred their Churnet Valley lands to the monks of the Abbey of St.Mary's, Croxden, they specifically reserved 'the old mines of iron and my old forges.' If they were old by 1290, the iron industry must have made a very early start, as by then there were five bloomery furnaces operating in the Oakamoor area. The early bloomery process consisted of the building of a heap of iron ore, limestone and charcoal over a saucer-shaped hollow of about twelve feet in diameter on which a thin layer of ganister had been spread. The six feet high pile was then covered with clay and turf, with a chimney at the top and some four equally spaced holes at the base for the bellows. Intense heat was necessary to aid the heated limestone to fuse the smelting ore. After about 24 hours the smelted ore would move to the centre of the basin, a glowing red bloom of about one and a half hundredweights, to solidify and cool down, before being cleared of partly burnt charcoal and slag.

In c.1236 there was a road from Cheadle proceeding over High Shutt to Old Furnace, before continuing by Stoneydale to Oakamoor. The Croxden Chronicles revealed that in 1291, 'Our wood of Gibbe Ruydinges was burned', that is burned for charcoal for the furnaces. The wood was sold in 1330 to R.de Holms, in 1345 to Jordan Skachare, and in 1367 to Didon of Waterhouses, who were probably ironmasters in the area. In 1337, 'Oak-Wall-Moor' was mentioned in a law suit when the last of the De Verdons of Alton Castle were handing over land. After the dissolution of the Abbey, the first name to be associated with the iron industry was Sir Walter Leveson, whose descendants were to be created Dukes of Sutherland in the nineteenth century. By the middle of the sixteenth century there was a hammer forge on the river used for forging small quantities of bloomery iron. There was an Assize Case in 1573 concerning this forge at Okam More in Alverton. The record reveals, 'Ralph Lee of Alverton, Yeoman, alleges that George, Earl of Shrewsbury, was seized of a messuage and Lands near Greendale called Okam More upon which land was built a forge or ironworks with other necessary houses, barns and buildings'. A Nicholas Lycette had an interest in these premises, eventually granting his interests to Ralph Lee. Then a Nicholas Woolley of Orton (Alton) and

Henry Copestake of Farley, Yeoman, claimed two barns. Lee claimed that his goods packed into the forge caught fire and were destroyed. After a deal of unpleasantness, Lee surrendered his interest in the premises back to Lycette, who eventually passed on his interest to a Richard Weston. Several other tenants followed until the death of the Earl of Shrewsbury in 1590, about the time that the bloomery process was abandoned. The Earl's affairs were taken over by the Countess who was Bess of Hardwick.

My ancestors were involved in the iron industry. In 1596 a Wilson made a living from the transport of charcoal, iron ore, limestone, clay and pig iron. On December 22nd 1593, Hankey and Wilson were paid 2/- for repairing the Forge bridge at Oakamoor which was carried down with the flood. This old bridge was made of wood. I do not know how my ancestors earned a living in the early years of the seventeenth century as the iron works closed, but they would have gained employment again by 1683 when the Foley family had enlarged forge hammers and a slitting mill at Oakamoor. In 1854, a Thomas Burndred wrote a letter to the *Staffordshire Sentinel* in which he described that in his youth he was acquainted with old men who had worked in iron in their youth. He wrote: 'The pigs were carried on mules' backs to Consall Forge through the woods; in winter the mud and dirt nearly reaches up to the poor creatures bellies. The pigs were then wrought with charcoal into bars and again carried on mules to Oakamoor and there made into tin plates. I remember the old tin mill being taken down'.

Mules were housed at local farms, one such being the Ranger Farm where a short length of a walled pack horse route is still intact. The mules carrying pig iron to Oakamoor would pass by the Old Furnace in Greendale where well worn tracks are still visible today. In 1761, the Oakamoor works came under the ownership of Iron Master George Kendall who installed a rolling mill for tin plate. A Swedish industrialist Johnn Ludvig Robsahm visited this enterprise and recorded a fine account of both works and working processes. Small extracts reveal, 'The rolls were only 15 inches long. The mill furnace was long and narrow. The iron in the furnace was carefully watched. Each bar was given five to six passes through the rolls. The tinning took place in pots and the tin was kept molten by a fire beneath them'. The year 1790 brought great change when the Pattens approached the Foleys with an offer to buy the Oakamoor works outright. The offer was accepted, bringing an end to iron and tin working at Oakamoor. The 'Copper Age' was to begin. I have but scratched the surface of iron. My late friend Herbert Chester was the real authority on the 'Iron Valley.'

In July, 2003, the Channel 4 Time Team came to the Iron Valley for digs at the Old Furnace site in Greendale and at East Wall Farm in the National Trust's Hawksmoor Nature Reserve. Experts in archaeology came from far and wide, anticipating exciting finds and good television. I found it most moving when on several occasions the name of Herbert Chester came from the lips of these experts, who relied on Herbert's work as their guide, proof indeed of the value of local historians. As the dig started in the orchard of East Wall Farm, thought by Herbert Chester to be the site of ancient bloomery furnaces, work started nearby on the reconstruction of a bloomery furnace. On the second day, the furnace began to blow, producing pig iron. On the third day it was used as a forge before it blew out.

Down at the Old Furnace, Phil Harding of the Time Team dug deeper and deeper into Rob Chapman's garden at Old Furnace Cottage. A good six feet down he identified slag from the Elizabethan blast furnace; by going even deeper he found evidence of mediaeval pottery and some bloomery slag of the thirteenth and fourteenth centuries. Carenza Lewis, a specialist in the mediaeval landscape at Cambridge University, said that hand bellows would have provided the air for the bloomery furnace, as the use of water power so early was rare. Could water have been used here? The area would have been alive and noisy with miners, charcoal burners and transporters around this smoky woodland iron works. Back at East Wall Farm, the home of Geoffrey and Margaret Burton, the 'Geo-phys' experts were excited as fantastic responses had been found in the orchard. An in-situ bloomery furnace was not far underground. How Herbert Chester would have chuckled! The diggers struggled to get through the slag, after which a painstaking trowel scrape slowly revealed the solid base and bottom portion of the high temperature heart of the furnace.

'Crunchy-bar', 'aero'-like slag was found around this furnace, suggesting that water power had indeed been used to drive the bellows that created such a high temperature necessary to remove such a large amount of iron from the slag. The experts agreed that the East Wall water powered bellows provided the missing link between the bloomery system and the blast furnaces that followed. Back at the Valley School which was used as the research centre, the micro-structure of examples of the slag were examined. Tony Robinson concluded by saying that the East Wall furnaces were tremendously efficient. Water power brought a 'step change' from Middle Ages technology, with the East Wall site being quite remarkable in this crucial step to the blast furnace, particularly since there had been furnaces on the site since the twelfth century. He ended by saying that the Old Furnace Cottage site was more humble. Then came a twist to the end of the story. Carenza had found a shard of Saxon pottery at the Old Furnace. Surely, therefore, they must have been smelting iron in these parts in the Saxon period? Tony concluded that they had shifted more slag in three days than thought possible, taking the iron story back to nearly 1000 years.

East Wall Farm in Hawksmoor Nature Reserve, National Trust. North Staffordshire iron ore was worked from soon after the Conquest, with the orchard to the left of the farm being the site of mediaeval bloomery furnaces. Consall iron ore was brought down the Churnet valley on mule back, to several wooded sites in the area such as East Wall, a mile upstream from Oakamoor where the Churnet had been harnessed to provide the power for hammer forges. Photo 1991.

Iron plates from the nearby Gibridding tramway of 1811, leaning on a 16th century stone ingot mould from the bloomery days, which was found in East Wall pool when it was dredged in the 1960s. By my right knee is a 'U' shaped drainage tile from 1840, about the time that the present farm complex was built. Digging under my feet would be difficult, as there is iron slag almost everywhere at this farm.

The Original Oakamoor Tin-plate Mill. The picture is signed 'B.B.', Beatrice Bolton, the daughter of A.S.Bolton, who was an artist. The original old painting must have been photographed, possibly by ASB in the 1880s, and subsequently copied by Beatrice in water colours.

The Old Furnace site in Greendale. Locals gather to watch the Time Team in action in July 2003. The house on the left is called the 'Old Furnace', while the site of the dig is in front of 'Old Furnace Cottage'. The experts concluded that the mediaeval bloomery furnace would have been in front of the cottage near to the stream, but situated a long way under the 'made up' garden, while the water powered Elizabethan blast furnace would have been, yes, you have guessed, right under the cottage! Have you got a cellar, Rob?

Left: The Time Team presenter, Tony Robinson, granted my request to be photographed with my wife, Ruth, between filming of the Old Furnace dig. Ruth said, "We love you Baldric," and thanked him for the enormous amount of pleasure that he had given to us all in his 'Blackadder' appearances.

Oakamoor Lodge, c.1895. Oakamoor Lodge was built by ironmaster George Kendall in 1761when he was manager of the iron works in Oakamoor. Several generations of the Wragge family lived there during the first half of the 19ᵗʰ century. In 1828, George Wragge junior became a partner in the Oakamoor copper works and was made works manager at £200 p.a., plus free rent of Oakamoor Lodge and grounds. He died in 1849, and in 1852 the house was purchased by Mr Wilson Patten of Lightoaks. Emma Wragge stayed on as widow and sitting tenant, along with Clement Ingleby Wragge, presumably her son, and other members of the family. Alfred Bolton, when on one of his many fact finding visits to Oakamoor, 'Dined at Mr Wragge's' on November 24ᵗʰ 1852. ASB's eldest son Thomas bought the Lodge from Wilson Patten, c.1878, and moved in with his bride Nina in 1880. The Lodge remained in the Bolton family until it was demolished c. 1953.

Geoff Burton, at his home at East Wall Farm, talking to field archaeologist Phil Harding of the Time Team. Phil reckoned he had been wearing the same clothes for eleven years. I know a 'two-three' round these parts who have worn their same clothes for longer!

The moment of truth. A mediaeval style bloomery furnace had been constructed at East Wall Farm, using nearby clay on its surface. Enormous hand bellows had been used to heat the ore and charcoal, before the furnace was 'tapped' and the slag drawn off. A part bloom remained in the furnace, which was stemmed with earthen clods for a while in an attempt to raise the temperature in the furnace even higher. Part of the bloom was forged into an implement the following day, giving all present an insight into the iron working times of centuries ago.

The 18th century smelting mill in Dimmingsdale, about one mile downstream from the Old Furnace, photographed in 1980. Dr Boucher, mills advisor to the National Trust, told me that the rusting machinery inside was c.1870 when the building was used as a corn mill. It has now been made into a house, with the remains of an enormous water wheel still in situ. The water level in the smelting mill pool has been lowered considerably, reducing its capacity, otherwise it would have had to conform with the requirements of the Reservoirs Act.

The Copper Story

Although 1790 was a watershed date for Oakamoor's transition from iron to copper, transition in the Churnet Valley evolved over a much longer period. Like two sections of an extending ladder, the copper story started much earlier and the iron story went on much longer than this date. Ironstone was still being extracted from the Ipstones and Froghall area during the mid-nineteenth century, and in 1871, Charles Bill who lived at the Woodhouse, authorised trials in Gibridding Wood. Five shafts were sunk, four of which fell into 'old men' workings. A.S.Bolton went 'to see where they were sinking a pit for ironstone on Charlie Bill's ground.' Prospectors poked around until as recently as 1923. Conversely, copper mining began in the reign of Queen Elizabeth I, when Cumberland copper was mined and smelted. By the 1680s, Cornwall's mines were to become the basic source for ore till the 1840s, when they were supplemented by Parys Mountain in Anglesey, by the Ecton Mine in the Manifold Valley and by Devon mines. By 1902, copper was supplied from America, by 1951 it was imported from Canada and Rhodesia.

Copper mines were dangerous places. The 'Gentleman's Magazine' of February, 1769, gave a graphic description of the conditions in the Ecton mine: 'Thus far into the Mountain, with the aid of lights, 'tis easy enough of access. The late Duke of Devonshire ventured to this platform, took a cursory view of the works, gave the miners ten guineas to drink, but returned immediately, not choosing to descend below. Indeed, such a horrid gloom, such rattling of wagons, noise of workmen boring of rocks under your feet, such explosions in blasting and such a dreadful gulph to descend, present a scene of terror, that few people, who are not versed in mining, care to pass through. From the platform, the descent is about 160 yards, through different lodgments, by ladders, lobs, and cross pieces of timber let into the rock, to the place of action, where a new scene, ten thousand times more astonishing than that above, presents itself; a place as horrible to view, as imagination can conceive. On the passage down, the constant blasting of the rocks, ten times louder than the loudest thunder, seems to roll and shake the whole body of the mountain. When at the bottom, strangers are obliged to take shelter in a nitch cut in the rock, to avoid the effects of blasting the rocks, as the miners generally give a salute of half dozen blasts, in quick succession, by way of welcome to those diabolical mansions. At the bottom of this amazing work, the monstrous cavern or vacuum above, the glimmering light of candles, and nasty suffocating smell of sulphur and gunpowder, all conspire to increase your surprise and heighten your apprehensions.' The copper manufacturer Thomas Patten of Warrington built a brass and copper factory in Cheadle in 1788, as this area had coal and water power necessary for this industry. Patten hoped to take advantage of the increased output from Ecton, but was disappointed as the owner of the Ecton mine, the Duke of Devonshire, built his own smelting works at Whiston. When Thomas Patten bought a tin plate works on the River Churnet at Oakamoor in 1790, he converted it to a rolling and slitting mill for brass and copper to supply his Alton wire mill. Oakamoor's 'Copper Age' had begun.

The Cheadle Copper and Brass Company transferred its wire production from Alton to the newly constructed 'Alton' wire mill at Oakamoor in 1829. The following year they closed the Cheadle works, transferring these activities to Oakamoor. My ancestors were heavily involved in this enterprise, as in a statement made to the Commissioners on the Employment of Children in 1842, Thomas Wilson, aged 74, was examined. He said: 'I have worked for this company 63 years; I think I am the oldest servant of the company, but I have two brothers who have just given over wire drawing, one is 82, the other 85; they have worked here ever since they were able, they began so long before me that I do not remember their beginning. There are twelve or fifteen men now upon the premises as old or older than myself, whose united ages amount to almost a thousand years. In my time a vast many men and boys have been brought up to the business; our ages are sufficient proofs that there is nothing unwholesome in the nature of it. I have seen a few accidents with the machinery, but these accidents in a general way are resulting from carelessness. I have never known any lives lost; our hours of work are very regular, and average twelve hours a day; if there should be any extra demand we make seven days a week or fourteen hours a day deducting two hours for meals. We all come at the same hour and go home at the same, there is no difference with any of us, when the bell rings it is a sufficient notice.

The boys in the works conduct themselves very well for anything I know to the contrary; they are all intelligent boys and attend at the desire of Mr Wrag, the church or chapel, and Sunday-schools; I believe they are better educated than they used to be; they have a better chance than they had in my time; my wages are a pound a week, I am paid like all the rest on every other Thursday, always in cash. Our workmen are well conducted, quiet, ordinary men, they behave very well to the boys upon the works, and to their children at home; there are no punishments of any kind; if a man misconducts himself, our masters will not employ him; they will not keep drunkards upon the premises to be bad examples to the young ones. I think we ought to be the thankfullest of men, for we have the best masters in England, God bless 'em. I cannot write, I never went to school as a boy; I can read the Scriptures Thank the Lord – I would have every child do that much'. The commissioners noted that the works were very extensive, and the rooms were very spacious, clean, light and well ventilated. In spite of good reports, the Pattens lost interest in Oakamoor, paid off all the men and had closed the works by 1851. They became 'gentlemen.'

The Oakamoor Works was put up for sale and, by 1852, a sale catalogue of the machinery included valuable steam engines, powerful draw benches, rolls, lathes, hammers, stamps and circular saws. The catalogue listed 655 items which never went to auction as Thomas Bolton purchased the works, stock and machinery for £7,750. The 'Bolton Era' had begun. Thomas Bolton had two sons in the firm, Alfred Sohier and Francis Seddon. Alfred was given the responsibility of re-starting Oakamoor. He arrived by the newly built railway and found lodgings at No.1, Star Wood Terrace, 'Earl's Row,' which was owned by Lord Shrewsbury of Alton Towers. My great-great grandfather, Richard Wilson, the key man for wire making under the Pattens, was brought back to Oakamoor to re-start the wire mill. These were the pioneer days of the electrical telegraph industry, with copper wire in great demand, particularly for submarine cables. Wire-drawing soon commenced, and by September, 1852, a consignment of wire was sent to the Gutta Percha Company to be covered with insulation. In the first five months of operations in Oakamoor 55 tons of telegraph wire was despatched. Over the next five years the demand for copper wire increased as many more cables were laid away from Britain's shore. The sales account for 1856 reveals that over 340 tons of wire was made and despatched, bringing in the sum of £41,361.3s.10d. Two years earlier Alfred had married Rebecca Dickinson Harris at Edgbaston Parish Church, and on returning from their honeymoon they received a rapturous reception from the workforce when they came to live in Oakamoor. The village brass band met them at the station, there were arches of flowers all over the road and over the gates of their new home, Sunnyside, and Mrs Bolton had to show herself several times at the door, as the Boltons were regarded as the saviours of the Works, securing employment for the people. Alfred became very involved with the needs of his employees, building a schoolroom in the works in 1856, a reading room in 1857, employing a full time evening class teacher in 1859 and giving lectures himself, the first one being "The Pleasures, Objects and Advantages of Science."

In 1856 experiments with the stranding of copper wire took place as single straight wires had been used before. What evolved was a wire with seven strands which was more flexible and easier to coil and handle than a multi-wire core that was not twisted. Lengths could be joined end to end with the bell hanger's splice, a major step forward indeed for the ultimate challenge of the day, that of making a cable that was strong enough to withstand Atlantic forces and containing a copper core of the highest possible conductivity. For the first Atlantic cable, 22-gauge wire was chosen, a finer wire than the 16-gauge used on previous cables. As I look at Richard Wilson's wire gauges in front of me now, one carrying his name, the other stamped C.C.B.Co., I can but reflect on the part they played in one of the major engineering feats of Victorian England. The first attempt to lay the cable, in August 1857, failed. It broke. In 1858, at the second attempt, the ships *Agamemnon* and *Niagara* started in mid-Atlantic and sailed in opposite directions. This attempt was successful and the first Morse code message was transmitted across the Atlantic on August 17th 1858.

There was great excitement in Oakamoor at this success. Ten days later an historic telegram from Queen Victoria to President Buchanan of America read, 'The Queen is convinced that the President will join her in fervently hoping that the electric cable which now connects Great Britain and the United States will prove an additional link between the two nations whose friendship is founded upon their common interests'. Was this the first reference to the 'special relationship' often quoted today? Twelve days later the cable broke, 'never to speak again'. Richard Wilson's wire book of 1864 reveals that work started on the second cable on June 3rd of that year. On completion, Brunel's *Great Eastern* was hired to lay this cable. Again, it broke. Yet more copper wire was ordered and it was not until May 1866, that the final order left Oakamoor, sufficient to connect with the then lost cable and a parallel one beside. The *Great Eastern* sailed again. *The Times* of September 2nd 1866, stated: 'The recovery of the cable of 1865 from the very lowest depths of the Atlantic seems to have taken the world by surprise'. These two cables were to be successful. Alfred Bolton decided to commemorate the occasion personally by purchasing a grand piano. Oakamoor men were to draw the wire for many more sub-marine cables and overland wires for the rest of the century and way into the next. The whole village felt secure.

Halcyon days indeed. An article entitled *Christmas in the Happy Valley*, written by a resident of Oakamoor, appeared in the *Staffordshire Sentinel* of December 31st 1887. The writer described the activities of the many clubs and societies that had sprung up in the village, yet observed that, 'One of the most powerful agents is certainly to be found in the constant employment which is provided for all at the copper-wire and metal works of Messrs Thomas Bolton and Sons. It is at these mills, which have during the year been considerably increased both in number of buildings and employees, that much of the copper wire produced and used by the English and other Governments for telegraphic purposes is made, and so highly is the material turned out esteemed that constant employment is found for very many hands besides those living in the village of Oakamoor. Since October the electric light has replaced the gas formerly used for lighting the works at night, and it is quite within the bounds of probability that the village may, ere another Christmas reaches us, enjoy the benefit of this wonderful invention in lighting up its dark places'. Figures for 1887 reveal: Population, 564; births, 15; deaths, 8; engaged at the works, 250; day school, 130 on the books; the Mills Sunday School, 64; Church Sunday School, 75; Primitive Methodist Sunday School, 24; Band of Hope, 102 members; Band of Mercy, 50; Choral Society, 25; Band, 20; Cricket Club, 53; Football Club, 46. Indeed, a Happy Valley.

But not always! As with many heavy engineering factories of the time, accidents lay very close. The *Staffordshire Advertiser* of July 12th 1890, proclaimed, 'Fatal Accident at Oakamoor Mills. On Wednesday an inquest was held at the Lord Nelson Inn, Oakamoor, before Mr T.B.Cull, deputy coroner, touching the death of Nathan Shaw, labourer, Cheadle, aged 27. Deceased, it appeared, was engaged on the night shift of Messrs Thomas Bolton and Sons copper mills. About two o'clock on Tuesday morning he left the mill, having occasion to go outside. He was observed to go through an outlet at the far end of the shed, which was not the proper way, but which had been recently used by the workmen. Not returning shortly, his companions went outside, and heard a splashing in the mill dam adjoining the works. They went for lights, and observed a hat floating on the water, and on the dam being run off the deceased was found quite dead about five yards from where he was seen passing. A verdict of accidentally drowned was returned, a rider being added that the jury were of the opinion that the way round the dam should be fenced by an iron railing or otherwise, in order to obviate as far as possible further accidents of the kind'.

In January, 1899, the local paper reported a 'Brace of Accidents. An accident of a rather serious nature has befallen Reuben Collier, foreman horse shunter in the employ of the North Staffordshire Railway Company. Collier was leaving the weighing machine house when, owing to the darkness, he stumbled over a piece of scrap iron, and was hurled forward with great force. His face came into contact with other scrap iron, and he sustained severe injuries to his nose and face. The other accident was one of scalding which occurred to Arthur Ratcliffe, Alton, who is employed in Messrs Bolton's works. Ratcliffe was going from one part of the works to another when, owing to the intensity of steam prevailing, he walked into a vat of hot water. He was quickly rescued, but received severe scalds on his legs'.

In March, 1902, there was a 'Terrible Death at Oakamoor Works. Caught by Revolving Shaft. While placing a belt on a pulley at Oakamoor works yesterday afternoon, William Berrisford's clothing was caught by a big revolving shaft. The youth was only 18 years of age. Berrisford was drawn in and his body was frightfully mangled, death being instantaneous'. There were more fatalities in the river. In July 1903, William Valentine Alcock, aged 7, was drowned; in August 1909, Samuel Benjamin Lowell, aged 18, was drowned near the wire works. One accident in my family occurred the same year when 'Thomas Wilson, foreman in the fine wire department, was struck with much force on the forehead by a hook which became detached from a heavily weighted pot which was being lowered into a receptacle. He received a nasty cut just above the eyes and was attended by Dr Bearblock, who stitched the wound'. My great uncle Jack Wilson's notes told of others. In December, 1906, A.Johnson had three fingers taken off under the forge hammer and ten days later W.Bullock had to have both arms taken off in the big rolls. I saw Will Bullock on occasions during his old age, but for years wondered why he was so badly maimed. Enough of this topic.

My great grandfather Caleb Wilson was foreman wire drawer during the last 30 years of the nineteenth century. He was followed by my grandfather, Richard.

Richard Wilson's notebook of February 1905, showing transactions in the wire mill, reveals that foremen had great responsibility to bear. They controlled all the activities, including the hiring and firing of men. On February 2nd, 27 men from Oakamoor, Cheadle and Alton were suspended. There are many familiar names on this list. Then, on May 25th, 'The four lads in Top Yankee are still acting stupid and cleared off home last night and Tipper had to shut the engine'. They were B.Perrins, H.Perrins, F.Perrins and E.Upton. The works manager, C.H.Child, fined them 2/6 each. On June 6th, Beardmore the strander was away ill. In October, Richard recorded, 'All my day men were kept idle owing to steam pipe bursting'. Time was not knocked off. Then, on December 13th, 'The watchman reports T.Swinson for drinking and being unfit for duty on nights. I have stopped him altogether'.

Alfred Sohier Bolton died on December 2nd 1901. He was immediately succeeded by his two sons, Thomas and Francis Alfred. In due time, Thomas's sons Michael Alfred, Edward John and David Colfox were involved in the firm. The years leading up to World War II saw the end of the Bolton family's connections with the firm, with the exception of David who continued for a number of years as head of the diamond die department. Thomas Bolton died in 1937, Frank Bolton resigned, Edward Bolton died, with Michael Bolton's departure proving an unpopular move with the workforce. Mr Michael was so well liked for his close affinity with the people of Oakamoor.

It is not my intention to write a history of the firm. This has already been done by John Morton in his excellent book of 1983. A brief dip into the activities of the Oakamoor Wire Works in Edwardian times, however, is revealed in an account in the *Uttoxeter Advertiser and Ashbourne Times* of June 2nd 1909. Commenting on the five places in which Messrs Bolton carry on their copper industry, Oakamoor, Froghall, Widnes, St Helens and Birmingham, the reporter stated that: 'Oakamoor is the centre of the wire making branch of the business, though the manufacture of copper tubes is also a very important department. The Rolling Mill is worked by means of two water wheels, and copper is rolled down to the desired width. Brass is treated in exactly the same way'. A visit was paid to the Drop Forge department, the Rivet department and the Wire Drawing department. The account continued: 'The firm are at present manufacturing some 400 tons of wire for a Japanese railway, and recently have supplied the German Post Office with 300 tons. The firm possesses an engine which has been in use over 100 years, and is still performing useful duty'.

Enoch Berrisford knew the works so well by this time as he started work in January, 1903. Enoch wrote: 'The first memory I possess which was associated with Boltons' Works was the sound of the old Mill bell. There were many functions at which it performed, besides being the signal for starting and ceasing work. Such things as Coronations, Jubilees, weddings and birthdays, and coming of age celebrations in the Bolton family. It was the messenger of both war and peace, in fact it was the forerunner to Broadcasting. It was indeed an 'institution' which evoked both respect and affection. A new and powerful manager had been installed at the Mill, we called him 'Togo', and one of his innovations to bring the Mill up to date was to replace the old bell with a steam hooter. My father and I received orders to install the thing. The old timekeeper was at his post ready to release it on the stroke of six in the morning, which he did. And was it a success? I should say it was as everyone laughed their heads off. It was the most hideous noise imaginable, it wailed and moaned and screamed like unto something in an agony of torment. Children were terrified and animals stampeded in the fields. It could be heard for miles across the countryside. After a day or two's use, a letter arrived at the office from old Mrs Bolton at Moor Court. It said quite briefly, "Discontinue using the hooter". That silenced it for ever'.

The unpopular manager, 'Togo', tried many ploys. When he approached a department, men were detailed by the foreman to keep on the move, lifting tools and metal from one place and placing them in another! Once 'Togo' left, it took about two hours to restore the department to a working unit. The showdown came when 'Togo' burst into a department to find the furnace men having a rest. They had just loaded several tons of copper into a furnace and were taking a well earned pause. The air became 'blue' as the furnace men had their say! 'Togo' was soon to leave T.B. and S. Enoch Berrisford went on to record, 'If a new man was introduced he had to go through his training. One new man was very gentlemanly in every respect. He never swore or anything like that. This, in itself, singled him out for special provocation. They were tormenting him one day beyond endurance. He prepared to leave the shop in a temper, and as he passed out through the doorway, he turned round and shouted 'Fart' at the top of his voice. That produced roars of laughter, but he had given them proof that he was a human being and he was accepted as a worthy 'gang man.' No more would he have been sent on errands looking for left handed spanners and glass hammers!

Two World Wars brought War Contracts to the Oakamoor and Froghall Works of Thomas Bolton and Sons Ltd. In July, 1915, a notice was posted on each site stating: "In order to enable our men to take a share in providing the money now required for the Country's need, and at the same time to 'lay by' something for themselves, we are purchasing on their behalf 'War Loan Coupons' of £5 each and 'Scrip Vouchers' of £1 each, and shall present one of the former to each of our employees over 18 years of age, and three of the latter to each employee under 18 years of age, who is still with us at the end of the year. Any men engaged after June 30th will be liberally dealt with. Thomas Bolton, Chairman."

This was a generous offer by a Management who recognised their services. After the Wall Street Crash of 1929, the 'copper bottom' fell out. Many men were laid off through no fault of their own. My father Richard was one, being out of work for 18 months. He almost gave up his struggle to pay his weekly mortgage of 2/6 a week for his bungalow, which was being mortgaged over 25 years. He eventually got a job as a clerk in the Transport Department on a weekly wage of £2.10s.0d., eventually holding the Superintendent's position for the last ten years of his working life till his retirement in 1962. In fact, Richard's retirement marked the end of centuries of my family's connection with the metals of Oakamoor.

As a boy during the Second World War, I would look through the windows of the old 'Alton' Wire Mill on Mill Road, where a scene of intense activity was apparent as workers were engaged in the War effort. I used to have my hair cut in a nearby office where one of the workers used to cut hair to supplement his income during the dinner breaks. During these breaks for 'snappin' there was a constant stream of workmen crossing the road to the Coffee Tavern for extra titbits. Just beyond the Canteen near the bridge I would stand watching a gigantic shaper chiselling out curls of 'blue' copper as it sought the required profile. There would be ground shuddering thumps of heavy machinery coming from within the Works, where men, and turban clad women, were striving night and day to keep the production lines going. As for the housewives, it was always unfortunate when the wind blew smoke from the factory's many chimneys on Washday Mondays! 'Gerry' planes never found us in Oaky. One bomb did, however, drop on the Ranger!

By the early 1960s it was decided to transfer the remaining activities on the Oakamoor site to Froghall. Once done, a major dismantling and wrecking session followed on this historic industrial site, with the felling of the big mill chimney on September 11th, 1963, witnessed by many old retainers. I was unable to attend owing to teaching commitments, but my father was able to take a series of photographs with my camera recording the event. This really was the end of an era. Industrial activities had held sway for 800 years. As I walk across what is now a picnic site, I feel such an affinity with those past generations who laboured in iron and copper. Part of my soul is there.

"Where'er we tread 'tis haunted, holy ground." Lord Byron.

The Big Mill Chimney in the centre of the works. Church Bank can be seen by Holy Trinity Church on the right.

Above: Two pioneer cyclists on Star Bank, c.1900. What day of the week might it have been? Certainly not a Sunday as the chimneys were in full throttle. Lets hope it wasn't a Washday Monday!

'Smokeamoor' on a post card dated 1906. In the foreground is the Admiral Jervis and the Coffee Tavern in Mill Road.

My Grandfather, Richard Wilson, with the notice recording that these coils of bronze trolley wire were the heaviest to be rolled at the time. Photo taken by Sam Ash on January 21st 1909.

FROGHALL MILLS, NORTH STAFFORDSHIRE, SUTTON ROLLING MILLS, ST. HELENS, AND BROAD STREET METAL WORKS, BIRMINGHAM.

REGISTERED OFFICE, MERSEY COPPER WORKS, WIDNES.   LONDON OFFICE:—88, BISHOPSGATE STREET WITHIN, E.C.

October 2nd./09. 19

FROM

THOMAS BOLTON & SONS, LIMITED,   TO   R. Wilson.

OAKAMOOR, NORTH STAFFORDSHIRE.

Re notice recently submitted to you in respect to your

obligations to Messrs Thomas Bolton & Sons Ltd. - You have

ignored this, and this is to give you notice that unless my

demands are complied with your services will not be required by

Messrs Thomas Bolton & Sons Ltd. after the 9th. instant.

Joseph Pryor
WORKS MANAGER.

Letter to R. Wilson from the Works Manager, Joseph Pryor. The bulk of foremen had their notice on account of not signing on. It must have been resolved, however, as my grandfather went on to receive his clock!

The Bronze wire mill built on the site of Patten's gas works. This 'Yankee Mill' was burnt out in a disastrous fire on January 6th 1921.

By 1922, the 'Yankee Mill' had been rebuilt but with two storeys, and used for continuous casting. It is the building with a new roof to the right of the Big Mill Chimney.

The Bottom Mill, T.Bolton and Sons Ltd, 1946.

Hydraulic tube piercer, T.Bolton and Sons Ltd, 1946.

The old fly wheel in the works. There used to be a row of houses on the edge of the works almost at a right angle to the Island. The axle of one of these enormous wheels protruded through the wall into the kitchen of one of the workers, such was the fight for space in this cramped industrial site. In fact, many buildings were built over the river, which disappeared near to the bridge, to emerge a considerable distance away.

Charcoal Burners in Hawksmoor. 'Charcoal Jack' had a hut near to Wood Gate bends, so that he could be near to his smouldering clod covered piles of birch wood. Now we make them into habitat piles for wild life.

Whiston Copper Works where the copper ore from the Ecton mine was smelted, between 1770 and 1890. Photo late Victorian.

Two aerial photos taken c.1949. The oldest part of this cramped industrial site is to the immediate left of the Big Mill Chimney. The Brass Wire Mill of 1792 was still in use, but the original Tin Plate Mill from the iron days had gone, as had the mill pools which provided the power for the two enormous water wheels that drove the hammer forge, rolls and other machinery. Above can be seen the Parish Church of Holy Trinity, built as a Chapel of Ease with the National School beneath, in 1832. To the left is the Oakamoor railway tunnel of 1849.

To the right of the Big Mill Chimney can be seen the factory extensions of the 1890s, built on the Middle Meadow in front of the bridge. A monster of a machine, the Robertson Piercing Machine, the largest in Europe, had a new tube shop built around it for its opening in June, 1894. Laid out horizontally, it had to take a continual battering as the ram exerted 2,400 tons pressure on a billet of copper, forcing it into a tube. A hydraulic pump used the water of the Churnet for power to drive this and three hydraulic draw benches. An octogenarian recently told me that "There was water everywhere!" The large foundation stones for this awesome machine can still be seen in front of the bridge. The 'Wing Line' can be seen at the bottom of the photo, with the Churnet, the cottages of Churnet View and Riverside, and the 'New Schools' of 1892 above.

Above: In the spring of 1963 the demolition gang moved in, salvaging as much as possible from the buildings on this ancient industrial site. At this stage the Big Mill Chimney presided over a scene of devastation. Much of the metal had gone, but the bricks remained. In the foreground is the roof of the Admiral Jervis with the Coffee Tavern roof projecting forward, the only building now left overlooking this old site. The 'Wing Line' was still in use as a number of open goods wagons can be seen. Inset: There was a frisson of excitement in the air when crowds gathered to witness the scene of the felling of the Big Mill Chimney. Nearby houses on the Island and the Gate House to the Knotty were evacuated. There were crowds on Church Bank and the Farley Road. Many old retainers were there to bid farewell to their Chimney. All were taken aback with the ferocity of the explosive charge when the plunger was pressed. The 'old lady' moved towards the village, as if bidding a fond farewell, before breaking into two sections as it fell, only to shatter into thousands of tar stained bricks as it hit the ground. The scene was then obliterated with an enormous cloud of dust and debris. In the silence that followed, old men wept. Part of each soul had gone down with that chimney. This central heart of Oakamoor is now a well maintained recreational park which is much enjoyed by villagers and visitors alike. Woe betide anyone who ever tries to dig into the middle of this emotive site. The Big Mill Chimney is at rest beneath the turf. R.I.P.

'The Old Brigade.' All gathered on September 11th 1963, to witness the felling of the Big Mill Chimney. From left to right, Samuel Berrisford, Fred Jones, William Jones, S.Harrison, Bernard Walker B.E.M., Joel Goodwin, N.W. Shaw, Richard Prince, John Keates, Enoch Berrisford, Walter Keates and E.Pointon. My father Richard would have been on this photograph, had he not been the photographer!

3   The Bolton Family

In the Black Country town of Walsall some 250 years ago, a whitesmith, a maker of edge tools such as scythes, reaping hooks, axes and hatchets, established himself in New Street. His name was Samuel Bolton. He married his wife Mary in 1748, after which they had two sons, Richard and John. Samuel Bolton died in 1781, leaving his business to his elder son Richard. Richard Bolton and his wife Elizabeth had seven children. The first three died in infancy, the fourth, Samuel, lived, the next one died in infancy, the sixth one lived, with the last, Thomas, born in 1790. It was not long before Richard moved his business to Birmingham which supported a burgeoning brass industry producing a greater demand for many articles of metal. He became a plater, tried two business partners, and moved his workplace, before starting a new career as a trader and dealer in metal products. He prospered. During this time Richard became a member of the dissenting community, worshiping at the Old Unitarian Meeting House in Bull Street. When Richard died in 1812, Samuel was not given control of the business. He died in 1818. With his brother's early death, Thomas assumed full charge. 'Thomas Bolton & Company' had begun. I refer to this Thomas as the 'first' Thomas, as he gave his name to the firm.

Under Thomas, the business expanded and moved to larger premises in 1823. By then he had travelled to America, where his legal representative, who became his friend, was William D.Sohier. Thomas by then was married to Sarah, and William Sohier became godfather to their first son, Alfred. Thomas was now an international trader in Birmingham metal wares and was fully aware of the growing need for fabricated copper and brass, with seamless copper tubes wanted for the boilers of steam locomotives. He then started producing goods as well as selling them. His business grew, enabling him to move his home into a fashionable area of Edgbaston, eventually sending Alfred and his younger brother, Francis Seddon, to University College, London.

Alfred returned to a different copper industry in which experiments in the use of electricity were taking place. There was a desperate need for copper wire for the telegraph industry. The Boltons took up the challenge in 1851 by expanding the wire making facilities at the Broad Street works, where they experimented with the stranding of copper wire. At this time, the Cheadle and Oakamoor works of the Cheadle Copper and Brass Company came up for sale. Thomas and his son Alfred showed no interest at first, yet eventually became particularly interested in the wire drawing facilities of Oakamoor. They visited the works for the first time in February, 1852. Alfred's diary recorded 'Interest taken in O'moor mill and purchased for £7,750'. Alfred Sohier Bolton had arrived in Oakamoor.

Founder Thomas and his sons Alfred and Francis made many visits to Oakamoor in order to supervise the re-starting of the works. Thomas, however, had begun to suffer ill health, and so Alfred became responsible for Oakamoor, with Francis continuing in Birmingham. Alfred kept journals throughout his life, right from his student days in London, and these have provided a fascinating account of his many experiments, innovations, successes, tribulations and developments in the copper industry of Victorian times, particularly in the field of electrical telegraphy. Although I will refer to some of his achievements as a brilliant engineer, my purpose is to highlight many of his attributes as a family man, benefactor and true friend of Oakamoor. During that first summer of 1852, Alfred became very involved with his workforce in Oakamoor.

It was at this time that he brought my ancestor Richard Wilson back from Wales as his foreman wiredrawer, a position he had held under the Pattens. The mill dam and waterwheels were restored, tall chimneys were renovated, the rolling mill was re-opened, and by September 'Oakamoor was busy sending off wire and getting ash dirt loaded'. The wire went to the Gutta

Percha Company. Activities had to cease on October 5th as 'river flooded and mill could not be worked'. Alfred experienced his first Oakamoor flood. He still had his mind on water a few weeks later as he 'went by rail to Froghall to arrange about sending telegraph wire by canal to London'. In November, 1853, news came from Birmingham that Thomas Bolton, was ill. Alfred wrote, 'Papa ill...much worse...died Dec.5th in his 64th year'. Thomas Bolton had been a 'highly respected magistrate of this borough and for 12 years an alderman'. The works in Broad Street and Oakamoor were closed for his funeral. The founder of the firm had passed on.

Happy times were not far off as there is a delightful account in Alfred's journal of July, 1854, when he arrived with his bride Rebecca at Oakamoor: 'Returning from honeymoon. – reached at about 2 o'clock, found Mama waiting at the station for us, – the station we found beautifully decorated with flowers and all the work people meeting us with a band of music which was playing –they had Mrs.Ingleby's carriage waiting for us, Beckie and I had to get into it and the men, about 80, drew us along with ropes to the gate leading to our house, in coming along we stopped opposite the works where Walter came out and presented Beckie with an address, when he gave us three cheers and we went on, by the works there was an arch of flowers across the road and a large flag with the motto "welcome home," in many places there were arches of flowers and a beautiful one over each gate leading up to our house, and little girls dressed in white with wreathes of flowers, holding bouquets and baskets of roses, stood each side the path as we walked from the carriage up to the house, during which they were firing guns and the band continued playing and did so nearly all the afternoon. Beckie had to come and show herself at the door many times, after showing Beckie our house, had dinner'. The house was Sunnyside, overlooking the weir. The Oakamoor spirit was apparent.

Down at the works a year later 'we were busy taking out paddle of Salt's water wheel, putting in new racks and pinions'. Stone was brought from Whiston to build a copper refining furnace. At Christmas, Alfred 'gave all the men a piece of beef, and a plum pudding each, and clothing'. In May, 1856, he opened a school in the works, the 'Silk Mill School,' and gave the first lecture. New workers' cottages were built. They stood almost at a right angle to the Island, but are now gone. November floods came, with 'water being higher than any of the oldest inhabitants could recollect'. In December, 1857, a reading room was opened at the works, to be followed a month later by a workers' party in the lower 'silk room'. Alfred read regularly at the reading room, once a week. Back at Sunnyside, in 1855, Rebecca had given birth to their first child, Rebecca Freda. Their second child, Alice Sohier, was born in 1856. Then, in 1858, there was great rejoicing when Thomas was born. He was the 'second' Thomas. As part of the celebrations, tables were fixed in the new refinery for a dinner for the men. On April 7th, 'Mother and Francis came, from Birmingham. 3 large cannon were fired on arrival of train. At dinner, about 200 men and women seated at tables – hot roast beef and mutton, 197lbs., cannon being fired at intervals, band playing in gallery. After meat they had 100lbs. of plum pudding, a cheese and 4 18gall. barrels of ale'. Over A.S.B.'s seat were the following lines –

"Where we refine, today we'll dine, a downright merry set
To drink good health, success and wealth to the welcome heir we've met.
And should he live, we know he'll give good reason to rejoice,
And drink to those who now propose his health with heart and voice."

The following year an annual works dinner was held in the refinery, with 300 present and many more coming after!

Throughout these years of the development of electrical telegraphy, copper wire was being sent to the cable makers, to be used in the heart of every cable to transmit messages by Morse code all over the earth. The 'Atlantic Cable' days, and those that followed, were halcyon days indeed for Oakamoor. There were early sub-marine cables, Denmark Strait, English Channel, Dover-Ostend, Corsica, Crimean, Falmouth to Gibraltar, Persian Gulf, the Far East and, of course, the Atlantic cables. Alfred Bolton travelled the country, gaining orders for wire, meeting pioneer businessmen, attending seminars, witnessing demonstrations, learning, learning, but most of his time was spent in the factory, in there with his men. He was beside my

Alfred Sohier Bolton, the 'Father of Oakamoor', taken about 12 months before his death in 1901, at the age of 74.

Rebecca Bolton with the head gardener William McKnight at Moor Court, c.1910. After the death of A.S.Bolton, his widow went into deep mourning. She would give her head gardener many books to read, particularly theology books, and proceed to have learned discussions with him as they toured the gardens.

ancestors, foremen wire drawers Richard and his son Caleb at the draw benches, he was in the casting shop, the tube mill, the rolling mill and at the steam hammer. There were nasty accidents: James Buttress had two of his finger ends badly torn with the large shears. The water wheel powered these shears. Copper was stolen; two men went to prison. In August, 1859, 'Susan ? came from London to look after the people here and manage school at works for girls'. She opened the school in the evenings, but left at the end of the year, after serving just one term, for a situation in London. By the spring of 1860, wash houses were being built for the new cottages. In December, A.S.B.'s mother died. Oakamoor Mills were closed for the funeral of the Founder's widow. All cottages in Oakamoor had their blinds down in mourning for six days. During this period, Rebecca had Alfred Colfox, who died in infancy, followed by Sarah Beatrice, born in 1861. In spite of his enormous business responsibilities, Alfred still found time to build a new house, Moor Court, in 1861, where their youngest son Francis Alfred was born in 1866, followed by Isabella Constance.

In January, 1863, the 'Refinery was lighted up'. This was by gas light, as the gas tank had been cleaned out in readiness. No wonder they used the refinery for many concerts, plays and dinners as it was the largest 'hall' in the village at that time. In this time of growth, my ancestor Caleb had a new annealing furnace built for him. Back at the refinery, the next social function was planned. Alfred recorded 'At works preparing Refinery for a dinner we were going to give men on March 10th, for the wedding of the Pr. of W to Alexandra of Denmark – general holiday – gave a dinner of beef and plum pudding to our workmen and wives, tickets about 240. Dinner was ready at 3 o'clock. We had about 236lb. of meat cooked and 23 puddings, 120lb., a whole cheese and a 36 gallon barrel of ale. Enough left to give a dinner to about 90 children as well. Cannon firing over stone quarry – over the entrance gates we had the letters AE + A illuminated in gas jets'. In September, 'Lord Shrewsbury went over the works'. By November, the

'Telegraph from works to house finished'. Over into 1864, the Mills Band 'came up to play for the first time' at Moor Court. Then, in March, 'Mr.Draper exhibited magic lantern with oxy-hydrogen light for benefit of sick club – the works band attended. There was a concert in the refinery'. Alterations and additions to the factory were on-going in those Atlantic cable days. Professor Holmes came 'about wire for his machines for lighting lighthouses' in 1866. By 1868, A.S.B. was doing so well that he 'bought a London carriage in B'ham for £155'.

Early in 1870, 'Moses Beardmore was much hurt at the works being dragged upon a wire block. One leg was broken and the knee of the other dislocated'. A year later, across the road behind the Admiral Jervis, 160 people attended a tea party in the works chapel. Later, 'Sarah James was found selling an iron refinery ladle to Williamson, rag and bone dealer from Cheadle. Lead ingot also missing. J.Johnson confessed to stealing other things'. Prison sentences followed for the two men. At the end of March, 1872, the first chaplain to the works, Rev.John Mills, preached his last sermon. 'Mr. Richards succeeded him'. The first wedding from Moor Court took place in September, 1877, when Alfred and Rebecca Bolton's daughter Alice married Charles Bolton Toller. To celebrate 'Alley's wedding, workmen and their wives and the tenants had dinner in the old schoolroom at the works'. Charles became a partner in the firm in 1881, along with Thomas Bolton and George Rathbone. This 'second' Thomas celebrated his 21st birthday in March, 1879. His father recorded 'Old schoolroom at works had been cleared and dining tables set out ready for dinner this evening. Cheadle Fire brigade came about 3.30 and presented an address to Tom. We then all went to the workmen's dinner fixed for 4 o'clock – after dinner I proposed health of Queen, after which address to Tom was read by Jos Kerry and presented to Tom with a gold watch on behalf of workmen...Hubert Greg, Edward and Oswald Rathbone and Harry Lee came while dinner was going on. Old William Mellor sang a song that he had sung at dinner when Tom was a baby. I stopped for first dance and then up to Lightoaks for dinner – F.S.B. stayed at works with some of the others'. And on went the works. A diary entry of July 4th 1881, read 'I went to Liverpool and purchased the Mersey Copper works'. Just like that!

During the 1880s, Alfred Bolton met and exchanged views with many great industrialists. In 1883 he met Mr Purtz, a German, 'who impressed upon me the necessity of having dynamos with the least possible internal electrical resistance for depositing metals successfully'. He met a Marquis and had a long talk with him about his copper works in the Provence de Grenade. He met the Telegraph Engineer of the L.C. and Dover Railway Company. A.S.B. made frequent visits to the Patent office in London. He met the Telegraph Engineer of the Great Western Railway Company. Back in the works in 1884, 'Men repairing top of large chimney all day and fixing lightening conductor'. The factory was busy. Travelling again, into 1886, Alfred 'Saw Mr.Ferranti who showed us the electric lighting plant under the Grosvenor', in London. Ferranti came to Oakamoor for further discussions, by which time A.S.B. was spending less time at Oakamoor. At the end of August, 1886, a family note among all his business affairs stated, 'Charlie and Ally left Oakamoor for their new house at Hawarden'. It was in this year, in December, that Alfred was elected a member of the National Liberal Club. The workpeople's annual dinner was moved to the new fine wire room, probably because it was still clean!

A year later, 'Young Walter Smith at the works was injured being twisted round a shaft in stranding room'. Four days later, 'After chapel called to see Walter Smith who was better, a nurse came last evening to look after him'. Electric lighting for Farley and the Towers was considered by the end of 1887. The band played on into 1888, now reformed as the Oakamoor Mills Brass Band. It played at Moor Court on Christmas Eve of that year. By the end of the decade, 'land for 8 new cottages was being levelled by the canal at Oakamoor'. Alfred left for America in October, 1889, to visit the Torrington Rolling Mills. He then went to Brooklyn where he 'saw our wire machines at work there – six benches, one man at each'. On returning to Oakamoor he put his mind to domestic matters, that of the lighting of Moor Court by electric light.

On March 1st 1890, Moor Court 'had electric light on in the house for the first time'. A few days later, W.D.Phillips of the North Staffs. Railway Company 'came to speak about land at Froghall which we propose for some new works'. Expansion was now moving up the valley, taking further advantage of the railway system for moving copper products. November 8th brought the much awaited opening of the Coffee House, 'beginning with a dinner at 4.00 after which I had to open it formally'. This Coffee Tavern in Mill Road, with its shop, reading room, games and committee room, served the Oakamoor people for over 70 years. In March, 1891, 'Mr Masefield gave lecture on wild animals of Staffordshire for Con's Band of Mercy class in schoolroom'. Constance was A.S.B.'s youngest daughter who founded the Oakamoor Orphanage. Mr Ferranti came to Oakamoor again in the autumn. Frank Bolton became a partner in the firm in 1892. In mid summer, 'Mr Robertson came from Manchester about patent for pressing out tube shells and I agreed in course of evening to give him £10,500 for it'. A new tube mill then had to be built on the middle meadow to house the Robertson Piercer, a monster of a machine, which was the largest in Europe.

In May, 1893, 'Robert Plant called about Litley Mineral Lease as I had given him notice that it must terminate if arrears of rent were not paid'. There followed a visit to Mr Blagg's office in Cheadle! July 6th 1893, brought the wedding day of the Duke of York and Princess May. The works closed at one o'clock and a cannon was fired from north hill. Over the next few years, Alfred Bolton's interest in local matters increased. 'Mr.Pearce, the Liberal candidate, had a meeting at Oakamoor at which I presided. Arthur Nicholson and Mr. Milner came with us'. In May, 1895, Alfred attended the first meeting of the asylum committee at Cheddleton, where most of the members came in a saloon from Stoke which was brought up the contractor's line to the site. Alfred Bolton's public service was at parish, city and county level. Early in 1901, Queen Victoria died. Francis Alfred Bolton recorded in his diary on February 4th that 'At 4p.m. a large number of the workmen processed with band through village to the chapel, Gampy [A.S.B.], Tom and I went at head of procession in funeral attire, where a special service was held for the Queen'.

Later that year, on December 2nd 1901, Alfred Sohier Bolton died, at the age of 74 years. When the flag was lowered to half-mast at Moor Court, my grandfather Richard wept, such was his respect for his squire. An outstanding Victorian had passed on. The funeral took place three days later at the chapel. I refer to F.A.B. again, who wrote '200 to 300 workmen formed a procession carrying the many wreathes which had been sent us. The bearers were representatives of oldest families in the village'. *The Staffordshire Sentinel* took up the story. Headlines, such as "A Large Employer of Labour," "Made the Wire for the Atlantic Cable," "County Councillor and J.P.," "Enthusiastic Educationist" and "Generous Benefactor," were followed by lengthy descriptions of his achievements. The funeral took place 'amid signs on every hand of genuine sorrow and regret. The whole village was in mourning. There was a complete cessation of business at the works at Oakamoor and Froghall, and at every house the blinds were drawn. On the churches, public buildings, and at other points flags were hoisted at half-mast.

The inhabitants of the surrounding villages poured into Oakamoor and joined with those of Oakamoor in taking part in the churchyard in the last sad rites over an esteemed neighbour and a beloved friend. The route of the cortege, especially in the village, was thronged with people. Presently the cortege made its appearance, and heads were uncovered in silent respect. Six hundred employees of Messrs Bolton and Sons from the works at Oakamoor, Froghall and Milton, and representatives from the firm's works at Birmingham, Widnes, and St.Helens, headed the procession, many of them carrying beautiful wreathes to be placed over the grave as a tribute to a highly-respected and generous employer'. R.Wilson and J.Wilson walked with heads of departments. There were six carriages of family mourners in the cortege, with Mrs.Bolton, her son Francis and daughter Freda, and Alfred's brother Francis, in the first. Waiting at the church was the MP, Charles Bill, many business friends, local gentry, JPs, Mayors, councillors, railway engineers, educationists, station masters and policemen. The church had been decorated with evergreens and chrysanthemums. After the funeral service, taken by his beloved works chaplain and minister Rev.Charles Denman, Alfred Sohier Bolton, family man, benefactor and true friend of Oakamoor, was laid to rest in the family vault, along side his infant son Alfred who died so long before.

The day after the funeral Frank Bolton and Charles Toller went to London for a meeting at the Euston Hotel with Holden and Bank Managers, which was 'a very stormy troublesome one lasting near midnight'. Martin Bolton, Frank's son, told me that A.S.B.'s personal and business property were hopelessly entangled at that time. Four days after this meeting, Frank had to go 'to law courts to file petition for Receiver and Manager to "hold" the business pending further arrangements'. The firm was in the hands of a receiver until affairs could be sorted out. Matters were further compounded by the fact that A.S.B.'s eldest son and 'heir apparent', the 'second' Thomas, had left his wife Nina and run off with the governess to live in America. Thomas did not attend his father's funeral. This is another story!

Meanwhile, Alfred's widow Rebecca went into mourning at Moor Court. She was a religious person who spent a lot of time reading. On the fourth anniversary of Alfred's death she wrote a letter, for private circulation, to the Men of Oakamoor and the "Mills." She referred to the 'unforgotten anniversary, the loyal steps that followed, and the loyal heads that bowed in the cemetery that winter's morning'. Memories continued. 'Oakamoor! Where, through fifty happy years master and men were as a father and children, one in interest, one in principle, one in effort, one in the bonds of mutual kindness, mutual sympathy, mutual respect'. The letter was signed 'Your old friend and neighbour still. R.D. Bolton'. Rebecca Dickenson Bolton spent the twilight years of her life in Bournemouth where she died, aged 91, on January 24th 1924. Her remains were brought back to Oakamoor for interment with her husband Alfred. As for Alfred's brother, Francis Seddon Bolton, he died at his home in Edgbaston on November 12th 1909, after a successful business career. Most of his life was dedicated to business, but he did become a Justice of the Peace and served as High Sheriff for Warwickshire in 1899. His memorial tablet in white Sicilian marble was placed in the 'Mills Chapel' in Oakamoor in 1910.

Alfred and Rebecca Bolton had seven children. Freda, born in 1855, lived most her life in Oakamoor and never married. She became very involved in village life, particularly in societies such as the WI During the latter part of her life she would walk down from her home at Woodbank, with her dog, to attend services at the family church. The dog always lay under her pew during the services. She died in 1947, aged 91, and was laid to rest with her parents. Second daughter Alice was born in 1856. As previously described, Alice married Charles Bolton Toller in 1877. 'Charlie' was put in charge of the Widnes works in 1885, eventually becoming the firm's buyer of copper for 40 years, before overbuying shortly before the Wall Street Crash. Tragically, Charlie felt responsible for losses and took his own life in 1929.

The 'second' Thomas was born in 1858. He was educated at Harrow and, like his father, went to University College in London for three years to study Engineering. He started work in Oakamoor in 1878. As eldest son, Thomas was groomed to be his father's successor. He experimented and introduced many innovations for the firm, one of which was a continuous wire drawing machine, and accompanied A.S.B. on many of his countrywide visits. In 1880, Thomas married Nina Rathbone, the sister of George Rathbone, a well known Liverpool merchant who had been working for the Boltons since 1876. Thomas and Nina had eight children; the first, Oliver, died at birth, the second, Oliver, died in infancy, after which six survived childhood. Thomas appointed a Governess, Miss Connie Brown, to teach his family at Lightoaks. Miss Brown used to accompany the ladies of the family on many outings, and when Nina started to withdraw from activities, staying in bed for long hours, the Governess spotted her chance with her master. Then came the family bombshell. Frank Bolton recorded in his diary on August 2nd 1901, 'Had terrible news this morning by telephone from Lightoaks, Nina had letter from Tom, who has been away since Wednesday, saying he should never return'.

Mr Ted Jackson recorded the story in 1960: 'Mr.Thomas Bolton left Oakamoor with Miss Connie Brown, a governess, who was rather ugly and of masculine appearance, but shared his musical tastes. Mr. Colfox, a friend of the Bolton family, went to America to fetch Mr. Bolton back. On his return, he wrote a letter to the foremen of the works thanking them for the kind reception and welcome they gave him. However, a sequel to this letter was that Mr.Bolton, as a result of the unkind treatment he received from his sister, Mrs.Bearblock, and to a less extent from his daughter, later told the foremen that he was going to leave Oakamoor again, and that this time he would never return. Mrs.Bearblock used to make it her business to be in the drive between Lightoaks and the Lodge at times when she knew her brother would be passing on his way to and from Oakamoor works, and deliberately snub him. When he left the second time, he brought his car to the veranda, loaded it over night, and went early next morning. After his return to Lightoaks the first time, Mr.Bolton had sworn never to play the piano again; in fact Mrs.Jackson did hear him once, but when he saw her he instantly stopped, got up and left the room, slamming the door as he went.

After leaving Lightoaks the second time, Mr.Bolton allowed his wife £200 per month, and gave her all sorts of presents, including a Daimler car, which cost £900 when purchased in 1913. This car was driven by Fred Plant. Mr.Thomas Bolton and Miss Brown had a daughter called Monica. Mrs.Rathbone Bolton told Mrs.Jackson that it was only his family troubles that prevented Mr.Bolton from being knighted for the part he played in the munitions industry during the Great War'. Thomas Bolton eventually re-married and went to live in Tunbridge Wells in 1905. He became chairman of the firm in 1909, a position he still held at his death in 1937. 'Very sincere regret was felt by all in Oakamoor' when they found out that Thomas Bolton had passed away. There was a full choir present at the Memorial Church where Rev.O.Morgans held a simultaneous service with the funeral service at Tunbridge Wells. The 'second' Thomas, a fine engineer and musician, had passed on.

The fourth child, Alfred Colfox Bolton, was born in 1858. He lived but six months. Young Alfred's memorial in stained glass is in the Memorial Church in Oakamoor. In the family it is referred to as the 'red window'. The fifth child to be born at Sunnyside in 1861 was Beatrice. Beatrice was aged 40 when she married 31-year-old Dr Peter Esdaile Bearblock in 1901. They moved into Oakamoor Lodge a year later, where Peterkin was born in 1904. They met when A.S.Bolton was a member of the asylum committee at Cheddleton, where Dr Bearblock was on the staff. I often wondered why the Bearblocks had an odd collection of servants; they had been patients at the asylum. Dr Peter became works doctor and doctor to the village. June Bolton told me that 'He was good at stitching up, but he didn't do births'! Beatrice allowed the windows of the Lodge to be covered in ivy, trees would grow out of the spouts, nothing at all would be cut down, and over a period of nearly 50 years, the house became dark and could hardly be seen from the road. Cats were everywhere! 16 on one count. When kittens were born, the race was on as to who found them first, Beatrice with the milk, or Peter with the bucket! Nurture or nature, you might say. Beatrice Bearblock died at the Lodge in 1948, aged 87; Dr Peter Bearblock died there in February, 1951, aged 80. Their story may well be expanded.

Francis Bolton, the sixth sibling and first to be born at Moor Court, arrived in 1866. He was taken round the village by his mother as 'Young Master Frankie', and when he grew up was always known as 'Mr Frank'. Like his father, and brother before, Frank was educated at University College, London, after which he began to learn the trade at Oakamoor. As an engineer, Frank became very involved in many experiments and innovations in the works, as a diary entry of May, 1887, reveals. 'Caleb Wilson and I tried the new fine wire machine with standard brass wire for 1st time, it ran very well'. By November 11th that year the new rolling mill was 'lighted by electricity'. With the opening of the new Froghall works in April, 1892, Frank was made a full partner in the firm. Although Frank Bolton was 'hands on' in the works, he also had many local interests, living a full social life all the time. He enjoyed shooting, fishing and photography. In November, 1888, he 'went up to the High Shut Toll Gate where met ferret and other keepers and beaters'. He won photographic competitions. The family instituted the 'Oakamoor Wakes' in 1890, by which time Frank was into cycling, followed a decade later by his becoming a pioneer motorist, eventually of national repute. Also in July, 1890, he subscribed to 'The 2 little boys, one at Kingsley, one at Cheadle, who were bitten by a mad dog last week started today with a trained nurse for Paris to undergo treatment of Mr.Pasteur'.

In August 1891, the works closed early and wages were paid for a 'Great fete day at Alton Towers, about 60 special trains. Horse racing, jumping and tight rope walking, etc.'. 1897 brought the first elections for the new Oakamoor Parish Council. Frank was elected, with his brother Tom topping the poll. 1902 brought further responsibilities when F.A.B. became a magistrate, sitting on the Cheadle Bench, and becoming High Sheriff in 1919/1920. During these years he was Lord of the Manor of Cheadle, following his brother Tom, but he sold it in 1919. Throughout Edwardian days the bachelor squire developed two obsessions; expensive motor cars and his nephew David Bolton. Ted Jackson's notes reveal 'F.A.Bolton monopolised David, making him his heir and paying for his education. David had only his breakfast at Lightoaks, his home, and then went to Moor Court for lunch and tea every day. F.A.B. built cars for David, Wasp, Ladybird and Slipper. David entered motor races at Brooklands and the Isle of Man, at which places he won several trophies. David always referred to F.A.B. as "U.F." Uncle Frank. "U.F." used to accompany David as far as Oakamoor station when he returned each day from Moor Court to Lightoaks. Miss Gladys Howell, the daughter of a tea planter, was David Bolton's girl friend, and F.A.Bolton was intending to build a house for David and Miss Howell when they got married. The house was to be sited somewhere in the grounds of Moor Court. As time went on however, Miss Howell and Mr.Frank became much more friendly, and on one occasion up at Lightoaks Mrs.Rathbone Bolton remarked to Mrs.Jackson, "It's plain to be seen, the uncle is far more in love than the nephew." Francis A.Bolton was 52 when he married Gladys Howell who was then 28'. They were married at St.Barnabas Church, Kensington, on April 25th, 1917. Although it was wartime, the wedding present list was formidable. Near the end of the list appeared 'Mr.D.C.Bolton – Miniature portrait'. I wonder who was featured in this present to "U.F."? Frank Bolton resigned as a Director of the firm in July, 1937. He had four children, with his son Martin farming at Croxden Abbey, eventually becoming a JP, and serving as High Sheriff for the County. Francis Alfred Bolton died in June, 1951, at the age of 85.

Constance, the youngest child of the family, was born at Moor Court in 1869. Ted Jackson recorded: 'Miss Connie Bolton had ideas about marrying a humble workman from the village, and used to get up early in the morning and practise cleaning grates with black lead so that the descent from a pampered daughter of the gentry to the wife of a workman would not be such a shock. She was given an orphanage as a present when she was 21, but it was later moved to Harwarden Street, Colwyn Bay. Miss Connie Bolton eventually returned to Staffordshire and lived in Leek where she joined the Salvation Army. She married one of the boys, named Billy Jones, from the orphanage and was subsequently known as Mrs.Bolton Jones: she had no honeymoon but sent her husband to college'. Constance ended her life in Bournemouth, where she died in November, 1929.

I have given but an insight into the lives of A.S.Bolton's seven children, there is much more to be written up, but in the meantime I would like to follow the line of the elder son Thomas, the 'second' Thomas, who married Nina Rathbone. They first set up home at Oakamoor Lodge, where five of their six surviving children were born, before moving into Lightoaks around 1893. This move established the 'Lightoaks' branch of the family, as opposed to the 'Moor Court' branch established by the younger son Francis. Thomas and Nina had five sons and one daughter, Margaret. The eldest was Michael, followed by Margaret, Edward, Gilbert, David and the 'third' Thomas, christened Thomas Tertius. Miss Constance Brown was the governess to this family. All five boys were sent to Abbotsholme school at Rocester, founded by Dr Reddie on the principles of education advocated by the German, Kurt Hahn. Abbotsholme was the precursor to Gordonstoun, believing in a vigorous education, outside! The five Bolton brothers were referred to as 'Bolton 1, 2, 3, 4 and 5', when members of the school.

When Thomas Bolton went off with the governess in 1901, Nina was left with her family. When the younger boys were naughty, she used to chase them round the billiards table with a carriage whip! Michael became manager at Oakamoor in 1905, and was made local director in 1911. Throughout his career Mr Michael became very popular with the men of Oakamoor, who were very sorry to see him leave the firm in 1937 when a new board took over. Michael was a fine musician and outstanding sportsman, and perhaps less of an engineer. For years, Michael played the organ at the family church, quite often in his 'Abbotsholme' shorts, part hidden under an overcoat in the winter. He would wear his hockey shorts when going for walks in the Lightoaks woodlands. He died in 1948, aged 65. Edward was sent to Birmingham in 1908, and then moved to the Froghall works in 1911 as local director when the Birmingham works closed. There followed a move to Widnes in 1924, with responsibilities for sales, but Edward died suddenly in 1939 at the early age of 52.

Gilbert Bolton was a fine musician, not interested in the firm, but as a pianist, organist and composer was heading for a career in music when, as a 2nd Lieutenant in the North Staffordshire Regiment, he was killed in action at the Battle of the Somme in 1916, aged 27. His memorial is the 'blue window' in the family church. Gilbert Benson Bolton is also named on the Abbotsholme School memorial, with 3 after his name. David came next, regarded by his bachelor uncle Frank as his heir. He started work at Froghall as engineer in 1911, eventually taking charge of the company's diamond die works which had been established near Bournemouth in 1920. This department was moved back to Froghall in 1933, still with David in charge, a position he held until the mid 1950s. David married Catherine Ratcliffe in 1919. Their eldest son, Pilot Officer Malcolm Bolton, died in action in 1941, aged 20, having left Cambridge to fight. David moved away from his home in Oakamoor, Barley Croft, for the remaining years of his life, dying in 1980 at the age of 89. The youngest of the family, the 'third' Thomas was never connected with the firm. He was the only one to be born at Lightoaks, in 1894. Thomas Tertius married, first, Caterina Eugene, daughter of the late Captain Eugene, Granddaughter of the Contessa Bentivoglio di Bologna and, second, Corysande. Mr and Mrs T.T. lived in the top flat in Lightoaks after the second war, before moving south. Corysande was a fine pianist who used to perform in Lightoaks musical evenings. The only daughter, Margaret Nina, married Geoffrey Holme in 1910.

Again following the line of the eldest son, Michael Alfred, Bolton 1, married Gladys Mary Higgin in 1907. They first lived at Wood Bank, eventually moving to Lightoaks a few years later. In their family of five, the only son Thomas was born in 1914. The 'fourth' Thomas was educated at Oundle, before moving on to St Catherine's College, Cambridge, where he studied Classics. As a keen rower, he took part in many races. Tom began working at Oakamoor in 1936, spending four years learning the trade before joining the Royal Air Force in 1941. He was posted to Singapore, but soon became a prisoner of the Japanese when Singapore fell. Tom suffered a harsh regime of labour, starvation and punishment for four cruel years. Nine out of ten prisoners did not survive; they died mentally first. Tom kept a small pen knife hidden away, used for survival when it became necessary to eat frogs and even a rat. Mercifully, the 'fourth' Thomas came home, but for years he lived the life of a recluse until, after much healing, he was able to take up poultry farming and rearing rare birds. When Thomas Bolton died at Lightoaks in November, 2002, at the age of 88, this last member of the copper dynasty to have actually worked for the firm, had passed on. June Bolton, Tom's youngest sister, with her cousin Tony, David Bolton's son, attended Tom's memorial service at St Catherine's College, Cambridge, in November, 2003, after which Tom's oar was returned to the college.

Alfred Sohier Bolton's great grand-daughter June, through the Lightoaks line, has Oakamoor at heart, and can often be seen walking the many footpaths in the Churnet Valley. Great grandsons Edward and Henry, through the Moor Court line, often visit Oakamoor when staying at Croxden. Along with Martin's wife Hazel, they meet at the family church, the Memorial Free Church, which is Alfred's Memorial, and where June is Chairman of the Trustees. I have but scratched the surface of the Bolton story; the half has never been told. The last word, for the time being, I leave to June's grandmother, Mrs. Higgin, who, after many years involvement with the family, said, "I shall never be surprised at anything a Bolton does!"

Members of the Bolton Family who lived in Oakamoor

Thomas Bolton, 1790 – 1853, who lived in Birmingham gave the Firm its name. Thomas and his wife Sarah had two sons, Alfred Sohier, 1827 – 1901, and Francis Seddon, 1828 – 1909. Alfred came to live in Oakamoor in 1852, while his brother Francis stayed in Birmingham. Francis had three daughters.

Alfred married Rebecca Harris, 1832 – 1924, in June, 1854. They came to live at Sunnyside in July of that year. Alfred and Rebecca had seven children:

1. Rebecca Freda, 1855 – 1947. Freda did not marry.
2. Alice Sohier, 1856 – 1941. Alice married Charles Bolton Toller.
3. Thomas, 1858 – 1937. Thomas married Nina Rathbone.
4. Alfred Colfox, 1858. Alfred died in infancy.
5. Sarah Beatrice, 1861 – 1948. Beatrice married Dr Peter Esdaile Bearblock.
6. Francis Alfred, 1866 – 1951. Francis married Gladys Mary Butts Howell.
7. Isabella Constance, 1869 – 1929. Constance married William Jones.

Grandchildren of Alfred and Rebecca, following the male line. The elder son was Thomas. Thomas and Nina had eight children.

1. Oliver, died at birth.
2. Oliver, died in infancy.
3. Michael Alfred, 1883 – 1948. Michael married Gladys Mary Higgin.
4. Margaret Nina, 1885 - ? Margaret married Geoffrey Holme.
5. Edward John, 1887 – 1939. Married Florence ?
6. Gilbert Benson, 1889 – 1916. Killed in action in the Battle of the Somme.
7. David Colfox, 1891 – 1980. Married Catherine Ratcliffe.
8. Thomas Tertius, 1894 - ? Married Caterina Eugene, and second, Corysande.

Michael, Edward, Gilbert, David and Thomas Tertius were Boltons 1 to 5 at Abbotsholme School. The younger son was Francis. Francis and Gladys had four children.

1. Penelope, 1918
2. Bridget, 1919
3. Martin Alfred Butts, 1923 – 2003.
4. Allison, 1925

On the female line, Charles and Alice Toller had three children.

1. Charles Richard Alfred, born 1878.
2. Alice Violet, born 1881.
3. Hugh Bolton, born 1883. All three were born at Woodbank.

Peter and Beatrice Bearblock had one son.

Alfred Esdaile Peterson, born at Oakamoor Lodge in 1904. This was 'Peterkin'.

Great-Grandchildren of Alfred and Rebecca. These number at least thirty. I will name those who have lived in or near to Oakamoor.

The Lightoaks Line. Michael and Gladys had five children.
Nora, 1911, Beatrice, 1913, Thomas, 1914, Violet, 1921 and June, 1925.
Lightoaks-Barley Croft, Oakamoor. David and Catherine had four children.
Malcolm, 1920, Anne, 1928, James, 1933 and Anthony, 1934. Pilot Officer Malcolm Bolton died in action in 1941.
Moorcourt-Croxden Line. Martin and Hazel had five children.
Kirsty, Edward, Rachel, Henry and Lisa.

Alfred Bolton, standing, with his wife Rebecca seated, possibly on the sports field for Queen Victoria's Golden Jubilee celebrations.

Sunnyside, built c.1805, where A.S.Bolton brought his bride in July, 1854. It is Grade II listed. Just for a few years around the Second World War it was used as the village police station. PC Cooper's roar used to frighten we boys when we got up to mischief, even though Mr Cooper's son Barry was a great friend of mine. Who, me? I didn't do anything!! PC Arthur Davies and his wife Betty lived here for a short while before moving into the newly built police house. In this photo of 2000 the house is receiving a sympathetic restoration.

Moor Court, shortly after it was built by A.S.Bolton in 1861. It is built in the Neo-Jacobean style to the design of the Victorian architect, William Sugden, of Leek. Additions were made in 1913 by F.A.Bolton, and it is now Grade II listed. A pointed niche contains the statue of St George. For 90 years Moor Court was alive with shooting parties, fishing, photography, golf, pioneer motor rallies, tennis, Jubilee and Coronation treats, garden parties, exhibitions and, above all, classic house parties. This all came to an

end when Mr Frank died in 1951. The house was put up for sale, but no one showed any interest for four years in those post war days, until the Home Office purchased the estate, turning the house into an open prison for young women. The notorious Mary Bell served time at Moor Court. The old Estate Agent, Mr Stephenson, said that he 'could not lay down his pen till Moor Court was sold'. After 30 years, the Home Office pulled out and the estate was sold in smaller units. The house was sold, and eventually bought in 1990 by Peter Thornley who has subsequently restored the interior. Moor Court and many of the houses on the estate are now used as residences for people with learning difficulties, founded by Peter Thornley.

Above: Moor Court, c.1870, showing the addition of a veranda on the south-west corner. A glass house has also appeared.

Left: West Lodge, formerly a lodge to Moor Court, shortly after it was built in 1861. The Lodge has now been extended in the same style. It is listed Grade II.

Above: Mr and Mrs Frank Bolton on the terrace at Moor Court on the occasion of peace celebrations in June, 1919. Most of the village attended for entertainment, races and games for the children, and tea. The Mills Brass Band played all the time.

Left: Francis Alfred Bolton, younger son of A.S.Bolton, c.1895. Mr Frank took over the running of Moor Court after his father's death in 1901.

The Cheadle Magistrates' Bench, taken in front of the statue of St George at Moor Court in 1950, with F.A.Bolton centre. Standing: S.E.Goodwin, T.Bagley, solicitor, W.Elks, my uncle, Spt. Fulton, ? S.E.Foreman, ? Cpt.Walker, ?Spt.Buxton, ?
Front: J.Barber, Mrs M.Philips, J.Hurst, F.A.Bolton, chairman, H.C.C.Collis, J.D.Johnstone, Mrs W.Fryer, justices' clerk assistant. Frank Bolton wrote in his diary on April 18th, 1902, 'I went to Cheadle at 12 and sat on the Bench for the first time. Mr Morton Philips and W.E.Bowers were the other magistrates sitting. Went over on bicycle. There were a number of cases and we did not get through till nearly 4 p.m.' A month later he sat with 'Jonny Willie Allen'. Frank Bolton served the Commission of the Peace for 48 years, with many of those years as chairman of the Cheadle Bench.

Thomas Bolton, 1858-1937. Thomas was the elder son of Alfred Sohier Bolton.

Nina Rathbone Bolton, 1859-1936, the wife of Thomas Bolton. Nina lies alone in the Bolton corner of the burial ground at the Memorial Free Church in Oakamoor.

Lightoaks, c.1890, before it was extended by Thomas Bolton. This Grade II listed building, erected in the early part of the 19th Century, stands on the foundations of a much earlier building associated with the Croxden monks. Pigot's Directory of 1828 records that John Wilson Patten lived there. Captain J.I.Blackburn, County magistrate, was there between 1834 and 1850. Kelly's Directory of 1880 does not mention Lightoaks, maybe there was nobody living there at the time, but the 1892 Directory shows that Major-General Thomas William Sneyd, JP lived there. Thomas and Nina Rathbone Bolton had moved into Lightoaks by 1894.

Throughout the decades, Mr and Mrs Michael Bolton hosted garden parties at Lightoaks. This photo of c. 1935, shows one such event for the Memorial Free Church.

Designed by H. Lowndes.   Printed by J. Lowndes.

Mr. & Mrs. M. A. BOLTON AND THEIR RESIDENCE, "WOODBANK," OAKAMOOR.

Mr and Mrs Michael first lived at Woodbank, before moving into Lightoaks.

Michael Alfred Bolton, 1883-1948. Michael was the eldest son of Thomas Bolton and grandson of Alfred Sohier Bolton.

The wedding of Dr Peter Esdaile Bearblock and Sarah Beatrice Bolton, the third daughter of A.S.Bolton, taken at Moor Court on June 1st 1901. Their son Peterkin was born at Oakamoor Lodge in 1904. Peter was doctor to the works until his retirement in 1942, when a grateful workforce presented him with a 'purse' of £78. In October, 1902, he was also appointed doctor to Cotton College by the new principal, Canon Hopwood. Dr Bearblock was seen round the village, in his chestnut brown suit and cloak, carrying his medical bag.

A Lightoaks wedding. Thomas Bolton's only daughter, Margaret Nina, married Geoffrey Holme on June 16th 1910. The wedding took place at Holy Trinity Church, Oakamoor.

Above left: The 'fourth' Thomas who died at Lightoaks in November, 2002, at the age of 88. Tom was the last member of the copper dynasty who actually worked for the family firm. He suffered badly, yet survived four year's incarceration in a Japanese prison camp after the fall of Singapore. Tom was the only son of Michael Bolton, the grandson of Thomas Bolton, and the great-grandson of Alfred Sohier Bolton. His lifelong interest in poultry and exotic birds enabled him to slowly get over his wartime experiences. Tom is seen here, near to the end of his life, feeding his poultry and fan-tailed pigeons outside the Lightoaks stables. Above right: June Bolton.

The Mills Chapel

In 1868, Alfred Bolton established a Works Chaplaincy by appointing Rev.John Mills as his first chaplain. By this time, Alfred Bolton had lived in Oakamoor for 16 years. He knew the place. He knew the people. The factory of Thomas Bolton and Sons had become famous in the field of electric telegraphy. Why, therefore, did he make this appointment? As the late Herbert Chester would have said, "Because…"

I think there were two causes. For the first one I must refer to Alfred Bolton's Journals of 1844, when still aged 17 he had left Birmingham in January of that year to further his studies in London. He left Birmingham on the 4 o'clock train and arrived at his destination by about 9 o'clock where he had to act as his own porter! During his student years in London, Alfred Bolton visited many famous places, on many occasions accompanied by his friend Colfox. The Tower of London, classical buildings, museums, tunnels, bridges featured, with a journal entry of June 5th stating, 'Saw a train come in the station in Drummund Street'. Pioneer days indeed! Every Sunday, however, Alfred Bolton would attend a religious service. Putney Church, St Pancras Church, St Martin's in the Fields where he thought the architecture was very fine, Baptist Noel's Chapel where he heard Mr Noel and was very much pleased, Westminster Abbey, and many more. Chapel services seemed to interest Alfred most, with Unitarian Chapels in particular finding great favour. One Sunday he visited the Unitarian Chapel at Hampstead where he heard Mr Kenrick preach. Alfred Bolton was obviously a very religious man with Unitarian sympathies, fertile ground indeed for what was to follow.

During the nineteenth century, many enlightened industrialists established Works Chaplaincies. Here lay the second reason for appointing Rev.John Mills as Chaplain to the workforce in Oakamoor. Alfred Bolton was aware of the grinding poverty existing around many mill towns in the north. He had seen poverty in parts of London. Although the factory in Oakamoor was situated in the countryside, he still thought the idea of a chaplain quietly moving through the workforce would benefit the men and their families. Rev.John Mills became very popular. He immediately started to hold services in 'a commodious room behind the Admiral Jervis,' as Plant's *History of Cheadle* reveals. After four years in the village, Rev.Mills established himself as a fine preacher and visitor of the sick. It was a sad day when he moved on, as a recently discovered citation reveals. The front page states: 'Address from the Choir of the Works Chapel to Rev.John Mills, April, 1872'. A gift of an Inkstand was presented, with the citation, written in rather flamboyant language of the time, ending, '..in the hope that your faithful labour may not have been altogether in vain'. Within four years the experiment of introducing a Chaplain to the Works had proved a great success. A bonus was that Rev.Mills' son stayed on in Oakamoor and became an accountant with the Firm.

The next appointment proved to be one of genius. A.S.B.'s diary of August 12th 1874, reveals, 'Mr.Denman came to act as minister in our chapel at Oakamoor'. The chapel referred to was the room behind the Admiral Jervis in Mill Road. Rev.Charles Denman was 26 years old at the time. Four days later he preached his first sermon. Within a fortnight, his fiancée, Miss Alice Searle, had visited Moor Court where Alfred's wife Rebecca had appointed her as Governess at £120 per annum. Two years later, in 1876, Charles and Alice were married. Alice was destined to bear seven children, three sons and four daughters, and to share his responsibilities and activities throughout their long connection with Oakamoor. Their early married life was spent at Sunnyside, with a spell of about eight years in Oakamoor Lodge until 1902, followed by a final move to 'The Retreat' at Farley.

Almost at the start of his ministry Charles was involved in the building of a new Mills Chapel. He would see the foundations prepared in 1876, the walls rise, the roof go on and the interior

The Admiral Jervis, nestling behind the Coffee Tavern, where Rev. John Mills started to hold services when he was appointed Chaplain to the Works in 1868.

The Oakamoor Mills Chapel, built by A.S.Bolton in 1876 and declared open on Easter Day, 1878. The architect was Edward F.C.Clarke of London. After the death of Alfred Bolton in 1901, it was re-named the Memorial Free Church, Oakamoor. It is listed Grade II.

The interior of the Mills Chapel, c.1900, when it was lit by oil lanterns and candles. Shortly afterwards it was lit by electricity generated in the factory.

Church garden party at Lightoaks, the home of Mr and Mrs Michael Bolton, in 1935. This annual social function used to alternate between Lightoaks and Moor Court. The event is now held at the Church, carrying on a tradition of over 100 years.

completed with its fine organ and east window by Powell, ready for the opening services on Easter Day, 1878. The Chapel was then available for use by any workman, villager or neighbour who sympathised with free worship with no sectarian limitations or control. The seeds sown in Alfred Bolton's life some 30 years earlier had now germinated; the Mills Chapel was alive. The choir of the Chapel faced each other across the chancel, singing the Te Deum at every morning service from then onwards, at the Founder's request. About ten years ago, centenarian David Pirrie, son of the School Headmaster, remembered these services. David wrote, 'It was the Te Deum, together with the *Authorised Version* of the Bible and the *Book of Common Prayer* with their incomparable beauty, which governed the form and contents of the services as I remember them. To a regular attender, the words of the Te Deum and the prayers, by constant repetition, became memorised, yet, miraculously, never lost their beauty and appeal. On the contrary, those qualities were enhanced as time passed'.

Music and worship went hand in hand with Rev.Charles Denman. Shades of Septimus Harding in the *Barchester Chronicles*? In June, 1881, three years after the Chapel's opening, he presented a Choral Festival in which the choir and soloists were accompanied by a string quartet and the organ. There were many sacred songs in the first part, with the second part given to a performance of Gounod's *Messe Solennelle*. Admission charges were reserved seats 1s, back seats 6d. In 1890, a reporter from the *Leek Post* experienced the 'dim, religious light' of this elegant building whose interior was tinted with the hues of a number of painted windows, the gifts of friends of the Bolton family. He referred to the fine organ, a carefully trained choir and an attractive musical service.

The Denmans' eldest son was George Searle. It must have been a proud day for the parents when George was commissioned a Lieutenant in the Army. Tragedy was to follow, however, as George died when proceeding to take up military duties in India. He is buried in Bombay. The Denman sisters were brought up to take a full part in the village life in Oakamoor. At an 'Open Air Fete and Fancy Fair' in 1907, Miss Marjorie Denman was inside a 'Palmistry and thought reading tent' and Miss Muriel Denman was in charge of the 'Rifle Range'. At this same occasion, Mrs Denman was in charge of one of the major stalls. The eldest daughter, Miss Alice Denman, was married by her father in the newly named Memorial Church in April, 1913, to Staff Surgeon R.S.Osborne, RN, Gilbert Benson Bolton was the organist.

As well as rearing a large family, Mrs Denman supported Charles in many ways, one of the most important being that of Superintendent of the Sunday School. The late Mrs Gwen Goodwin who lived to the age of 99 remembered Mrs Denman holding Sunday School in the day school, starting at 10.15am and then on to church for morning service. Once a year they had a written examination, the questions from the Bible being compiled by Mrs A.S.Bolton who also marked the completed papers. Ten marks were given for each correct answer. Mrs Goodwin went on to describe how Mrs Denman was very strict and placed pupils several feet apart so that they could not copy from one another. One year the children were taken on an outing to Dovedale. They went in horse drawn brakes and when they arrived they played games, with some of the children climbing Thorpe Cloud. Before returning home they were given a cup of tea, a bun, an orange and a small bag of sweets. Those days were happy days around 1903.

Rev.Charles Denman served Oakamoor through happiness and tragedy. There were many happy occasions when he would baptise a new baby into the Christian church. The first baby to be baptised in the newly opened chapel was John, son of John and Eliza Pattinson, Joiner of Oakamoor. Names included Kerry, Buttress, James, Howlett, Toller, Mills, Swinson, Bolton, Walker and many more in the first five years of the Chapel's life. By 1900, over 100 babies had been baptised. The Chapel was registered for the solemnization of marriages on December 6th 1879. Many weddings were to take place. The first burial ceremony performed by Charles Denman was on February 26th 1881, when David T.B.Davies was laid to rest in the new burial ground. Only 20 of the first 100 burials were of people who had reached their three score years and ten. Infant mortality was rife. Of the first eight burials in the Church grounds,

Above: The Bolton Family with Rev. Charles Denman photographed at Moor Court on June 6th 1919, on the occasion of the baptism of Penelope Bolton. Penelope's mother, Mrs F.A. Bolton, is kneeling on the left. Penelope was to become Lady Wilson.

Above left: Rev. Charles Denman, the beloved Pastor of the Mills Chapel. Above right: The East Window by Powell, the Victorian stained glass expert. All the windows in the Church possess stained glass, with the majority being memorial windows. The 'blue' window, in memory of Gilbert Benson Bolton who fell in the First World War, is etched in blue glass inspired by The Happy Warrior series by G.F. Watts of c.1884. F.A. Bolton's memorial window was executed by Hugh Easton, famous for the Battle of Britain window in Westminster Abbey.

five were children. Their ages were 9 weeks, 3 days, 6 days, 2.5 years and 3 months. Charles Denman gave love and support to these families.

On March 21st 1902, the local paper recorded a terrible death at Oakamoor Works. The account stated that while placing a belt on a pulley, William Beresford's clothing was caught by a big revolving shaft. Beresford was drawn in and his body frightfully mangled, death being instantaneous. William Beresford was only 18, full of life and highly popular with his workmates. Charles Denman comforted the family. The War Graves Commission has two graves recorded in the burial ground. One from the First World War is that of Reginald Birks, aged 20, who died at Frensham Military Hospital of battlefield wounds. Charles conducted a Military Funeral for Reginald, on February 21st 1919, comforting his family as he had done so for many families over 45 years.

Besides leading worship at his beloved Mills Chapel, Charles Denman was involved in nearly everything in village life. He was Vice-President of all the clubs and societies of the day. In 1887 he was Vice-President of the Oakamoor Floral and Horticultural Society's Thirteenth Annual Show and it is recorded that he contributed 2/6 to the funds in 1886. To put this in perspective, most members contributed 6d. or 1/-, while the President A.S.Bolton contributed £2.

It is recorded that through his long ministry, Rev.Charles Denman brought peace, contentment and continuity to the people of the Chapel, and it was this fact that made the period so noteworthy. David Pirrie recalled three names who had supported the minister through the years leading up to the First World War. By just being there, by their regular attendance and quiet dependability, they conveyed a wonderful sense of calm continuity which was more effective than any amount of 'action.' The first was Tommy Powell, the bell ringer and organ blower, who started ringing 20 minutes before the services began. He rang the bell, first, for 10 minutes, then, after a 5 minute interval, for the remaining 5 minutes. Although he started ringing each period 'by his watch,' he knew from long experience exactly how many strokes of the bell were needed for each one. The second person was John Alkins, 'Faithful Johnny,' who sang tenor in the choir and was never known to miss a service. The third person was David Pirrie's father, the organist and village schoolmaster, Charles Pirrie. On entering his 40th year of residence in Oakamoor, Charles Denman was presented with a testimonial, part of which read: 'Not only has he been the valued minister of the 'Memorial Chapel' but also the unremitting and sympathetic visitor of the sick and friend of the village, and the generous, scholarly helper of many a young student'. On October 1st 1919, Charles Denman took his last funeral service in the Chapel. Numbered 143 in the register, it is sadly that of a ten-month-old child, Thomas Dutton of Carr Bank Cottages, Oakamoor. A few months later, on June 2nd 1920, the village's beloved and respected pastor died, aged 73.

The *Staffordshire Sentinel* of June 11th 1920, carried a funeral account of the passing of the late Rev.Charles Denman. An extract reveals that: 'Oakamoor was a veritable village in mourning when the mortal remains of the beloved pastor were laid to rest in the picturesque burial ground attached to the Oakamoor Memorial Chapel. In accordance with his desire, the coffin was borne by the hands of members of Mr Denman's congregation from The Retreat, Farley, to the Oakamoor Chapel, the bearers being R.Plant, W.Plant, W.Lovatt, J.Wilson, T.Wilson, J.Alkins, G.Alkins, J.Swinson, G.Swinson, F.Walker, T.Scott, A.Pattinson, B.Tipper, H.Ainsworth and W.Ainsworth'. The account goes on to reveal that: 'All creeds were represented at the burial of a man whose gentle Christianity and genuine goodness earned him the love and respect of all. They included the Very Rev.Canon Hymers of St.Wilfrid's R.C.College, Rev.A.E.Dudley, Vicar of Oakamoor, and representatives from all surrounding churches. The children of the Oakamoor Day Schools were arranged along the approach to the Chapel, the boys reverently uncovering and saluting the coffin as the funeral procession passed. The officiating clergy were Rev.E.Moore Atwood, Canon of St.George's, Jerusalem, and the Rev.Henry B. Green, son of the former Vicar of Oakamoor. The organist was Mr.Charles Pirrie. The building had been draped in purple by Ladies of the Bolton Family. The casket had been supplied by Messrs.J.Pattinson and Sons, who most satisfactorily conducted

Sunday School Queen Rebecca Wilson with her retinue at the Church Garden Party, 1971.This Edwardian tradition still continues.

all the necessary arrangements'. Rev.Charles Denman was indeed a remarkable man who served his Lord and Maker in our village for 46 years.

Subsequent ministers at the Memorial Free Church have given much to the village, some staying for up to 12 years, as did Rev.Leonard Fountain, but it has not been possible to break the 46 year record established by Charles Denman. He just happened to take up his position in Oakamoor in its halcyon days of the electrical telegraphy industry which lasted for several decades. Two world wars changed the social pattern, and as the twentieth century progressed, life practices evolved even more. Happily, incumbents have reflected the age in which they lived, offering stimulating challenges to the congregations. Rev.Oliver Beard (1946-1949), sadly a sick man who had to have a leg amputated whilst at Oakamoor, was a scholarly preacher. He was followed by a young Rev.William Unsworth who, again, was a good preacher and pastor. Rev.A.A.MacDonald Thomson had two spells with us, amounting to about 11 years before finally retiring in 1959. Rev.John Powell gave seven years conscientious service to the village, before dying of cancer in 1966. Rev.Alex Johnson (1969-1977) gave eight years fine service, before the eccentric missionary, Rev.Leonard Fountain came from the jungle in Nigeria where he had founded a school. Len, a vegetarian who drank only water, became confused with the tax system and slept on the bedroom floor! He did not follow the normal conventions of life, but many people followed him, as was said of the young Montgomery, out of curiosity. Together with his wife Muriel, they loved Oakamoor. Rev.Keith Boughy, C.of E., came in 1994, and, like Len, was a fine preacher. Keith always preached a well prepared sermon, gaining recognition nationally by having his name on the Good Preachers Guide, an honour which indicated that any visitor who came to hear him preach would be guaranteed a good sermon. Rev.Brian Dingwall came in 1999, after a career in the Social Services, followed by four years at Aberdeen University. Brian came from a background in the Church of Scotland and along with his wife Esther, has done excellent work, particularly with the children. The present minister is Noel Clarke, B.A.Econ., M.A.Hons., from the Presbyterian Church of New Zealand and the Church of England. A dip into the characters of a few incumbents is sufficient for now, but whether named or not, all have contributed to the Christian ethos of our village.

Music has played an important part in the life of the Memorial Church. There is a fine pipe organ which has been well maintained and played by some fine organists. Several have been members of the Bolton Family, with Michael perhaps being the longest serving. He was choir master, too, achieving a very high standard with his members. Harry Kidd played for four years, before being succeeded by a young Peter Redfearn. Peter became a fine organist who sometimes practised in the middle of the night, such was his enthusiasm for the instrument!

Perhaps Peter's greatest achievement was to persuade Christopher Dearnley, Organist and Master of the Choristers at St.Paul's Cathedral in London, to perform the inaugural recital on the organ after a major restoration, completed under Peter's stewardship. Son of the Vicar of Oakamoor, Christopher attended our village school in the late 1930s, became a railway buff by watching the steam trains pass through Oakamoor during his childhood, and so it was easy for him to return to the village in June, 1972. Sadly, Peter died in 1992, aged 55. My wife Ruth has been the 'volunteer organist' since, with Michael Redfearn as the choirmaster. In the spring of 2002 a morning service was successfully broadcast on BBC Radio Stoke. Members of the Bolton Family still worship at the Church, with June Bolton, Chairman, and Henry Bolton serving as trustees. This beautiful little church, with its origins in the factory in 1868, is still alive.

Interior, Easter 1978, on the occasion of the Church's centenary.

Rev.Leonard and Mrs Muriel Fountain with Chairman of the Trustees, Martin Bolton of Croxden Abbey, on the occasion of Rev.Leonard Fountain's retirement from the Pastorate in 1990. Len looked like an Old Testament prophet as he walked for miles round the district, befriending all sorts of people on his way. As a missionary for 30 years, he had formed many unusual habits, giving the impression that he was 'three parts in the wind'! At the age of 78 he decided he would like to take a sabbatical in order to go on holiday to, of all places, Papua New Guinea where he could again get a final feel for his lifelong missionary zeal. Nobody would take him seriously in a Hanley travel agency; they thought he was a crank and left him sitting there. As was usual, Muriel went to convince the agency that they were genuine. The holiday was arranged, and off they went, each with a minimum of belongings in a holdall.

Rev. Keith Boughey with members of the Wedgwood Family on the occasion of the dedication of the Wedgwood Memorial plaque on August 11th 1996. The plaque in Portland stone and Wedgwood blue records thanksgiving for the lives of Major Cecil Wedgwood DSO and his wife Lucy who worshipped at the Church from Edwardian days when they would often walk from The Woodhouse, via East Wall, to attend services. Major Wedgwood fell at the Battle of the Somme in 1916, aged 53. Also recorded are their daughters Phoebe and Audrey,

and Audrey's husband, Lieutenant Colonel Geoffrey Makeig-Jones MC. The sculptor was Will O'Leary who has work in Westminster Abbey. Family members seen with Rev. Keith Boughey and Miss June Bolton include sisters Mrs Cecilia Hampshire and Miss Anne Makeig-Jones, also Sir Martin Wedgwood Bt. and Lady Wedgwood.

Above: Rained off in the Millennium Year. Dilys Baker (Elks) returned to the village where she grew up to attend this Village Fayre. Jade Hughes, presenter, can be seen with Rev. Brian Dingwall, Esther Dingwall, Douglas Charlesworth and Peter Wilson.

Right: Exterior, c.2000.

5 Primitive Methodism

I come from a family of Protestant Dissenters. In 1838, my great-great-grandfather, Richard Wilson, registered a house in The Square, Oakamoor, as a Meeting House for Primitive Methodists. If a 'Dissenter' to the established Church wished to preach or hold religious services, he had to obtain a licence under the Toleration Act of 1689. Politicians were keen to enforce this Act because they were afraid of large gatherings gaining a revolutionary momentum as they had done in France. Fortunately these fears were not to be realised in England. It was purely religious fervour that boiled up in the Staffordshire Moorlands east of Mow Cop in 1800, spilling into the Oakamoor area within a few years. How did this dramatic revival start?

The two leaders of this religious revival were Hugh Bourne (1772-1852) and William Clowes (1780-1851). Bourne grew up on farms to the north west of Stoke-on-Trent and was converted to Christ at a Love Feast, a form of communion, in which he found himself a member of the Methodist Society in Burslem. 'And this lovefeast I shall ever remember. In it the Lord manifested it to me that it was his will for me to be a Methodist.' Clowes was born at Burslem, his mother being related to Josiah Wedgwood. He had an adventurous early life in Hull where he drank, gambled and fought, but on returning to Burslem in 1805, he also was converted and joined the Tunstall Wesleyan Methodists where he formed a friendship with Bourne.

Two early attempts at revival waned in 1802 and 1806. Bourne needed further impetus, which was to be found in the influence of an American travelling preacher called Lorenzo Dow, who used to hold open air religious meetings called 'Camp Meetings.' The revivalists resolved to hold a Camp Meeting themselves at Mow Cop on May 31ˢᵗ 1807. This first Camp meeting was a tremendous success, supported by between two and four thousand people formed around several preaching stands. Afterwards, Bourne wrote, '..the people of God were greatly quickened, the wind was cold, I perceived that the Lord was beginning to work mightily'.

The Wesleyan Methodist Church at this time was, in many ways, becoming more like the established Church as its members gained higher social standing in the community. They disapproved of Camp Meetings, eventually to exclude Hugh Bourne from their fellowship in 1808. Bourne then started to spread the Gospel through the Staffordshire Moorlands, via outlying farmsteads, eventually coming close to Oakamoor when he arrived at Ramsor (Ramshorn) in May, 1808. Very soon Ramsor Common, an evocative wild area from where Mow Cop Castle could be seen, became the site for several Camp Meetings. One held on May 3ʳᵈ 1810, had important consequences. It began at eight o'clock in the morning and ended at six o'clock at night, attended by the 'magic' Methodists James Crawford and Mary Dunnell in a large congregation eager to hear the preaching of William Clowes on his first visit to a Camp meeting. For this, Clowes was excluded from the Methodist plan. My ancestors would have been at this gathering.

It was not until 1812 that the community called themselves Primitive Methodists, due to the suggestion of brother Crawfoot who had heard John Wesley preach in Chester in 1790. Wesley had said, 'Fellow labourers, wherever there is an open door, enter in and preach the Gospel. If it be to two or three under a hedge or a tree, preach the Gospel. And this was the way the primitive Methodists did'. The newly formed Society of Primitive Methodists created their first preaching plan for the Tunstall Circuit in 1812. The second Cicuit to be created was the Ramsor Circuit, established in 1822, with the Societies at Ramsor, Whiston and Alton included.

By 1838, several houses in Oakamoor had become registered for the holding of cottage meetings, Richard Wilson's being one, something which was to bring trouble within a few

The first Camp Meeting of the Society that eventually called themselves Primitive Methodists took place in a field on the Cheshire side of Mow Cop Castle on May 31st 1807. Mow Cop already had religious associations going back to the burial chambers of the Iron Age, it was a wild and dramatic place and also common land, three factors that contributed to its choice as a suitable place for an intense and mystical religious revival.

years. At this time, the Pattens were the owners of the Oakamoor Brass Works. Richard Wilson was their foreman wire drawer. For several years, Richard had become the victim of some religious persecution before being hounded out of Oakamoor by two Anglican ladies in the village who took great exception to the fact that he held Methodist meetings in his house. Pressure was brought to bear through his employers so that he was obliged to either give up his religion or his job. Richard gave up his job and his house and went to Holywell in North Wales where a similar range of industrial activity was available. The Bolton family bought the Oakamoor Works from the Pattens in 1852. Alfred was soon ready to reopen the wire drawing department, but the key man for wire making was not there. The Boltons, however, persuaded Richard to return and continue as head of the wire making department. I sometimes think that if Richard had refused to return to Oakamoor, I might have been Welsh!

My great-grandfather Caleb continued the family's interest in Primitive Methodism. He had his eldest son Richard, my grandfather, baptised in the Primitive Methodist Chapel at Alton on March 9th 1867. My grandfather was full of fun. The Ebeneezer Primitive Methodist Chapel had been built in Oakamoor in 1859, and on one occasion the young Richard took some bees in a jam jar into a service. After a while he let them out, causing confusion in the congregation. As the years went on, Camp Meetings were held down by the river in Jimmy's Yard. The Wesleyan Methodists built a chapel near the foot of Carr Bank in 1860, reflecting the fact that the Wesleyans too had a following in Oakamoor.

In the early years of Primitive Methodism Hugh Bourne became aware of the folklore and superstitions that were rife in the remote hamlets of the Staffordshire Moors. Witchcraft was abroad. Witches were the head labourers under Satan and Clowes became terribly troubled with a Ramsor woman who he believed would prove to be a witch. The moorland people had a vivid fear of hell, and the Primitives drew on this fear with deathbed conversions common. Clowes experienced a spiritual intensity when fighting the Devil, describing it as a 'spirit of burning' as he put his faith in the strength and the power of the Lord. By late Victorian times the Primitives had consolidated and had built many chapels, 'Prims' as they were affectionately called. The Oakamoor Primitives were a respected body of people who played an active part in the village. On one occasion in December 1889, Rev.W.Mottram gave an interesting address on the life-personalities of the characters of *Adam Bede*, Seth Bede and Dinah Morris, from George Eliot's celebrated novel *Adam Bede*. Rev.Mottram was born at Waterhouses, found success in London, and had returned to Oakamoor to speak about his friend George Eliot and the characters on whom she had based her novel. They were all found around Ellastone Common, often visited by George Eliot. The Prims hosted a large audience on this occasion. The Mills School log book records that on May 10th 1880, 'The attendance is rather smaller today on account of a tea meeting at Threapwood Primitive Methodist Chapel'. Later in the

Old Furnace Farm at Greendale near to Oakamoor where the Primitive Methodists first met in 1830, before building the Threapwood Chapel in 1835. When this farm was sold in 1982, a box of old hymn books from this early period appeared for sale.

Oakamoor Primitive Methodists at a Camp Meeting in Jimmy's Yard in 1900. My grandfather was there, with my Aunt Marion Wilson one of the three girls on the railway track. Behind the congregation is the lock keeper's cottage and stabling in use by 1811 for the Froghall to Uttoxeter Canal. The 'Knotty' truck, used as a pulpit, is on the track laid in the bed of the disused canal. A United Songs of Praise was held exactly on this spot for the Golden Jubilee of 2002, but on this occasion local corn merchant Bill Moss provided one of his lorries as a pulpit.

year the Mills School closed for the afternoon when the Oakamoor Prims had their Sunday School Treat. Children's Tea Parties were annual events, as were the major festivals and regular worship. Ten years later in August 1890, a Tea Meeting and Service of Song was held 'in connection with the re-opening of the Chapel,' probably after alterations. A service of song entitled 'Lost in the Wild Woods' was given to a crowded audience. The traditional Camp Meetings were still to continue into Edwardian times, 100 years after they were founded, but on a smaller and local scale.

By the mid-1960s few people were supporting the Oakamoor Prims. It was decided to close the doors, but only after one of its Moneystone members, Jessie Corbishley, had been married by Rev.Derek Holtham, Methodist Minister in the Cheadle Circuit. Actually, this was the first and only wedding to take place in this little Chapel for 100 years! The Swinsons and the Wibberleys continued for a short while afterwards. The Oakamoor Methodists now worship across the road at the Memorial Free Church, but for years the respective congregations had visited each other for many services, with members laid to rest in a shared burial ground. The organ, the pipes of which my father had 'gilded' some 40 years earlier, was donated to the Morrilow Heath Chapel. As a boy I remember attending services in several local Primitive Chapels, Alton in particular. Imagine the scene through the eyes of a seven-year-old. After eating Sunday dinner my parents would attend an afternoon service. Entrance was gained through a door at the front, the pulpit faced you from the other end. Everything was brown varnish; the pews, the pulpit, the door, the wainscoting, almost the lot!

The preacher called us to worship, the brown harmonium was peddled until it became full of wind and rocked. The congregation sang heartily, Rose Tideswell 'ripped', the sun shone on me during the sermon and the brown clock ticked. You could smell the varnish, the flies buzzed incessantly on the window pane and the little boy wanted to go to sleep! Yet the spirit of the Lord was there, a fact that was not apparent to me until I was older. At each end of the Oakamoor pulpit there were two tall wooden posts that used to support candle holders. One local preacher sometime in the 1930s became so animated that he knocked a candle holder off one of the posts. 'Well', he said, 'Way met us well 'ave th'other un', and knocked that off as well! In my early days I always enjoyed the Harvest Festival services at the Prims, remembering with affection Preacher Austin Gilbert who seemed to preach and sing louder than most. Oakamoor, too, had its somnolent moments, but the spirit of the Lord was also in that place. What a heritage. The Prims on the hill is still there, but successfully converted into a house.

The ladies of Oakamoor Prims outside their Chapel on Carr Bank, c.1920.

Peter and Ruth Wilson outside Ramsor Chapel, 2002. It was not until 90 years after the founding of Primitive Methodism that the Ramsor Society, like many others, could afford to build this Chapel in 1897. A.S.Bolton laid one of the foundation stones. Until then, services had been held in the Critchlows' and other family farms surrounding Ramsor Common. This Chapel closed in 1969.

The Chapel of Ease

In 1830 Oakamoor, although not an ecclesiastical parish at that time, had a population of 671. The village was situated in three parishes, Cheadle to the west of the River Churnet, and on the opposite bank, Kingsley to the north and Alton to the south of the Star Brook. Few of the houses that we know today were there, with no school and no place of worship. As the population was expected to increase, due to Thomas Patten extending the Brass Works in Oakamoor, the Established Church made the first move to build a 'chapel of ease' in this outpost of the Cheadle parish. The Assistant Curate, John Horatio Cotterill, saw the need for a church in this industrial village and set about raising money for this cause. By linking the building of a chapel of ease with the building of a school, further funds could be applied for from the National Society.

The National School features elsewhere, but in applying to the National Society for funds, the Rector of Cheadle, Rev.Delabere Pritchett declared that there was no Protestant School whatsoever, and Lord Shrewsbury had lately built a school room at a short distance from Oakamoor where he understood 50 children were instructed at his Lordship's expense. They were almost all the children of Protestant parents but were obliged to attend the Roman Catholic Chapel on Sundays and learn the Roman Catholic Catechisms on other days. This would not be if there was a Protestant School. The application was successful. The National Society made a grant of £70, Thomas Patten donated £100, plus land and stone for the building and other members of the Patten Family gave the organ and the bell. The architect J.P.Pritchett, a nephew of the Rector, drew up the plans, with Trubshaws of Great Haywood engaged as builder. On completion of the building, Oakamoor's first place of worship was consecrated as a Chapel of Ease above the National School by Bishop Ryder of Coventry and Lichfield on August 18th, 1832.

The following day, baby Joseph Collier was the first to be baptised in the new Chapel. Sadly, the burial register reveals that the first funeral was for this same child on May 24th 1833. Even greater sadness came when Rev.Cotterill who had done so much to establish the Chapel of Ease, died on December 5th 1833, at the early age of 28. Five more curates were to serve the Chapel until Oakamoor was made an Ecclesiastical parish in its own right in 1864. During this period, 19 members of my family were baptised and 10 buried. The first Vicar was Rev.John Henry Killick who was instituted in 1865. It was now possible for weddings to take place in the Chapel of Ease as it had become Holy Trinity Parish Church. The first marriage to be recorded was December 23rd 1865, between William Goodwin and Hannah Plant. The fourth wedding, a year later, was of a member of my family when Joseph Birch married Caroline Wilson, daughter of Richard Wilson, wire drawer.

In 1875, Rev.William Cass Green came to the living, destined to serve for 30 years, during which time he achieved many things and also had many upsets, the most difficult when a paternity charge was brought against him. Rose Bank was his vicarage. One of the first things Rev.Green did was to put his mind to raising £9,000 towards the building of a new vicarage and the endowment of the living which at that time was worth only £75. By 1880 the new vicarage had been built. Later, he was to add a vestry at the Church. Over a three-month period in 1883 Rev.Green had a major difference of opinion with Alfred Bolton when he tried to re-open the Oakamoor National School, an episode described elsewhere. By 1889, the Vicar wrote a flowery pamphlet in support of Alfred Bolton who was contesting the County Council Elections. Part of the letter read, 'As Vicar of Oakamoor for the past 13 years, and as a strong Conservative in Politics, I yet feel that I am doing but a bare act of justice in asking both Conservatives and Churchmen alike to place Mr. A.S.Bolton in the County Council of

Oakamoor Village Cricket Team, c.1890, with Rev. William Cass Greene in the frock coat and tall 'shiner.'

The Parish Church of Holy Trinity in Oakamoor in 1906.

Stafford'. After referring to 'great industry' in the village, William Green referred to Alfred Bolton's expertise as an employer, his caring attitude to the people, adding that 'the education of the young is an important item in the work of his life.' Alfred Bolton was elected, heading the poll in the Caverswall Division. Kelly's Directory of Staffordshire for 1892 states that the Oakamoor Living was now worth £267.

Ten years on, in 1902, the Vicar of Oakamoor experienced a very difficult and unfortunate period in his life when a paternity charge was brought against him. A newspaper account of the day revealed that a hearing took place at Leek Police Court before Major-General Phillips (chairman) and Messrs A. Nicholson, W.S. Brough, A. Ward, J.P. Sheldon and R. Wright. A domestic servant living in Leek applied for an affiliation order against William Cass Greene, claiming that he was the father of her child. She had entered the defendant's service when she was 15, left, and returned to work at the Vicarage in 1898. After another break, she entered his service again in January 1901. She complained that the defendant had been familiar with her on several occasions during this period. Whilst in service in Leek she had told her mistress of her condition and named a young man in Alton! Under cross examination it transpired that this servant had been familiar with many men. Frances Greene, the wife of the defendant, said that she had found her domestic servant troublesome, but did not know that she was not moral. She had fits of idleness, however, and was not truthful. Frances Greene went on to say that during the 35 years that she had been married she had never seen any acts of impropriety on the part of her husband.

In his evidence, William Cass Greene had said that there was not a word of truth in his having had any intimacy with the applicant, and he said he would swear before the whole Bench, the whole world and before the throne of God he had never had anything to do with that girl. He had never heard such an avalanche of lies since he was born. Richard Weston, Vicar of Burntwood, Lichfield, spoke of William Cass Greene's excellent character. Elijah Jackson, four years churchwarden at Oakamoor, did likewise. Perhaps the greatest support for the Oakamoor Vicar came from Rev.Charles Denman, Nonconformist minister at Oakamoor. Charles Denman knew William Cass Greene well. They had both come to Oakamoor 27 years earlier, Charles as the Industrial Chaplain, William as Vicar. Charles Denman spoke as to the excellent character of the defendant. It was also reported that the charge had made the Vicar ill. Dr James Thomas Hall, surgeon, practising at Alton, said that he had attended the Vicar on several dates and that he owed him about 30 shillings for the previous year. The Bench retired to consider their decision, and after being absent for about ten minutes the Chairman announced that they had decided to dismiss the case. Rev.William Cass Greene's ordeal was over.

Rev.William Cass Greene immediately set about raising money to pay for essential repairs to Holy Trinity. A poster of 1903 states that on examining the church roof, it was discovered that all the beam ends, both lean to and cross beams, were decayed under the lead covering. The whole roof was therefore found to be unsafe, as some of the cross beams had fallen as much as four inches from the horizontal. All the lead work was found to be so decayed as to be useless. The tower roof was found to be in the same condition, and the entire renewal had so far cost £118. Then the heating apparatus had to be renewed. The organ was in sad need of repair and the lead lights of the west windows had been condemned by the architect. £150 at the lowest was needed. The Vicar and Churchwardens set to work by forming a Repair Fund Committee of about 20 members who first planned a Sale of Work for the cause. Those of us who care for old churches know what a challenge this was for the congregation. Three years later a local newspaper announced the death of Rev.William Cass Greene on July 8th 1906, at the age of 64. The news was received with great regret among his parishioners and many friends of all denominations, to whom his genial qualities, his eloquent preaching and warm-hearted sympathy had long endeared him.

Rev.Arthur Wellesley Greeves followed. His first task was to complete the massive renovation started by his predecessor. This he did, adding much new furniture which included oak

Oakamoor Vicarage situated up the Farley Road, soon after it was built in 1880.

Rev.F.T.S.Powell and Mrs Powell with Rosemary, outside the Vicarage in 1924.

choir stalls, a screen, a pulpit and new communion plate. The First World War came, bringing devastation to Oakamoor families. None was hit harder than the Greeves Family who lost not one, but two sons in this most terrible of wars. A contemporary newspaper account describes a Memorial Service late in 1917 for Oakamoor soldiers who had fallen in the War. 'Great sympathy has been shown with the Vicar of Oakamoor, Rev.A.W.Greeves, and his family in the double bereavement which has befallen them in the deaths of Lieut A.F.W.Greeves and Lieut J.W.Greeves, both killed in action'. There were special services in the Church during the day, culminating in one of the most moving services ever to be held in Oakamoor. Not only were the Vicar's sons remembered, but also Lieut G.B.Bolton and Ptes B.Salt and T.Fearns. Five wreaths were placed on the chancel screen and litany desk. An opportunity was given to all parishioners to attend by the thoughtfulness of the Bolton family and the Rev.C.Denman, who announced that there would be no evening service at the Bolton Memorial Chapel. The organist for the day was Mrs Greeves. She was assisted by Charles Pirrie who played The Dead March from *Saul*, after which the Last Post was sounded by Mr.W.Shipley, a member of the choir.

A large number of parishioners attended this service, together with many from Foxt with Whiston, where the Vicar had served for ten years. There were representatives from other neighbouring parishes, also from the St Giles Lodge of Freemasons, Cheadle, led by Mr T.B.Cull. The preacher was Rev.Percy Greeves, M.A., Vicar of Kempstone, Bedford, who took as his text the 13th verse of the 116th Psalm, 'Right dear in the sight of the Lord is the death of His chosen'. At the close of his sermon he read out what his brother Arthur had intended to say about Oakamoor's Thomas Fearns and Bertram Salt, had he preached that night. ' To their honour, be it said, volunteered to fight, and if duty demanded it, to die for their country. They died, and God bless them for it through the long reaches of eternity'. Of Lieut Gilbert Bolton he said, 'Some of you knew more of him than I did, for you watched his life developing from childhood. Still, I saw sufficient of him to recognise his gentle spirit, his cultivated nature, his refined and aesthetic taste, yet, notwithstanding a native sensitiveness, he was ready when duty called him to wade through the blood and filth of war to an heroic death. The first from Oakamoor to be mentioned in dispatches, General Haig wrote of his gallantry, we are proud that the King himself expressed his high appreciation of the services rendered by Lieut G.B.Bolton'.

The preacher continued, 'The other two young officers who have made the supreme sacrifice are my own nephews. Very different in many respects, they were both alike in love of home and parents, in their frank and gay good humour, in their devotion to duty and in their fearless courage when the call came'. Many attributes were described of each brother, including the reverence they had for their father, the deepest affection and admiration they had for their second mother, that they were both destined for the Church, with the thought that the younger one in particular would have made a model parish priest. Rev.Percy Greeves concluded that his nephews were, 'In the near presence of our Heavenly Father'. Rev.Arthur Greeves, beloved Vicar of Oakamoor, never got over his double tragedy. He died in 1919, grieving for his two lost sons who fell in the Great War.

The London Gazette of July 22nd 1932, announced, 'That the said Benefice of Oakamoor and the said Benefice of Cotton shall be permanently united together and form one Benefice with cure of souls under the style of The United Benefice of Oakamoor with Cotton.' Rev.K.F.Jones was the first Incumbent of the United Benefice. Some time in the 1930s, my father Richard was approached by the Warden, John Heath of Stonydale, who reverently blurted out that, 'The 'O' had come out of 'Oly, Oly, Oly' and a very important service was due'. My father did not have the time to carve another wooden 'O', so he quickly painted one to match. Nobody noticed the difference, in fact they haven't done so since. Please leave it; it is a bit of human history! The 'Dancing Vicar' came in 1957. A friend of Victor Sylvester, Rev.F.R.Powney removed the iron pillars from the crypt and replaced them with wall to wall girders, so that he could hold dancing classes in order to make money. For a number of years after 1972, Oakamoor has had Priests in Charge. The Vicarage was sold in 1979 and is now a beautifully kept house. I hope I have given a flavour of the Holy Trinity story.

I must comment, however, on a lay person who served Holy Trinity for close on 90 years. Miss Jessie Collier was an outstanding servant of the Church. She first played the harmonium in the Crypt for Sunday School in 1910, becoming a Sunday School teacher in 1914. By 1916 she was deputy organist, becoming the organist in 1919, a post which she held for 70 years. Miss Collier was elected a member of the P.C.C. in 1923, taking up duties of secretary in 1938. At the age of 90, Jessie climbed the 21 stone steps to the organ loft, with still no intention of retiring. She served Oakamoor as a day school teacher, taught for many years in Alton, and still found time to work for Oakamoor in many other capacities. Service to Holy Trinity came first, however, and it was no surprise that she was presented with the 'Royal Maundy' by Her Majesty the Queen in Lichfield Cathedral. Jessie Collier died in July, 1995, in her 95th year. Holy Trinity, Oakamoor, which started its life as a 'Chapel of Ease,' has served the village for over 170 years. It is now in the Alton group of Churches, with Rev.Michael Last as Vicar.

Rev.Keith F.Jones and Mrs Jones, with Dr Peter Bearblock and Mrs Bearblock at a Church Bazaar in 1932. The two children are Peggy Ryder and David Leake. Mrs Bearblock was Beatrice, the third daughter of A.S.Bolton.

The interior of Holy Trinity Church in 1957, showing the new Altar in memory of Elsie Elks, née Collier, who died in September, 1956, after serving as Sunday School teacher, Church Councillor and as a chorister for 50 years.

The National School

Just over a decade ago I gave a series of talks on the History of Education in Oakamoor, leading up to the centenary of the present Valley School in the village in February, 1992. The first talk, on the National School, was given in the National School by candlelight; the second, on the Mills School was given in the Mills School by oil lamp; the third on the New Schools was given in the New Schools by electric light. I was educated in the village school, as were my daughters Rebecca and Susanna. My wife Ruth taught there for many years. Reversing through the generations, my father Richard was educated in the New Schools, my grandfather Richard was educated in the Mills School, and my great-grandfather Caleb was educated in the National School. Previous generations never went to school.

The National Society was founded in 1811 with the aim of placing a National School in every parish in the land. By 1827, the *British Critic* proclaimed that, 'Education with religion is the greatest good which man can bestow on man; education, unless grounded on religious principles, may be a curse instead of a blessing'. *A Short History of the National Society*, by H.J.Burgess and P.A.Welsby, has proved to be a valuable source of information on the early years of the movement. The book revealed that for centuries, education in England had always

A rare photograph of the two Oakamoor National Schools, c.1864, provided by Mrs Dilys Baker, Miss Collier's niece. The first school of 1832 is situated beneath the 'Chapel of Ease', with the Boys' entrance and Girls' entrance either side of the window. The 1856 school can be seen beyond the 'Chapel of Ease', with its door and bell tower clearly visible. Oakamoor became an ecclesiastical parish in its own right in 1864, with the Chapel becoming the Church of Holy Trinity. The Second National School was knocked down in 1944 as it had gone beyond repair and had become unsafe. The stone was used to build the boundary wall to an extension of the burial ground. My school friend Dilys attended the consecration of this graveyard on July 17th 1945. Apparently, Mr Pyatt, the Schoolmaster, was not too pleased at Dilys having the afternoon off to attend the ceremony, which was conducted by the Bishop of Lichfield.

been Christian education, with the Church being the patron and sole provider. There was a break in the seventeenth century when, under the Puritans, the State took charge of the schools. At the Restoration, Universities and Grammar Schools were to remain under Church control, but for the poor there was little provision apart from a few charity schools.

For a century the charity schools increased to some 1,400 containing 220,000 children in 1729, before declining. Towards the end of the eighteenth century the Sunday School movement was founded, but what was really needed was a widespread network of day schools. At the beginning of the nineteenth century, two Christian gentlemen had discovered a new, cheap and efficient method of education; the monitorial system. Andrew Bell and Joseph Lancaster proclaimed their ideas, Bell insisting on instruction in Liturgy and Catechism of the Established Church, Lancaster insisting on the undenominational approach of the Quaker. Sadly, these sound Christian men failed to appreciate either the sincerity or the difficulties of the other during a period of religious intolerance. Lancaster founded the British and Foreign School Society in 1807, while Bell, after returning from India in 1797, introduced the 'Madras System' into as many parochial schools as he could. When was Oakamoor's turn to come? We were not a parish, nor had we a church.

By 1830, Oakamoor still had no school. At that time, however, due to the expansion of the Cheadle Copper and Brass Company's Works at Oakamoor, there was a growth in population as more jobs became available, justifying the erection of a Chapel of Ease to be served by the clergy of Cheadle. By incorporating a National School with this new building, a substantial grant was obtained from the National Society. On a visit to the Society's headquarters, then in Church House, Westminster, I came across the original application form for aid towards the building of a National School in Oakamoor. The form had been filled in by Rev.Delabere Pritchett, Rector of Cheadle, but by then was in poor condition. The application, dated June 10th, 1831, was for a school for boys and girls at Oakamoor in the Parish of Cheadle. The population was then 671, but a note added that it was to increase very rapidly owing to the Works of the Brass Factory being greatly extended. The number of children, between 7 and 13, requiring cheap or gratuitous instruction was not less than 35 boys and 35 girls. The Rector went on to write that there was no Protestant School whatsoever. 'Lord Shrewsbury had lately built a School Room at a short distance from Oakamoor, where I understand 50 children are instructed, the greater part of which at his Lordship's expense. They are almost all the children of Protestant parents, but are obliged to attend the Roman Catholic Chapel on Sundays and learn the Roman Catholic Catechism on these days. This would not be if there was a Protestant School'. The new building would be used for Sundays and weekdays, and would be supported by subscriptions; 2d. per child per week. The Chapel of Ease about to be erected, along with the schoolroom beneath, would accommodate 150 children. The estimated annual charge for Master and Mistress, books, etc., was £60. The stone building which would be freehold for ever measured 30' long, 14' wide each for boys and girls, and 11' 6" high to the ceiling. Six square feet of floor space was allocated to each child. The entire estimated cost was £175; that is £50 for the ground, £100 for the building, with fittings up to £25. By declaring that the school would be united to the National Society, a grant of £70 was made.

Oakamoor National School was opened as Oakamoor's first school in the autumn of 1832. The Society considered 'that a common schoolmaster or excise man, a book-keeper, and in general, any person of good character, who can read distinctly and write fairly, may become qualified to conduct a school upon the Madras System'. Married couples could be in training together and even W.S.Gilbert describes how the reformed Sir Despard Murgatroyd and his wife came 'to rule a National School'. Oakamoor's first Head Teacher, therefore, would hold qualified status. He would sit at a high desk from where he could survey the whole school. There would be several aisles in front of him. Each aisle separated classes on the basis of ability, not age. Monitors, older children, were spread around to pass on prescribed rudiments. The morning session began with prayers and collects. After prayers, the first aisle did Arithmetic until 10a.m., then learning of religious exercises until 10.30a.m., followed by writing until

11a.m., and, finally, reading until noon. With three aisles, each did work in a different order. A similar arrangement took place in the afternoon, with perhaps some practical work akin to Oakamoor's industries.

Learning by rote was the order of the day! 1841 saw the inauguration of the Pupil Teacher system, in which boys of 15 were paid as assistant teachers while they were being taught how to teach. By 1846, a boy or girl of 13 accepted by an inspector could start a five-year apprenticeship at a salary of £10 a year and rising to £20. The Master, or Mistress, was paid to instruct the pupil teacher who, at the end of the five years, would compete for Queen's Scholarships which provided them with College training. A modified Pupil Teacher system still existed in Oakamoor a 100 years later when it was recorded in the New Schools log book in July, 1940, that 'Miss Daphne Swinson ceased as pupil-teacher'. I remember Daphne as she taught me.

In the Cheadle Parish Directory of 1851 it is recorded that the brass and copper manufacturing firm of John Wilson Patten was still the proprietor of Oakamoor Mills. Captain John Ireland Blackburne lived at Lightoaks, Eli Bowers was a lime burner, and Rev.William Hendrickson was incumbent of Oakamoor and Cotton. His 'perpetual curacy' was valued at only £57. Beneath his Chapel of Ease, the National School was at bursting point, with 160 pupils on the register. Three years later Rev.George Mather of Huntley Hall, the incumbent of St Chad's, Freehay, wrote to the National Society with a view to building a second Oakamoor National School. The return letter said, as far as I could decipher, 'there is not a word in my papers in this office as to a deed or for a school having been erected'. What a start, but start they did! Plans were drawn up for larger premises. Over time, the plans were lost, eventually to turn up in the roof space of the New Schools in the 1970s. The plans reveal a schoolroom measuring 32' by 18', with smaller rooms for boys' coats and hats and girls' bonnets and cloaks; one door for boys and one door for girls. The desks, 12 in number, were 6' long and 1'3" wide, fastened to the floor, with benches on one side, and an aisle of 1'6" between each row. There was a stoke hole and copper at the back.

Meanwhile, in the autumn of 1856 there was a dispute between the Curate and the Committee, concerning prayers and the dismissal of a teacher. The Bishop became involved, but the dispute must have had many ramifications as the Lord President of the Council of the National Society was called on to pass judgement on all other matters. At least the National Society had woken up to the fact that they had had a school in Oakamoor for the previous 24 years! Planning continued, with the first stone of this new school being laid by Miss Patten of Lightoaks. Her father had given the land, plus a very handsome donation towards the building of this school. The Architect was Thomas Fradgley of Uttoxeter, whose planning and building cost £537.14s.4d. A Government grant of £196 was paid in 1858.

A few years after the opening of the second Oakamoor National School, an unscrupulous secularist named Robert Lowe became Vice-President of the Council for Education. Burgess revealed that Lowe abolished the various maintenance grants, replacing them with the 'Payment by Results' system. An annual grant would be based upon the result of an annual examination in the 'Three Rs' by Government Inspectors. By linking the income of the school and schoolmaster with the children's proficiency in the 'Three Rs' alone, they also crippled the teaching of other subjects, and in particular undermined Religious Instruction. For just a few years, the National Society had a common cause with the British and Foreign School Society, the Church of England Education Society, the Home and Colonial School Society, and the Wesleyan Education Committee. How things were to change again when the 1870 Education Act opened the door to the progressive secularization of English Education. A period of denominational strife began. 'Everything for the flesh and nothing for the soul: everything for time and nothing for eternity', wrote the seventh Earl of Shaftsbury in his diary. Oakamoor National School, along with many others, was starved of Government grants. It struggled on for another few years, until it finally closed, for good, on June 2nd 1876. Alert to this threat, Alfred Bolton opened the Mills School in a disused part of the factory in 1871. This school was opened as a 'British School' based on the parallel system advocated by the Quaker Lancaster.

Meanwhile, Lord Shaftsbury was still railing against the decision of the Government to end the grants to church schools. He proclaimed that 'Any education system without a moral and spiritual content will produce a race of clever devils'. The one cause for regret was that, nationally, disunity between English Christians led to the ending in 1870 of an educational system that had hitherto been an almost exclusivey Christian enterprise. Reflecting the national scene, Oakamoor suffered its share of unhappiness, yet I feel that the children of our village did not suffer educationally because they always had a school to attend. Like an extending ladder, during the overlapping years when both schools existed, our children gradually moved from one school to the other, hopefully shielded to a certain extent from the arguments that raged around them. It was not until the Education Act 1944, that a spirit of harmony and co-operation between the churches started to return.

When I began to research the history of the Oakamoor National Schools in 1989, I went looking for second-hand memories, all that could be hoped for of a school that then had been closed for 113 years. I approached three nonagenarians still living in Oakamoor. I spoke to my father's cousin, Mrs Nelly Reeve, who was by then 91 years old. She said, 'My mother attended the school behind the church. She used to walk from Farley with Vida Howlett's mother'. Learning this, I then went to root out Vida Howlett who was living on Carr Bank as Mrs.Colin Cope, aged 93. She told me, 'My mother went to the National School behind the Church. She was born in 1868 and attended the School for about three years until it closed. Two sisters ran the school then. Each wore a thimble on one finger. They would hit people on the head with these thimbles. My father went to this School when he could afford to pay. He missed out a lot because of this and so could not write very well'. My third visit was to Mrs Chrissie Byatt, née Goodwin, who was 92. Her mother, too, had attended the National School, but she went on to say, 'She couldn't have been there long as when she left at 11 she couldn't write her name. She was immediately hired out to a local farm for 1/- a year where she had her keep, bed and food, but no payment. It was not until she received a pension that we taught her to sign her name and write, that after a family of 12'.

In 1883 the Vicar of Oakamoor, Rev.William Cass Greene, attempted to re-open the National School. This started an almighty row that lasted for three months. Rev.Greene wrote to the National Society, 'I am anxious to establish a Church of England School in this Parish. Formerly a school did exist, but owing to some action of my predecessor, the Gentleman who employs nine twelfths of the population, opened a secular school, and this action compelled the trustees to close the Church School owing to the want of scholars and funds'. It is sad that right from the start Rev.Greene blamed Alfred Bolton rather than the Government of the day for causing the demise of the National School. He continued, 'I have approached the Dissenting Squire, who has a Chapel and a resident minister here. Three times during my incumbency have I asked Mr.Bolton to allow at least the scriptures to be read, but on each occasion he has refused. The building we have is adequate to hold 70 scholars. It is filled with maps but will require a new set of books and repairs'. The specification for repairs revealed that four closets needed attention, walls cemented and limewashed, doors varnished, seats and desks repaired, the roof repaired and the drains restored.

Rev.Greene enlisted the support of the Vicar of Alton who claimed to have 'learnt by experience how hopelessly ignorant in all religious matters the children attending the present day school are'. One or two children had been transferred to Alton School and Rev.Moncrief wrote that 'in every case I found they did not even know the Lord's Prayer and the Ten Commandments'. The application for aid was supported by the Archdeacon and the Bishop of Lichfield. P.Ford and Sons, Masons and Builders of Uttoxeter, quoted £33 to effect the repairs. My great uncle Henry Wilson of Farley, who was a 'Maker of all kinds of Ornamental Bands and Iron Work, including Wrought Iron Fencing, Woodmen's Axes, Hooks, Etc., also a provider of Quarry Tools, a Fitter of Hot and Cold Water Piping and a General Smith', quoted £7 to fit a heating apparatus. Rev.Greene sent all the details to the National Society, applying for £80 for the School and £70 for the first year's stipend of a Master. He even offered to go to London to support his case. Rev.Greene also wrote that he had recently become the Chaplain to the Earl of Shrewsbury at Alton Towers who owned land in Oakamoor, and so material help was hoped for.

A letter dated June 19th 1883, from the secretary of the National Society brought Rev.W.C.Greene down to earth. It said, 'I fear that you have quite mistaken the extent of the Society's resources. The Society does not make grants towards teachers' salaries and could only vote a small sum in aid of the cost of repairs'. Rev.Greene immediately replied with a forceful letter of annoyance, and his obvious desperation was shown in that he made several disparaging remarks about the Mills School, as this was where the Government grants were now paid. Sadly reflecting the bitter denominational strife of the time that existed at national level, it was localised in an attack on the Mill Owner, not the Government of the day. 'A Church population of entirely poor people have had their school closed for some ten years by the action of a Radical Unitarian Birmingham Secularist Manufacturer', claimed Rev.William Cass Greene. The fact that the Mills School was by then thriving, with over 100 pupils on its books, obviously exasperated the Vicar. Two days later he received a reply from the Society saying that as the necessity for awarding such grants had ceased, the Committee had decided to discontinue them. In a final desperate plea, Rev.Greene wrote, 'Rescue these children from a secular school'. He was really annoyed with the National Society when they awarded Oakamoor £15 towards the repairs. Case closed. The row over the National School pinpointed the gulf which then existed between the Established Church and the Non-Conformists in the nineteenth century.

The schoolroom was used less and less over the next 35 years, and when Rev.Albert Dudley came to Oakamoor in 1919 he set about tidying up the old 'Top School'. It was finally brought back into use for meetings, clubs and the Sunday School. Craft classes were held, the boys working in raffia and the girls sewing, after which they held a little sale. By this time the floor was black oiled and if you dropped anything it became dirty. Miss Collier told me that Rev.Dudley, a bachelor, had his mother living with him, with two housekeepers. After a while his mother died and he thought it 'not right' to live in the Vicarage alone with two women! He wrote to the Bishop, suggesting that the old National School should be made into a vicarage where he could perhaps live alone. Bishop Kempthorne refused, and so Rev.Dudley resigned the living to become a missionary. He did marry in the end, as he met his wife-to-be on the mission field.

The building decayed further until, in 1937, Rev.C.Dearnley faced up to the fact that the Old School by this time was in such poor condition that it was probably beyond repair. He wrote to the National Society asking for advice on what to do in the matter. He received no response. It was obvious that they did not want to become involved in any expense. Two years later Rev.Dearnley sent them the deeds of the Old School, inferring that they were still responsible for its upkeep and repair. This time a reply did come from the National Society, claiming that under the *School Sites Act*, 1841, the land should revert to the estate from which it was granted, should the premises cease to be a day school. It followed that when the school closed in 1876, the property should have reverted to J.W.Patten, but no reversion was claimed. Legal arguments ensued between the National Society and the Lichfield Diocesan Trust that the Bishop may have acquired a title. Eventually, a letter went out from Lichfield saying, 'The Bishop agrees'. The blind Vicar, Rev.E.R.Grant, was given permission in 1944 to raze the old building to the ground. This was the end of Oakamoor's Second National School, built through necessity in 1856 to accommodate the rising tide of children born in Oakamoor during the pioneer years of electrical telegraphy, but fated to close 20 years later when starved of Government grants. The land is now consecrated as a burial ground.

Through its long history, the National Society has kept alive the principles of Christian education. It is a matter for thanksgiving that this worthy Society served our village for 44 years during the middle part of the twentieth century.

As the Education Act, 1870 sounded the death knell of the Oakamoor National Schools, it heralded the founding of the Oakamoor Mills School. However, the story really started earlier than this. Since his arrival in Oakamoor in 1852, Alfred Bolton involved himself much more with the needs of his employees than the previous owners of the Oakamoor Mills. Some 15 years before founding the Mills School, Alfred established a school for his work people in the village. The 'Alton' Wire Mill in Mill Road, built by the Pattens in 1827, decreased its wire drawing activities after some 20 years and the building was used for a number of years by the Leek silk industry. Silk workers from Brosters of Leek travelled by the Churnet Valley Railway, opened in 1849, to work in silk in the vacant mill. When the silk industry withdrew in 1856, Alfred opened his school for adults in the old wire mill. He called his venture 'The Silk Mill School'. He appointed a full time teacher in 1859 and, by 1870, a Miss Graham was the Head of the 'Silk Mill School'.

Also by 1870, it was generally acknowledged that elementary education should be provided for all. In his book, *A Century of Growth in English Education*, H.C.Dent wrote: 'During the 1860s alone, half a dozen parliamentary bills had perished in the attempt to find an agreed solution, as had many others previously. All had died in the flames of sectarian strife'. With the 1870 Act, warring factions mobilised, one side attempting to preserve denominational schools, the other to make elementary education unsectarian, free, compulsory, and universal. The strife had reached a new intensity when it hit Oakamoor. Our National School was doomed and seeing the inevitability of the situation, Alfred Bolton immediately applied to the Department of Education for the new Government grant in order to create a new foundation. He already had a building used as a school for his work people. The birth of the Mills School was imminent. The undenominational approach of the Quaker Joseph Lancaster appealed to Alfred Bolton, particularly as the British and Foreign School Society had already established the first training college for teachers, in Borough Road, London. It was from this college that in 1871 the first head of the Oakamoor Mills School was to come.

Charles Barton took up his appointment as Headmaster at the beginning of January, 1871, some three weeks before the formal application for grant aid was made. Alfred Bolton must have been confident in the success of this application as he had already started lessons in the school, and was able to describe it as an established organisation, albeit for a few weeks! Thomas Bolton and Sons owned the building and were responsible for making necessary regulations. The schoolrooms were described as being part of a building, the other part of which is not used, and were used for a night school from 7 to 9p.m. on three evenings weekly. This would be the 'Silk Mill School', still in use, with Miss Graham as head. The main room for both boys and girls was 32' long, 26' wide and 12' tall. There were six windows and an open pitched roof containing two roof lights. The ventilation was described as 'Abundant'. You bet it was, in a building originally used as a wire mill! The next column on the form was headed 'Offices'. Were they separate for boys and girls, and with separate approaches? The confident reply was 'Yes'! 'Offices' did not refer to headmasters by the way, they were Victorian euphemisms for earth closets! All boys, girls and infants were under the same management, there were no debts, and any deficiency in income would be met by Thomas Bolton and Sons. Charles Barton, the first Head, was born on December 13th 1847. He was never apprenticed as a pupil teacher but spent one year employed at Seacombe School, Liverpool, before entering training at Borough Road, London, on January 7th 1869, 'quitting' in December 1870. He had 'Obtained a certificate of 2nd Division of 4th Class' in December of 1869, and was waiting the result of his last examination of December 1870. An Annie Riley had been appointed but had not yet commenced work in the Infants' department. As well as the three 'Rs' girls were taught plain needlework as part of the ordinary course of instruction.

Right from its foundation the Mills School kept records. The log books in particular reveal a fascinating insight into the social history of the village of Oakamoor from 1871 onwards. The Mills School opened at two o'clock in the afternoon of January 9th 1871. Charles Barton registered 13 pupils. Who were these children? The Admissions Register named Walkers, Warringtons, Wilsons and Tippers. Would you believe it! The three Wilsons were Caroline and Lizzie, my great aunts, and Richard, my grandfather, all children of Caleb and Margaret Wilson who had twelve children in all. The children had been transferred from the Oakamoor National School. It is also interesting to note that most of the first-day pupils came from foremen's families. Although they had come from the Church school into an undenominational school, no parent claimed exemption from religious instruction. The Scriptures were taught. In fact, of the 713 children who were admitted to the Mills School during the first 22 years of its existence, not one parent claimed exemption for their children from Religious Instruction. Interesting, too, were the reasons given when children came to leave school.

Again, in the case of my own ancestors, Caroline and Lizzie were 'Required at Home', obviously to help with a large family, and Richard went to 'Work in the Mill'. He was 12$^1/_2$ years old. Another reason for leaving for Alice Warrington was 'Gone into Service'. The Admissions book makes interesting reading. One entry of October 29th 1893, was Rose Long who gave her address as 'Orphanage', Oakamoor. This building still stands. Furniture arrived at the school soon after it opened. The girls received their first lesson in sewing from Mrs Rebecca Bolton, Alfred's wife. A few days later the 'Routine was disturbed by the smoking of the chimney which needed sweeping'. This was soon done, and after two more weeks an Infants' School started on February 6th. February 21st brought the first holiday, that of half a day for Shrove Tuesday. The first visit from one of Her Majesty's Inspectors came in August. Subsequently, more time had to be given to Arithmetic as it was found that children were most backward in that direction. A few days later the log book states, 'Attendance somewhat thinned by the occurrence of the Wakes'. The first year ended with 'Some difficulties with the cold, the old stove being worn out.'

The day the Mills School opened religious intolerance began to ferment. It took only five days to surface. In a letter to the *Staffordshire Advertiser* of January 14th 1871, 'Anxious Enquirer' wrote, 'I have read with a considerable amount of surprise of a tea party in this village in a large room described as the Works Chapel. One object of this social gathering was to inaugurate a new day school which was 'greatly needed' in Oakamoor'. The writer was a subscriber and supporter of the National School in the village. He challenged the Founder of the Mills School 'to prove that a new school is greatly needed'. Alfred Bolton responded that, 'These schools were absolutely necessary to ensure a good education to our work-people's children. Families of all denominations may conscientiously avail themselves of our schools as no question of religious difference is there raised'. A week later the Vicar of Oakamoor, Rev.John H.Killick, picked up his pen. He wrote, 'Any parishioner's child has had the opportunity of attending either of our schools for the small sum of 2d. per week, whether he or she attended the Church Sunday school or not, but no Nonconformist has ever contributed a single subscription towards their support during the whole of the five years that I have been connected with them'. Letters were received from many sources. Three previous masters of the National School wrote too.

John Bennett admitted that the children of Nonconformists were not allowed to attend the day school at all, W.T.Walker was ordered by Rev.Killick to charge 2d. per week for those who attend the Sunday School, 4d. for those who did not attend, and 3d. for those residing out of the village, and H.Walton reported that in his time it was still 2d. per week for the Sunday School attenders and 3d. for the rest. Dissenter Joseph Walker said he had to pay 4d. per week, and dissenter Edward Tipper paid the extra money for a while until the Mills School opened. All this seems so trivial now, but in the context of Victorian England, some poor families in

Oakamoor, 1861. The Square to the left, Starwood Terrace to the right. Directly above the man standing in the middle of the road, behind some conifers, is the Wesleyan Methodist Chapel of 1860. To its right is the house that was knocked down in order to make more space for the Mills School.

The Mills School, centre right, c.1885.

Oakamoor could not afford to send their children to school at all. One family sent a son; at home he told the rest. These letters were too much for the Vicar, as the Advertiser of February 11th carried a long tirade in reply. In the overblown style of the day he wrote, 'I have no wish to be otherwise than perfectly candid and straightforward; I hate deceit and underhand dealing as much as any man', and after raking over the fees argument yet again, he described the letters from dissenters Joseph Walker and Edward Tipper as 'most dishonest productions'. By now the Editor of the *Staffordshire Advertiser* had had enough of the Oakamoor rumblings and wrote, 'Any more further correspondence must be paid for'. The final words to be printed, however, were from Thomas Bolton and Sons who wrote in support of their two workmen, Joseph Walker and Edward Tipper, bringing an end to the saga.

During September, 1872, Oakamoor Wakes took place. On opening school the following day, only two turned up, and so Charles Barton 'deemed it advisable to defer till tomorrow'. On the morrow 33 turned up, still not good enough as he wrote, 'Attendance being very unsatisfactory, I would take the Village children a-black-berrying, which had the effect of bringing them together, and of giving me the opportunity of urging the importance of their punctual attendance next week'. Poor attendance was noted on many occasions during the early years of the Mills School. One day in 1873, we read, 'Progress seriously impeded by the paucity of numbers present. Most of the children were picking bilberries'. A year later we read, 'A great number of children have been troubled with a complaint known as Mumps'. Seasonal fruit picking was a part of country life; childhood illness was a scourge. When my uncle Caleb was a boy he was often kept away from school in the winter, his mother claiming he was 'delicate'. Nelly Reeve, née Wilson, who as a child lived in Farley, was kept at home in the winters of her early years. With a twinkle in her eye she once told me, 'Delicate you know, delicate'. My family had suffered infant deaths, as had others. One phrase of conversation between families was often, 'How many have you buried?' So it was not a disdain for education that kept them away, but survival. It was pure fright of killer diseases. Caleb lived to 90; Nelly to 94!

The first Head, Charles Barton, ceased his connection with the school at Christmas, 1874. By this time Alfred Bolton was considering building a second school away from the old mill classroom at the bottom of Mill Road. Mr F.Osborne came in January, 1875, and by August of that year received an HMI's report stating that: 'The children are well disciplined, write very well, and read and spell very fairly on the whole, but their arithmetic is very bad, being utterly wanting in accuracy, tho' not without knowledge of principle'. There was a sting in the tail after the second visit in March, 1876. The Inspector wrote, 'The Infants have hardly been taught at all and no payment can be made under Article 19(B) (a) unless the Infants are properly taught'. As these were the days of 'payment by results' this teacher came unstuck. He had the sack and left the following day. A John Wood came a week later in place of a master who had been appointed yet failed to turn up! He stayed but a few weeks.

Eventually, a Mr S.G.Height was appointed, commencing his duties on May 15th. His first comment was that 'the slates are in a wretched state'! As numbers in the school were growing, Alfred Bolton had by now settled on a site for a new building. At the bottom of Carr Bank stood the Wesleyan Methodist Chapel of 1860. A large Georgian house which must have been in poor repair stood nearby, as it was recorded in July, 1876, that Walter Tipper's house was pulled down. Work started on the new school building which was situated at almost a right angle to the Chapel. The Star Brook squeezed between this and the site of the old house. The great day came for the children to leave the first home of the Mills School in the noisy smoky mill and cross the Churnet bridge into their new 'Mills School' in the heart of the village. On October 11th, Mr Height wrote, 'We commenced work in the new schoolroom this morning. The children seem very happy and very much enjoy the new building. Great interest was taken by them in decorating the room with beautiful flowers suitable for the occasion'. There were 59 scholars present. Fees were 2d. per week; for large families 2d. a week for the first three children, 1d. thereafter. The children were encouraged to be thrifty. A Clothing Club and Bank were started, with 1/- being the largest amount that could be received each week, with the stipulation that the amount paid on the first occasion must be continued throughout the year. It was decided 'there cannot possibly be any deviation from these rules'. If 1d. a week was promised, 1d. must be paid. This was early training in budgeting and commitment for life.

Some three months after the new schoolroom had opened a Miss Evans was appointed as mistress in the Infants' Department, which was housed next door in the Wesleyan Chapel. A month later the Mills School had become very popular, with 93 children being taught reading, handwriting, spelling, needlework, arithmetic, grammar and geography. Mrs Bolton promised prizes at Christmas 'for those who acquit themselves most successfully'. Although an Inspector's report for 1878 revealed good discipline, many weak points in attainment had been identified. S.G.Height suffered a deduction of one tenth of his salary 'for faults in the instruction of arithmetic'. He left very suddenly, having fallen foul of the 'Payment by Results' scheme, or so it seemed. A cryptic remark by a new head, James Murphy, in April 1879, recorded, 'I am to request that you will at once state specifically what charges the Managers have to bring against Mr Height on the score of immorality'. Scandal indeed? Then in the autumn, news came through to the school that HMI Rice-Higgins was dead. No emotion was recorded! Right through 1880, childhood scourges of measles, mumps and scarlet fever were rife. Alice Whiston, one of the infants, died. The school was closed early on May 31st so that the children would be able to attend the funeral of their little friend. Other occasions brought joy. Attendance was low when children were taken to a tea party at Threapwood Primitive Methodist Chapel, when a circus came to Cheadle, when the hay had not been gathered in, with complete closure for the Primitive Methodist Annual Treat. A one-off treat came to the children when dinner was provided for them in the schoolroom to celebrate the marriage of Mr.Thomas Bolton on November 10th. 1880 ended with another outbreak of measles which closed the school for several weeks. Early 1881 provided severe weather. An HMI's report recorded 'poor in most subjects', causing James Murphy to have to give in his notice. At the end of the year two hanging lamps were provided by Mr Bolton for the school. 'The Temperance Society have liberty to use the same', states the log book, 'using their own oil and wick and providing the same for any of Mr Bolton's meetings. If a Night School be instituted, the school provides its own oil, etc. for the same'. Alfred Bolton gave so much to the people of Oakamoor, but he didn't provide everything, lest a dependency culture should prevail. I feel that the moral of the Mills School lamps has a relevance today.

Early in 1882 Elias Handy took charge of the school, destined to preside over a series of misfortunes. May 10th brought two cases of fever to Oakamoor, to Arthur Swinson and Miss Mellor. Neighbouring children were withdrawn from the school on doctor's orders. Polly Thompson became ill with fever, measles struck, more cases of fever developed as the weeks went by, and by October so many children were sick that the school had to be closed for six weeks on account of the rapid spread of the fever. There were still more cases in 1883, when it was found out that a boy who had been in school before Christmas was recovering from an attack of scarlet fever, having returned with his hands and feet in the process of 'peeling'. The school was ordered to close again and did not open till the end of March. By then there were 117 children on the register. For once, the authorities were kind. Although the school had been closed for 16 weeks, the full grant was paid. That epidemic lasted for almost a year.

Then, a few weeks later whooping cough became prevalent, and many children became very ill. The social life went on, with a Band of Hope trip, Cheadle Wakes and the Oakamoor Flower Show to attend. Illness continued into 1884. Frank Gibson became ill with fever, mercifully to survive as Frank became the Lightoaks Estate woodman. I remember him as an old man working on his cleft oak fencing, some of which still survives. At the end of April, assistant teacher Mr Thomas became ill with rheumatic fever. He died on May 2nd. Then came the inevitable poor result of an inspection. In the autumn the fever was still rampant and the school had to close for another five weeks. Dr Hall allowed the school to open again in October, only after certain houses had been disinfected. Stumbling over into 1885, the school had a disastrous

Elias Handy, with possibly Mrs Handy, c.1885. Elias Handy experienced much misfortune in his three years at Oakamoor. I think he looks a little sad. To his left on the back row is Burton who was to become a pupil teacher.

inspection, with even the 'offices' described as dirty. The issue of a full teaching certificate to Mr Handy was withheld. Poor Elias Handy. He had served the children of Oakamoor through almost three years of illness and disasters. He must have been utterly fed up and dejected when he disappeared from Oakamoor for good.

In the spring of 1885 George Elam became Master of the Mills School. After first being 'occupied in getting into my house', The Glen, the new Master recorded that he found the children in a very noisy backward state. By mid-April he wrote: 'My time has been wholly occupied in classifying the children and instituting a stricter discipline and a neater more careful way of doing slatework. I have frequently punished in order to secure this result, and shall continue to do so if necessary, as I am of the faith that 'Order is Heaven's First Law', and a little well done is better than much half done. Another reform I have carried out – I have abolished home lessons. I firmly believe these to be a delusion and a snare, giving trouble to parents, over pressure to the child, and above all causing annoyance, anxiety, and a weary waste of valuable time to the teacher'. George Elam had revealed his philosophy.

George Elam was a musician. So was A.S.Bolton's eldest son Thomas. It was only a matter of months, therefore, before the first 'Juvenile Concert' was presented in the school. A newspaper report of the time describes the patronage of A.S.Bolton and Mrs Bolton, with Thomas Bolton in the chair. Anthems, part songs, solos and operatic choruses were gone through by the children. They sang 'The Union Jack of Old England', 'Laugh and Grow Fat', and many others, with Mr Elam singing 'The British Lion'. The children and their conductor were congratulated. The evening closed with the singing of the National Anthem. A second concert came at Christmas. The children sang many items, both serious and comic. Thomas Bolton sang 'The Village Blacksmith', and Mr and Mrs Elam sang the duet 'What are the Wild Waves Saying?' The local newspaper reported 'Perhaps the greatest success was achieved by the amusing song of a select few of the boys, who appeared as well blacked 'niggers' and acted accordingly, entitled 'Shoo-fly', with chorus'. Political correctness was over a century away! The term ended with prizes, merry games and dancing for the 134 children.

George Elam standing with his class by the corner of the Mills School, c.1889. The newly built house for the Master, The Glen, can be seen to the right. George Elam made a considerable impact on Oakamoor, as a musician and outstanding teacher.

George Elam and Thomas Bolton got on well; music was the common factor. Thomas founded the Oakamoor Orchestral Society, holding a bazaar which raised £45 to start off the fund for the society which he believed would act as a real power for good in the village. He also hoped to form a choral body. As a violinist, Tom led the orchestra whose members included an Alkins, Walkers and Wilsons. J.Shipley, a member of the Earl of Shrewsbury's Band at Alton Towers, played cornet solos. After their first concert in the Mills School, The *Staffordshire Sentinel* reported that: 'The pieces were all fairly well played' and that this orchestra was 'an organisation almost unique in village life'. By April, 1886, a third children's concert was produced. Thomas Bolton took part. At the end the Chairman, A.S.Bolton, gave 'a well deserved tribute of praise' to Mr Elam. Pointing out three classes of men – 'First those who fulfil the bare requirements of their employers, escaping all they can; second, a better class who fully do the need-be, but think it troublesome to go beyond; and third, those who throw their whole heart into the part they take up in life and have no limit to their endeavours but the limit of power', he congratulated the village on having a worker of the last description in command of its children, and earnestly urged upon all parents the recognition of the wear and tear of such labour, and their appreciative support of it as the teacher's best reward. I feel that this is a classic Victorian Vote of Thanks. The proceeds of George Elam's concerts went to pay for outings for the children. In July, 1886, about 65 elder scholars went to Rhyl, but think of the train journey!

That same month two assistant mistresses, Miss Fox and Miss McRae, were dismissed after a formal complaint to Mr Bolton on their inefficiency and unsatisfactory work. High standards were required. As far as some of the boys were concerned, high standards and good sense started at the trouser bottom and worked upbank! S.Whiston was caned for speaking in an improper manner to Burton the pupil teacher. The log book reveals that: 'I have laid the cane smartly across Wm.Salt's back for continued laziness and shirking of duty. The effect was magical, a couple of sums being afterwards worked in one tenth of the time usually occupied by him'. 'This morning I punished Jessie Leake for impertinent conduct'. 'Sent Fred Kent home this morning to clean his boots'. In a case of bullying in which a boy's ears were pulled until they bled profusely, 'I administered a well deserved correction which I trust will prove efficacious' to another boy. At bonfire time 'I have severely punished Hamlet Leake for throwing a firework into the fire during schooltime to the great danger of the children sitting near, when I had left the room'.

Early January, 1887, brought bad weather. 'This week has been so stormy', George Elam wrote, 'snow having fallen to a tremendous depth, attendance record utterly ruined. More than one third absent. How is it ever possible for a country school to produce results equal to a town school with such conditions as we are obliged to work under? When will "My Lords" make things more equal for us?' These were still the days of 'payment by results' and numbers on the register. Despite frustration, April brought the best Inspector's report so far. 'The discipline and tone of the school are very pleasing and the children are bright and clean and cheerful at their work. Percentage of passes high', wrote the Inspector. Numbers on the roll were increasing and the seed was sown for a new school. How would Alfred Bolton respond? Meanwhile, activities in the Mills School flourished. Oakamoor Cricket Club held a concert in which the Cheddleton Handbell Ringers and the Alton Jubilee Minstrels took part. Soloists included T.Bolton, E.Bolton and G.H.Elam. There was an amateur dramatic performance of 'Tom Cobb; or Fortune's Toy', a farcical comedy in three acts by W.S.Gilbert, put on in aid of the Oakamoor Coffee House fund. A series of fortnightly entertainments for the people during the winter months contributed to the same fund. A fourth school concert brought the year to an end in which a full grant had been paid. Mr and Mrs Bolton distributed illuminated certificates to the 62 children who had passed in every subject in the Inspection.

Severe winter weather was experienced in 1889, with no school till the middle of February. A month later there was still nine inches of slush lying around. This period escaped illnesses, but with ever increasing numbers and repeated appeals for enlarged premises, Mr Elam wrote: 'It is hopeless, with seven different standards in one room. I find the overcrowded state of the large room acting very severely upon my constitution. The strain lately has been very great, owing to the large first class containing over 40 children which is under my personal care and the increased difficulty of carrying out oral lessons in the numerous standards. Neuralgic headache has been my daily companion for nearly a fortnight, induced, I am convinced, by over pressure'. New children were being brought to the school, but the final straw came when 'On Monday I admitted a child who was seven last September, had been nowhere and knew nothing'. For George Elam, serious illness followed and the school had to close. In the new year George made an attempt to prepare for a concert, 'but was utterly prostrated by the effort'. He was obliged to go away from Oakamoor for the benefit of his health. The mumps came, and stuck; the school had to close again.

By May 1890, George Elam had returned in time for another inspection. The Mills School emerged as an excellent school in spite of the previous term's misfortunes. '98% passed the exam; 4 only failed, two from Alton, who have merely visited us, and as the days of miracles are past, it was impossible to teach them in their absence!' At the end of June Mrs Elam became seriously ill. A week later one of their children died. This was a dreadful year for our village schoolmaster and his family. 1891 started with a different kind of epidemic. We read, 'The third Standard seem to be troubled with an epidemic of bad language. Jas.Woodward has been the offender, having been guilty of using very obscene words indeed. As he is an all round bad lad I have followed out the instruction of the wise-man and have not spared the rod'. Furthermore, the atmosphere in the crowded rooms was 'better left undescribed' with 180 children on the books. Pressure again built up on the teachers with George Elam and his family going away to Leamington 'in the hope of finding better health than I have had lately, in fact I am at the end of the tether and nearly breaking down'. Staff illness, disease, and intense cold brought the year to an end.

George Elam spent eight years in Oakamoor. He gave conscientious service to the village, raising the standard of the school before seeing the children into the New Schools. On going

Teachers and pupils of the Mills School in 1889. At that time there were 180 children crammed into the school by the brook, prompting Alfred Bolton to start planning for the New Schools.

Bessie Parsons, the formidable Infants' Teacher, with her class of 1914. Bessie served our village for 31 years, a remarkable record. Sadly, she died 'in post'.

on to another school he received many gifts, but as a family man, George, like many Oakamoor families at the time, had known tragedy. He had buried a child, his wife had been ill and he, too, had become ill. In spite of difficult conditions at times, George Elam made a considerable impact on Oakamoor, entering wholeheartedly into village life, yet almost like Moses had led his people to the Promised Land. It was left to his successors to develop the New Schools.

At Christmas 1891 there was a massive party for the children of the Mills School. A note was kept of the provisions needed: '1 and a half lbs. Tea, sufficient only; 8lbs. Butter, Barely sufficient; 11lbs. Sugar, Sufficient; 8 gallons Milk, Too much; 6 plain loaves, 4 seed loaves, 4 currant loaves, Only sufficient; 7 plum loaves, Too many.' This list was for 180 children, wonderful for a party but now impossible as a school. What an enormous relief it was a few weeks later for the older children to be transferred into the New Schools. The Mills School was to carry on as the Infants' School, under a formidable mistress called Bessie Parsons. Bessie Parsons was born in 1863. By the time she left her previous post at Thrapston British School she was 28 years old. Once the older children had moved up the hill, 44 infants remained under her charge. One of the first things she did was to order two dozen wands for Drill. A few weeks later Mrs Bolton came to school and heard the children sing. Mrs Bolton must have been delighted with the progress made in the new Infants' School as she granted them a half day's holiday with a party at Moor Court.

The Infants must have had a wonderful time as further treats were recorded. A holiday was granted on account of the choir trip, one for the Sunday School Treat, two weeks in September for the Wakes, and a Christmas Party at the end of the year. In January, 1893, a harmonium was received at the school which made the 'Drill' lessons much more interesting. Then a stove, in place of one of the fires, was placed in the room. Practical cookery lessons for older children took place in the adjoining room, the old Wesleyan Chapel of 1860. By then there were 70 children in the school, 32 being under five. Harry Perrins aged 6 had been on the register for 9 months and had made only two attendances, as his parents said he was too delicate to attend school. Harry lived to a great age! Florrie Wilson, my great aunt, and Mary Alkins, both aged 14, commenced as monitors that year. Dairy classes must have been a nuisance as Miss Parsons complained about more churns taking up space in a crowded room. The school grew in numbers, possibly attributed to the fact that Bessie proclaimed that 'None was to go up to the New Schools, whatever their age, until attainments were reached'. A gallery was constructed to accommodate more children.

Childhood illness was still a scourge. Other members of my family were kept away from school because they were 'delicate'. Albert, Marion and Richard Wilson, my father, had missed lessons, as had children in the Alkins and McKnight families. Bessie Parsons understood, however, as she had shared the anguish of parents when they lost a child. Her red ink inserts in the admissions register remind us of this. One of September 15th 1899, states that 'F.Smith died yesterday of Diphtheria'. I then checked my family records for the last quarter of the nineteenth century, only to find that *nine* Wilsons died in childhood, five of them under three years old. My grandparents, along with other contemporary families, were terrified of losing another child to one of the killer diseases lurking around.

In Edwardian times the building was used by many societies in the evenings. The village brass band rehearsed there. On one occasion Miss Parsons complained that 'After last night's Nigger entertainment, the new desks were scratched and a cupboard chipped'. Inspectors continued to complain about the 'offices' and the stove pipe, yet 'The children were taught well'. Chicken pox and ringworm made an unwelcome appearance. In 1990 I received some memoirs from my aunt, Gwen Wilson, née McKnight, then aged 90. She was taught by Bessie Parsons and well remembered her washing drying round the stove fireguard! 'In 1906 the heating was by a large black stove which used to belch forth smoke and smuts. There was a three tiered platform at the road end. The children sat on long forms to long desks. We wrote on slates with squeaky slate pencils. I remember Tommy Whiston spit on his slate and clean it with his sleeve, but we were provided with little sponges. Most of the children had a handkerchief pinned on their dress or jersey. I spent very little time at school because of illness. I missed out over a year so missed valuable basics in arithmetic, but I remember two comical episodes. 'Bobby' Barrow arrived at the door with a very subdued little boy tucked under his arm. His mother was having difficulty in dragging a kicking screaming son to school, so P.C.Barrow simply picked him up and did the necessary. Another time, someone from the Works had to come to rescue Jimmy Tidmarsh who had stuck his head in the railings and couldn't get it out. The same Jimmy fell over the low wall into the brook and cut his head badly. First Aid was given in the Works surgery'.

The year 1907 came, with a February snow storm in which only 18 children managed to get to school. During one dinner hour Evelyn James, aged four, fell from the school wall into the brook. Life went on as normal, beating to the rhythm of annual social events and the seasons. November 21st 1907, brought an extraordinary event, when a holiday was given on account of the King's visit to Alton Towers. All the children were assembled and marched into Dimmingsdale, near the smelting mill, accompanied by most of the school managers and some friends. King Edward VII appeared from the Serpentine Drive, the National Anthem was sung, and three cheers given as the cars passed by. How wonderful for these children to see the King in those pre-television, pre-wireless days. My father described this exciting day to me on many occasions when I was young, of how he waved to the King, and of how the whole school was caught in a thunderstorm and sheltered under a rock until the rain ceased to fall.

As for the King, he had the Dowager Duchess of Londonderry with him, one of his 'fancy ladies', and apparently the Earl of Shrewsbury sent his Countess packing from Alton Towers on that occasion when the Royal Party came. The final years of the Edwardian Era followed the normal pattern of music competitions, special holidays, whooping cough, influenza, visits from school inspectors, severe snow, intense heat and staff away with the Infant teachers' plague, back ache! The one thing that caused most comment, however, was the smoking stove pipe. The school was often filled with smoke, when men were sent from the Works to attend to it. Children had to march in the yard until 9.25, waiting for the chimney to be swept. A Drill Inspectress was not amused and advocated 'plenty of romping games', presumably outside. It was not until 1915 that the offending stove pipe was removed.

No mention of the outbreak of the First World War was made to the children. Bessie took them to Farley Lane to watch haymakers at work. In May 1916 a parcel was sent to Wandsworth Infants' School. It contained bluebells, marsh marigolds, cuckoo flowers, forget-me-nots and daisies. The Infants then corresponded with this London School. In 1917 the children were taken for a short walk up the Star Road to watch the ploughing of the new Allotments field. The only mention of war activities was after the Armistice of 1918, when a holiday was given as the North Staffordshire Regiment had distinguished itself in battles. Bessie Parsons followed the natural flow of country life with the children of the Mills School during those war torn years, shielding them as much as possible from the turmoil beyond their understanding. By desire of King George V an extra week's holiday was granted in August, 1919, to celebrate 'Peace'.

After this, the long desks were thrown out and dual ones brought in; frog spawn was brought in; Leslie Bould fell in the brook whilst crossing the plank from the school yard to Mrs Pattinson's garden, in fact life's activities continued. On April 3rd 1922, it was recorded that 'Miss Parsons never turned up'. On July 3rd the dreadful news came of Miss Parson's death at Dewsbury. Bessie Parsons gave her soul to the children of Oakamoor, over 31 years of remarkable service. About 10 years ago I met Ivan Finney, who has since died. I said to Ivan, "You went to school in Oakamoor, didn't you?" His face broke into a happy smile. "Yes," he said, "I went to the school by the brook, and Miss Parsons, Oh, she was alright!" From a man of North Staffordshire, this was high praise indeed.

After the death of Bessie Parsons, Miss Gwen McKnight was Infants' teacher with eventual help from Miss Mary Warrington, student teacher. Miss Warrington commenced duties as a certificated assistant in October 1926. Mary had 40 in her class and she once told me that by the time she had finished blowing noses, wiping clean and drying up, she just managed to get in a bit of teaching where she could! By 1929 the winter temperatures were so low that the Infants were transferred to the New Schools for several months. The schoolroom was used in July by the school dentist who worked all day on extractions over a period of three days. The Mills School limped on into 1931, but the end came on September 1st 1932, when the Infants were finally transferred to the New Schools. On occasions the pupils came back to the old school. In 1950, when dry rot repairs were needed in the New Schools, the old Wesleyan Chapel was used with its open fire protected by a fire guard, with the Mills School being used for the 'Scholarship' examination.

In January 1959, when the top school heating apparatus failed, down the hill again went the pupils, little knowing that this was the last time Oakamoor children were to occupy the school by the brook. It was not the last time they had to move, however, as major structural alterations in the New Schools, in 1960, drove the children further back to their original roots. With Mr David Pyatt they were housed in some disused offices in the declining factory at the bottom of Mill Road, just a few yards from where Alfred Bolton started his original school. This particular generation of children who just happened to spend six months of their primary school lives in the old copper factory, perhaps knew better than anyone else what the 1871 generation of children experienced. The intensity of industrial noise would be less than the former, being perhaps more like echoes from the halcyon days of Oakamoor's involvement with the electrical telegraphy industry. The Mills School by the brook still survives and thrives as our Village Hall.

Oakamoor, c.1935, about three years after the Mills School closed. Either side of World War II the old school was used by the British Legion. It became the Oakamoor Village Hall in 1959.

9

The New Schools

On January 29th 1892, a despondent George Elam was still in the Mills School. He wrote 'Illness is still rampant throughout the village and there are still cases of scarlet fever'. In the memoirs of a scholar of the time, John Robert Goodwin wrote: 'I was born at Oakamoor in 1884 and began school at the age of 3 years in the little rooms near the bridge over the brook, which accommodated standards 1 to 7. I well remember forming up by the old school and marching up the drive for the opening of the new school which was designed in advance of its time with a stage at one end and a gallery at the other, and this led to choral, orchestral and amateur dramatic societies being formed with great success under the leadership of Mr.Tom Bolton, to be followed later by his son Mr.Michael Bolton'. The march up the drive took place on February 1st. A happy note records: 'This is a red letter day with the school for we have begun work in the new premises. There is a strange unearthly stillness about the place in comparison with the necessary noise which attended the work in the old school and everybody feels the improvement very much. The work of the school will certainly be carried on more comfortably'. From now on education was free. Within two weeks, however, bad weather and illness struck. Mr.Elam recorded 'If we have a continuation of this sort of weather, this log book seems likely to become little beyond a record of illness, bad weather and bad attendance. The school was never before in such a deplorable condition. Children who are at school are ill and many would be better in bed. The teachers are all out of sorts'. Meanwhile, down in the Infants' School, Miss Parsons had lost her voice! At this time there were 192 children on the books. Right from the opening the Societies were itching to use the new facilities. As early as February 25th a programme of music was presented; songs, violin and 'cello solos, duets and trios. Doors were opened at 7.30, with carriages at 10! By July the Dramatic Society got going with two plays; *Ticklish Times* and *Done on Both Sides*, the parts played by Tom and Frank Bolton and their friends. George Elam left Oakamoor at the end of the year.

J.J.Ireson came in the new year as a temporary teacher. He found that a whole week's work in school had been rendered almost impossible by 'workmen being abroad in connection with the Theatrical Entertainment'. He then recorded 'with sorrow that having had experience in schools in Lancashire, Yorkshire, Durham, Essex, Surrey, Denbighshire, Shropshire and several other counties I never met lads who were so generally insolent as these and who were so completely supported in their misconduct by their parents. Even the girls, a few, are inclined to be saucy'. Perhaps Mr Ireson had lost his touch? George F.Duncan was soon to follow and he found that 'behaviour is languid in the extreme and punctuality unknown'. Miss Jane M.Duncan, probably the Head's daughter, started at the same time. 1894 started with measles and influenza, but neither stopped six boys being absent 'on the plea of beating for Mr Bolton's shooters'. A pantomime and a dance took place in the spring and the children improved, only to lapse again after the summer holiday when Mr Duncan wrote 'The children feel that if they come to school, they have done their whole duty. There is a feeling amongst the parents too that the children are merely casks to have the educational liquor poured into them here'. To waken them up, Musical Drill was handed over to Sergeant Leake! Meanwhile, the Dramatic Society put on *The Private Secretary*, a three act farce. The cast included W.Coates, W.Alkins, J.Wilson and, of course, T.Bolton and F.Bolton. The Upward and Onward Association met, and the year ended with the School Concert, which included a choir of 80 voices conducted by George Duncan, readings by Mrs Bolton, and Magic Lantern Views of General Gordon. A.S.Bolton was the chairman.

Mid-January 1895 brought the hardest frost that Oakamoor had ever known. The winter was so severe that the Dam froze over. By late spring the Head's daughter became ill. I do not

The New Schools, built by Alfred Bolton, shortly after opening in 1892. Besides being one of the village schools, the building was used as a social centre for village societies, with its stage and orchestral pit at one end and a minstrels' gallery at the other. All pupils climbed the steps by the wall on the left when attending school; only the staff used the drive on the right. It is a great pity that the bell tower was removed in 1962. Apparently, it 'moved in the wind' but surely it should have been restored?

know what the illness was but, sadly, Jane Duncan died on August 16th. Her grave is outside the main door to the Memorial Church. George Duncan carried on and produced his next concert in November. It was a 'Service of Song' entitled 'Round Europe', with a choir of 70 voices. There were '45 Illustrative Magic Lantern Views' which accompanied the choir. Shortly afterwards a School Cricket and Football Team was formed with Oswald Tipper as captain. The Head felt 'It is hoped by organising children's games it will abolish roughness, to improve the children mentally, morally and physically'. In June 1896 a large number in the V, VI and VII Standards left as they were all over 14, or had obtained labour or attendance certificates as 'these children have been a drag to us; they began wrong and could not end well'. George Duncan left a month later.

On October 19th 1896, a formidable Master took over the New Schools. The log book recalls 'I, Charles James Pirrie, commenced duties this morning as Headmaster in this school'. He held a First Division Certificate. Little did people know what was to come. After several weeks of tightening up discipline he still found 'listlessness and a general want of energy' prevailing. He found the lighting was bad, believing that the electric lamps needed overhauling. Electricity was supplied by the works on the old 100 volt system, very advanced when most schools in the land were probably still lit by oil lamps or gas. The 'abominable condition of the boys' and girls' offices' were dealt with by 'a man sent from the Works'. The previous Head had started the 'Oakamoor Mills Evening Continuation School', but the French Class had dwindled to 7, 'partly on account of overtime but more on account of the band, which is playing almost every night, and to which many of the boys belong'. Charles Pirrie renamed this venture 'Oakamoor Mills Evening Classes' offering Commercial Arithmetic, specially designed to be serviceable to those engaged in the Works, Commercial Geography and Carpentry and Carving.

At a 'Social Evening' in 1898 there was a demonstration on X-Ray Photography, Chemical demonstrations, with 'the social character of the evening fully sustained by vocal and instrumental music and exhibitions of photographs'. One evening in 1899 there was 'inadequate light owing to neglect of duty by the man in charge of the dynamo in the Works'. By October 1901, it was decided 'to dispense with the Evening School on account of the poor response'. I assume that all the men would be tired out with their long hours in the Works and the women would be at home with large families. All other societies thrived, however, as a week after Mr Pirrie came to Oakamoor, the New Schools was the venue for the operetta *Snow White and the Seven Dwarfs*. A School Bank was formed, with children receiving interest of 1d. or more on every 1/- saved. On June 4th 1897, the school was closed for the Queen's Diamond Jubilee. An Inspector's report a few weeks later recorded 'Considerable improvement'. In August external air grates had been broken by boys throwing stones. Richard Alcock, Samuel Berrisford and Archie Goodwin were all punished with the cane. This was but a foretaste of what was to come. On August 23rd a new school for Roman Catholic children opened at Cotton, with 11 children being transferred. In May 1898, the Bishop of Lichfield accompanied by other clergymen visited the school shortly after the scholars had left. Not a bad time to visit! The autumn brought a heat wave.

Societies continued to use the New Schools. An 'Entertainment' was put on in aid of Oakamoor Good Templar Lodge. A group of ladies and gentlemen gave songs and recitations in a popular concert which ended in true Victorian style with a quartet singing 'Twilight now is round us'. Singers were Alice Leake, Dorothea Denman, Thomas Bolton and William Coates. There was a 'Grand Morning Concert' which included a piano trio and vocal items. A 'Variety Entertainment' was presented to aid in the purchase of an American Organ for the school. Part I was musical, in which Master Michael A.Bolton was one of the performers with a pianoforte solo by Mendelssohn, with Part II comprising a 'Comedietta in One Act' entitled *Petticoat Perfidy*. All these took place in 1897. November 1899 brought the death of Sergeant Leake 'after much suffering from cancer. The deceased Sergeant has for some eight years acted as Drill Instructor'. The century ended with a rendering of *The Messiah*.

The twentieth century began with one of the heaviest snowfalls for years. Many children had to miss school. In the spring two local policemen addressed the children, warning them against interfering with birds' nests and eggs. Mrs A.S.Bolton, Mrs Thomas Bolton and Miss Bolton visited the school to inspect the garments completed by the girls. They expressed great pleasure at 'the general excellence of the work'. A log book entry of May 23rd 1900, states 'We shall have a holiday tomorrow in honour of the double event of Her Majesty's Birthday and of the raising of the Siege of Mafeking'. The School under Charles Pirrie was fiercely patriotic. About the same time the Oakamoor Nigger Minstrel Troupe was very popular in the district. One concert in aid of Oakamoor Cricket Club started with a full chorus singing 'Scarlet and Blue', followed by a series of songs, some of which were 'The Water Melon Party', 'Servin' 'em all alike', and 'Hooligan's Mule'. The Minstrel Entertainment ended with 'A Nigger Sketch, entitled Mischievous Moses', in which Jack Wilson took the part of Mrs Fizzy! The Dramatic Society put on two Farcical Comedies, 'A Marriage Noose' and 'Meadow Sweet'. Between the two productions several humorous songs were performed, one of which was 'When Father laid the Carpet', sung by T.Barker. The year ended with a performance by the Orchestral and Choral society of Mendelssohn's *Elijah*. With four semi-professional soloists, an augmented orchestra of 18, and a large choir, all conducted by Mr Herbert Drury, this performance brought great acclaim. Trains left Oakamoor at 10.30 and 10.50, the former for Leek and the latter for Uttoxeter and intermediate stations. Could any village in England at that time beat this? The year ended in the day school with Prizes, with particular mention of Annie Alkins who had attended 8 years and 8 months, and William Alcock who attended 6 years and 6 months, without once being absent!

Programmes of Entertainment were a feature during the Edwardian Period. A concert in April, 1901, started with the orchestra performing 'The Lost Chord', continued with many

Songs and ended with 'The Fashionable Coon' sung by Mr C.Woodward. The Minstrels were to give many performances which generally included comic songs and sketches, bone solos by John Critchlow and ending with 'If the Missus want to go'. Another concert in aid of the Cricket and Football Clubs included 'I can't think ob nuthin' else but you Lu Lu', sung by Jack Wilson, as part of a programme of 25 items. Two concerts took place in February, 1903, 'In Aid of the Oakamoor Parish Church Repairs Fund, with items by the Band, the Orchestral Society and the Oakamoor Handbell Ringers. 1903 ended with a 'Concert devoted to the Choir Fund of the Free Church'. The conductor was Mr C.J.Pirrie, the accompanist Miss Madge Wilson. The performance of orchestral items and songs was so massive that a note at the bottom of the programme said 'Owing to the length, the Audience is requested not to demand encores'. Well, some amateurs never do know when to stop!

Down in the day school in 1901, Charles Pirrie was flexing the cane. He wrote 'Clarence Gordon was punished this morning for endeavouring to cheat, two strokes; as he was afterwards found to have been wasting his time he received several strokes of the cane over his shoulders. His sister went home...her mother came to school...she departed, making use of sundry threats as to the course she intended to pursue'. 'Over the shoulder' was a euphemism for thrashing the buttocks. On May Day, Miss Beatrice Bolton was married to Dr Peter Bearblock. A day's holiday was granted to the children with 'a treat on Bee-Low'. The Alcock Brothers from Ross Cottage were punished for playing truant. On December 2nd 1901, the death was announced of A.S.Bolton, JP After paying his respect, Charles Pirrie wrote 'While his death will be a calamity to the whole district, Teachers and scholars alike feel that they have lost a kind and generous friend'.

On June 2nd 1902, news reached Oakamoor that Peace had been declared in South Africa. Amid the general rejoicing the children were given a day's holiday, followed three weeks later by a whole week's holiday for the Coronation of their Majesties King Edward VII and Queen Alexandra. At the end of the year the beginnings of a school library were formed, with contributions from Mrs Bolton, £1, Rev.C.Denman, Mr S.Berrisford, and others. In 1903, under the new *Education Act*, Foundation Managers had to be appointed. They were T.Bolton, F.A.Bolton, F.A.Mills and W.Coates. In the summer, seven scholars left; 'one scholarship, several for work and one little fellow, Valentine Alcock, was unfortunately drowned in the Churnet during the holiday'.

At an October meeting the Managers agreed on the salaries for the teachers. They were: Mr C.J.Pirrie £185 p.a., Miss B.Parsons £75, Miss S.D.Beels, Miss C.F.Duncan and Miss G.A.Stanyer £50 each. The salary of the Caretaker/Stoker, G.Swinson, was £9 p.a., with the estimated cost of fuel, light and cleaning, including six new oil lamps, would be £30 for the winter six months. The letting of the 'large' school was 10/- per night, lights and piano not included, 20/- per night for outsiders, lights included but no piano. The use of the grand piano was 10/-. The fee for outsiders was 25/- if electric lights were used. An Inspector's report at the end of the year stated that 'slate work should be abolished; more work on paper is desirable both on educational and upon hygienic grounds'. There was a sting in the tail of 1903, however, as a twelve-week epidemic of mumps struck.

On the social side, 1904 came in with the 10th Annual Dance of the Oakamoor Tennis Club, held in the New Schools on January 8th. Under the patronage of Mrs T.Bolton of Light Oaks, dancing was from 8 to 3. Stewards were Dr Bearblock, Mr F.A.Bolton, Mr C.Weiss and Mr T.Bolton. Tickets were Ladies 1/6, Gentlemen 2/-. A few weeks later, Oakamoor Orchestral Society held their First Annual Ball. Florence Kerry's Programme reveals 22 dances, with partners' names written in. Many were the 'young bloods' of the day, but the name of her eventual husband, Samuel Walker, was yet to appear. Most people today would have no idea how to start with Polkas, Quadrilles, Lancers, Schottisches and the like! How sad. In the Day School, Charles Pirrie 'Admitted Harry Perrins of Greendale, aged 7, – never been to any school'. Later in the year Mr Pirrie was taken very ill, with the failing heating system aggravating his condition. In October a Violin Recital was given by Herr Schuller, upon

Left: Charles Pirrie with his staff of 1924. Standing, Miss G.Mc Knight, Miss M.James; seated, Miss K.J.Collier and Miss Ault. Miss Ault used to arrive by motorbike!

Below: The Class of 1906, with my father Richard Wilson in the striped blazer, sitting on the front row. The teacher may well be Miss Stanyer.

Mr. F. A. Bolton's Breshian Violin. Part II was given to a One Act play *Who is Who?* or *All in a Fog*, with the Bolton Family playing some of the parts.

The year 1905 turned out to be a dreadful one for Charles Pirrie. He wrote 'I have not been in school since the last entry, March 10th; this was on account of the sudden, serious illness of my dear wife, an illness which unfortunately terminated fatally'. The Pirrie grave is in the Memorial Church grounds. On May 24th 1906, Empire Day was celebrated; 'Attention drawn to the size, importance, etc., of the British Empire, and the responsibilities it entails. Patriotic Songs sung. Cheers for H.M. the King'. A Grand Concert of that time reveals the existence of the Oakamoor Male Voice Choir, a banjo soloist and many groups of vocalists. Mrs Chrissie Byatt, née Goodwin, told me that she was in the New Schools at that time. She thought that Mr Pirrie was a wonderful Head, but he always favoured foremen's children. 'One day, my brother Clarry, he had St. Vitus's Dance, couldn't do an essay for Mr. Pirrie as he had been away ill. He was told to go and wait in the porch but everyone knew that this meant the stick! My sister, realising the situation, asked to be excused. Mr Pirrie, without thinking, let her go. She ran home and fetched my mother, who went rushing up to the school. She flew into the room and grabbed Mr Pirrie by his beard. He then bustled her out, while the class sniggered, and locked the door on her, leaving her skirt and petticoat trapped in the door. He did not unlock the door till after school'.

So much went on in Oakamoor during those Edwardian Days that I can but reveal a flavour. In June, 1907, the Alfred Bolton Scholarship Fund was established, in his memory, the purpose being to give financial help to pupils of sufficient talent to be educated at a High School. By 1908 an examination had taken place and the Scholarship of £15 per annum was awarded to Eveline Wooliscroft who studied at Leek High School for three years. The Honours Boards are on display to this day in our village school, but were 'lost' in an attic for a number of years, being out of favour for political reasons, until a more enlightened management restored them for their historic value. The Mills Brass Band gave performances for the Pleasant Winter Evenings Association, whilst the school went on with its annual routine which included diphtheria, scarlet fever and measles. A P.W.E.A. Concert in April, 1908, consisted of mainly vocal items, 25 in all! J. B. Collier, the Band Master, sang 'Something in the bottle for the morning', Jack Wilson sang 'Swing me higher, Obadiah' and a young Master Albert Wilson sang 'Little Black Me'. In a contemporary newspaper report on another concert in the series, we read 'All these artists were well supported by the very able accompanying of Mr Gilbert Bolton: who appears to have a special gift in this direction'. While studying at the Royal Academy of Music, Gilbert composed a piece of music for violoncello and piano, dedicating it to his friend, 'cellist Albert Wilson. Gilbert lost his life in France in the First World War. A few years ago, my daughter Susanna, a professional 'cellist and Royal Academician, played this composition at a musical evening at Lightoaks, the house in which it was composed over 70 years earlier.

Early in 1909 a Cookery Class was started for 18 senior girls who spent each Friday in the old Wesleyan Chapel, under the charge of Miss Brooker of Uttoxeter. Three girls took part in an exhibition of the 'Calwich Abbey Amateur Art Society', where Fossie H. won a prize for needlework. In April, the Dove and Churnet Valley Musical Competitions took place at Denstone College. The School Choir was placed first in their class. On July 28th, Charles Pirrie was married to Miss Bell of Foxt. The teachers and scholars gave them a handsome present: meat and fish carvers.

When aged 90, my aunt Gwen Wilson, née McKnight, told me of her days as a pupil in the New Schools in the latter part of the Edwardian decade.

'Arithmetic lessons in Standard I seemed to consist of reciting tables, then having to get four sums worked correctly in pen and ink. They had to be correct or there was a thump on the back. Too many wrong and it meant a visit to Mr Pirrie's desk! These were nightmare lessons for the backward ones. Reading lessons were very boring because we all had to proceed at the same pace. We each read one paragraph out aloud. Recitation meant all the class chanting together with 'expression'. Geography lessons meant Miss Stanyer pointing to places on the large map while we recited the names. Miss Stanyer's hand pointer used to come down with a whack at wrong answers. I did learn all the headlands, bays, rivers and cities. I can still recite them all, for what good it ever did me. Drawing lessons were more boring than reading. Imagine spending a whole lesson drawing one small flower or leaf in pastels on a paper 6in by 4in. History was better because the large picture thrown over the easel could give imagination a chance. I often rode with Boadicea, cutting people down with the knives on my wheels.

When the whole school assembled for prayers and hymns, shoes were inspected. No hymn books were used, so the words used by younger children at first were rather strange. One memory is of my next in line singing 'hokey pokey fight' for 'put the foe to flight'. Standards II and III had lessons at the lower end of the big room. We sat together in dual desks. I learnt the number basics, and so arithmetic lessons no longer had me dreading every morning. Miss Stanyer used me to help some of the backward children. I stopped being bored in reading lessons; I had caught up by now. In Standard IV Miss Haynes was a very strict disciplinarian. Slaps and thumps on the back seemed a way of life for slow learners. The boys were now daring to be naughty. Three boys who earned the admiration of the milder girls were Herbert Swinson, Billy Stubbs from Moneystone, and our own Oaky hero Freddy Buttress. Miss Haynes pinned Freddy in the corner with a hooked map pole, after having suffered some nasty kicks. Someone fetched Mr Pirrie of course, who frightened us to death with his angry roar. Arithmetic lessons now consisted of working sums from cards. Wrong answers meant punishment, the worst one of course was being sent to Mr Pirrie. In Standards V, VI and VII Mr Pirrie gave us a thorough grounding in English grammar which stood me in good stead later on. If only Mr Pirrie hadn't shouted so much and had not been so handy with the cane I would have really enjoyed it'.

Sphor's *Last Judgement* was performed in April, 1910. On May 13th, there was 'National mourning on account of the lamented death of His Most Gracious Majesty King Edward VII'. Near the end of the year the 'Board of Education recognised that this school is suitable for 254 children'. In March, 1911, Harry Barker, the son of the Station Master, was drowned in the Churnet. His body was never found. A full week's holiday was given for the Coronation of George V and Queen Mary on June 22nd. The year ended with a performance of *Elijah*, this time conducted by Mr Michael Bolton. Evening classes had started again by 1912; by 1913 'The Offices were often dirty, caused by rats travelling up and down and conveying the filth on their feet'. The Dramatic Society presented *Are You A Mason?*, a farcical comedy in three acts. The year war broke out reveals 'war' for Mr Pirrie. In March, 1914, there was a law case, *Mrs.Howlett v. Mr.Pirrie*. Mrs Howlett won and was awarded 2 guineas. The log book reveals 'war' in the classroom. 'I approached him with the cane in my hand. He seized hold of the cane with both hands, and there was a struggle for its possession, during which he several times kicked at me. On getting the cane free, I gave him 3 or 4 strokes over the back. He then seized a hockey stick and threatened to hit me with it, using much impudence the while. This necessitated further punishment, and 3 or 4 additional strokes of the cane were administered. This had the effect of putting an end to his violent behaviour'. Pirrie v. Whom?! The boy was the 'Oaky hero' Fred Buttress, aged 12. War was declared on August 4th and by early September it was recorded: 'Wakes cancelled, owing to the European War. The Oakamoor Mills are excessively busy, and the holidays are not being observed by the workmen; no flower show or sports are being held'.

A few weeks later the older girls began knitting socks for men at the front. 12 pairs, 2 pairs of mittens and a cholera belt were dispatched. Three more consignments were sent within two months. Mr Pirrie entertained the children to tea in early December on the occasion of his daughter's wedding. The pattern of school life continued through 1915 until we read in early January the following year 'It is with deep regret that I record the death of Mr.T.Mills, corresponding manager since the foundation in 1871'. Thomas Mills was the son of Rev.John Mills, first Chaplain to the Works. By Empire Day 'The flag has been saluted, patriotic songs sung, lessons given on size and importance of the British Empire'. By the end of November the

Oakamoor and District War Savings Association had a fair number of children as members.

Moving forward to February, 1917, the children presented a pantomime *Babes in the Wood*. In the orchestral pit were 11 instrumentalists, 4 of them Wilsons! Close on 40 children were on stage, all conducted by M.A.Bolton. Proceeds were in aid of YMCA Huts for the welfare of the Men at the Front. Massive whist drives had been held in the school for years, like the one in aid of Oakamoor Photographic Society a few years earlier. One whist drive held in the Schools in November was in aid of the North Staffs. Infirmary. Two hundred and seventy-six people took part in raising over £40. The first social event of 1918 was a Presentation Evening for Charles Pirrie who had served Oakamoor for 21 years. F.A.Bolton, JP spoke words of appreciation, after which Mr Pirrie responded. He was presented with a 'purse' of £34. In May, RSPCA badges were sold in aid of attending horses wounded in the War. They were in the shape of butterflies, hence 'Butterfly Day'. The children took part in an autumn scheme for harvesting blackberries. Over a week, 8cwts. were dispatched by train to a jam factory. Armistice Day was soon to come.

In January 1919, Nurse Leigh of the Oakamoor Nursing Association 'examined the condition of the girls' heads. 8 unsatisfactory out of 37'. This was a nit hunt! An extra week's holiday was granted in the summer 'at the request of H.M. the King in recognition of Peace'. Again, by the request of the King, on November 11th 'two minutes silence was observed for the first anniversary of the Armistice. Two captured German rifles were allotted to the school as War Trophies'. When the 1920s came in people realised that it was good to be alive. It was the time of Art Deco, the YHA took off (in 1930) and the Jazz Era began. In response, Oakamoor struck up with a series of pantomimes that raged for several years. The first one, *Little Red Riding Hood*, was staged in February, 1920. It was written by Commr H.C.Anstey with M.A.Bolton as Musical Director. In the pit was the village orchestra with a cast of 24 on stage. Performances took place over a week, with an extended audience taking advantage of late trains on the 'Knotty' to journey home. Memories of these pantomimes kept a whole war generation alive well into old age. As a boy during the Second World War, I found it such a thrill to coax Harry Lucas, the pantomime dame, into mini repeat performances whilst waiting to be served in Sarah Weston's grocery shop. These pantomimes between the War and the Wall Street Crash, were remarkable.

May 1921 brought further experiments with British Summer Time. This did not suit the school as 'children are running about the lanes and fields at hours of the night when they ought to be abed and asleep; they are consequently listless and sleepy in school hours'. The Boy Scouts went camping under canvas. One, Cecil Goodwin, developed scarlet fever. In October, 8 senior boys, all Scouts, commenced a course of boot repairing. Early in 1923 a statement was made from the Parish Church pulpit that the Commandments were not taught. Mr Pirrie 'wrote to the Vicar that the children were expected to memorise them'. The Empire Day message from the King 'was delivered by gramophone'.

In late January, 1924, Mrs Rebecca Bolton died, aged 91. The children lined the drive to the Memorial Chapel for the funeral. On November 11th, the children attended a brief service at the newly erected War Memorial. One entry in the punishment book of the time was 'for waylaying a lady teacher after school and abusing her in the presence of a crowd of children and some adults', Albert Seaton received 'Six strokes on the hands and several over the shoulders'. The cane still reigned! At the end of September, 1925, Charles Pirrie retired after serving 29 years as Head of the village school. F.A.Bolton wrote to him expressing thanks and gratitude for his valuable service.

As for some memories: Mrs Nelly Reeve, née Wilson, aged 91, said: 'The first day in the Big School I was so frightened that I kept my coat on; I couldn't undo the top button. Mr.Pirrie would swish down with the cane. One day, obviously in a fit of frustration, Fred Buttress blurted out, "Don't like you Pirrie." Mr Pirrie picked him up by the coat collar, thrashed him with the cane and threw him across the room. He was cruel. I was so terrified that it made me cry. Still, he got them on'! Mrs Vida Cope, née Howlet, aged 93, said: 'Mr Pirrie frightened

Miss Jessie Collier with her Class, c.1928. Back; George Ryder, L.Cox, Charlie Walker, Roland Mellor, Doug Salt, Horace Dulson, Eric Alcock. Middle; Dolly Tipper, Tess Bradbury, Dorothy Lemm, Lilian Peake, Freda Waring, Winnie Roberts, Freda Roberts, Margaret Perrins, Kitty Mosley. Seated; Jack Bold, Edwin Wright, Violet Plant, Violet Cox, Margaret Hodgkinson, Sam Harvey, Jesse Leake. Front; Arthur Walker, Edwin Wright, George Forrester. I think some names might be a bit out!

Miss Mary Warrington with her Class of 1932, taken in front of the girls' porch. Back Row: Miss Warrington, D.Byatt, G.Warrington, B.Bottom, V.Ryder, L.Plant, E.Heath, A.Swinson,   ?, P.Burton, K.Fearns. Second Row: N.Plant, J.Jackson, D.Bryan, T.Pyatt, G.Plant, M.Gibson, J.Forrester, M.Forest, ?, S.Summers, B.Alkins, E.Forrester, J.Kent. Seated: ?, E.Wright, E.Mellor, M.Alcock, E.Dixon, B.Roberts, J.Parry, A.Alcock, B.Cope, J.Perrins,   ?, E.Leake, M.Ratcliffe. Front: D.Dulson, G.Kent, B.Ryder, B.Harvey, M.Warrington, D.Plant, J.Roberts, M.Goodwin.

the living daylights out of everybody; he used to clout people on the head and shout a lot. Could he shout! Every time, Polly Fearns used to faint'. Barbara Warrington, née Bottom, observed that: 'Freda Walker used to faint. I used to think, however did she manage it, lucky girl, as I could never manage it'! Bill Cope remembered: 'Old Pirrie went mad. He used to bang the blackboard with his fist and fly off the end with the chalk'! Albert Wilson said: 'He was mustard, lad'! Modern day psychologists, discuss.

The autumn of 1925 brought another musician to Oakamoor when organist and pianist Harry Edge became Headmaster. His 'breaking up' concert at Christmas included 'cinema entertainment' for the first time. The funds from this concert were used for the construction of a first wireless set, constructed with the assistance of the older boys. It was brought into use early in 1926 when 'at 3.15 the school listened to a wireless concert for schools'. The school was unable to take part in a Music Festival at Stafford because of a railway strike. There were 134 on the books. On October 1st Miss Mary Warrington commenced duties as Infants' Teacher. Children's pantomimes were produced, with the pupils on stage and the village orchestra of 17 in the pit, conducted by Harry Edge. The first one was *The Legend of the Water Lily*. With music still to the fore, an audience of 200 parents much appreciated a 'Music and Dancing Demonstration' in May 1927. In July, Oakamoor experienced one of its dreadful floods, with many children absent as they were unable to get down stairs. In January, 1928, the 'Old Pupils' Association' was formed.

An electric stove was installed to provide pupils with a hot drink, but a 'violent stench in the girls' porch' was caused by a dead rat. By December, 'H.A.Chester should have started as assistant but for some reason he has not arrived'. Herbert, local historian, had the flu. 1929 began with a dance in aid of old boy W.H.Kerry who had suffered great financial loss in a disastrous garage fire. All were sorry when Harry Edge left.

The next man to come, Eric Russell Raby, lasted but a few months. He claimed he could play the organ at the Memorial Church, and couldn't, he embezzled Hebert Chester's salary and was found to be a bigamist. After a visit from the Deputy Director of Education, F.A.Bolton gave him the sack! Late in 1930, Fred J.Dale commenced his duties. In the 1931 Stafford Music Festival, Oakamoor came 1st for singing and 2nd for country dancing. At the end of July all the senior children left as they were transferred to Cheadle Senior School. The school said goodbye with great regret. The Oakamoor Floral and Horticultural Society held their Annual Show, with Elsie Bradbury as Rose Queen. In September, the school became a Junior Mixed and Infants School, with 101 on the roll. In the 1932 Stafford Music Festival, Oakamoor gained three 1sts and two 2nds, as a result of Miss Collier's efforts. A year later they gained two 1sts. and three 2nds. Herbert Howells was the adjudicator. At the end of 1934 school milk was first supplied under a Government scheme. Fred J.Dale left in 1935, to be followed by Mr W.L.Brown. Mr Brown continued with the County Music Festivals, the school plays, the open days and the normal yearly routine. This was punctuated with the death of George V and the Coronation of George VI leading up to the Second World War. In September, 1938, 'Dr.Wilson visited the school to lecture the children on Gas Masks. The Air Wardens visited the school and gave the children their gas masks. Nurse Gray now inspecting the children'.

The log book entry of September 12th 1939, said 'WAR'. Leslie Brown was made Billeting Officer for Oakamoor. He wrote 'Lateness of opening due to outbreak of War. As Billeting Officer I have billeted 84 mothers and children in the village. 11 Manchester children commenced, 7 Germans and 1 Czech, one girl from Salford, one from Lichfield, one from Middlesbrough, and 4 Oakamoor children.' I was one! We had a Manchester family staying with us in Stonydale; their teapot was brown. One boy was frightened to death down the Dale as he had seen a cow peering through a gate and he dare not pass. He had never seen a cow before; he did not know what it was. That same boy tried to walk across a weed covered pond, again not knowing there was water underneath. To cope with the crisis at school, Mrs Williams, a new Infants Teacher, commenced her duties. I remember her as being very kind.

More evacuees came. Eight Czech refugees attended school in the mornings only. At a school whist drive held in the Works Canteen, refugees attended, including one Czech teacher. Spirits had to be kept up at all costs. At the beginning of 1940 Mrs Williams returned to Manchester and pupil teacher Miss Daphne Swinson took her place. In April Mr J.Dawson, my uncle, came to inspect our gas masks. I remember Gas Mask Drill. Edna Goldstraw, who had rather a small head, had to have a 'Mickey Mouse' gas mask, a red one with a face like a mouse. When it was forced onto Edna's head, she used to roar and roar inside the mask, and all we naughty boys could see was a streaming red face within! My gas mask was a black one in a rectangular cardboard box which I had to carry everywhere I went. One of the first morale boosters for the war effort was in late April when an 'Olde English Fayre' was held to raise money for the purchase of an Ambulance for the Forces. £500 was needed. There were eight 'Olde Shoppes' in the main hall of the school, with a 'Chamber of Horrors' under the stage prepared by my cousin Mary Dawson. The opening ceremony was performed by Col G.McAlister; the chairman was Dr P.Bearblock. An orchestra played selections during the afternoon, with the day rounded off with a whist drive and dance. The ambulance was duly bought. On May 10th 1940, the news was serious. Many parents were quaking at the thought that Hitler would invade.

By Empire Day, 'The Marseillese and National Anthems were sung together with suitable hymns. A collection was taken for the Overseas League Forces Tobacco Fund, the magnificent sum of £1-8-0 being forwarded'. We were all encouraged to save and the response was excellent. I took 2/6 a week. An air raid shelter was built near to the school gate, roughly where

Exhibition of furniture and wood carving from my father Richard Wilson's Evening Institute Class of 1933. He was the only apprentice that wood-carver Marcus A.Cope of Leek had, prior to the outbreak of the First World War, which sent my father back to the Oakamoor Works. The style is 'Neo-Jaco'.

Country Dancers, 1933, who won a second certificate in the County Music Festival. Back; Ethel Dulson, Hilda Swinson, Phyllis Swinson, Dolly Tipper, Ethel Jordan. Front; Marjorie Perrins, Daphne Swinson, Ethel Dickson, Thora Pyatt.

School, 1936. Back; Miss Warrington, Clive Inskip, Roy Wright, Roy Plant, Brian Ryder, ? Norman Weston, Kenneth Bond, Lawrence Jordan, Gilbert Johnson, David Wilson, Allan Butress, Mr Brown. Next; Margaret Parry, Sheila Hamilton, Joyce Brough, Mary Clowes, Laurie Cope, Betty Hamilton, Gwendy Whitehead, Rosemary Unsworth, Jeanette Perrins, Norian Dunsden, Emma Alcock, Florence Bettany, Eileen Edge, Barbara Walker. Middle three; Margaret Hathaway, Sheila Critchlow, Joan Swinson. Kneeling; Leslie Kerry, Betty Perrins, Agnes Johnson, Marion Swinson, Flora Miller, Nada Bottom, Mona Burnett, Carol Wilson. Front; Dennis Ratcliffe, Fred Organ, Sydney Goldstraw, Wilfred Wright, Harold Cartledge, Lawrence Goldstraw.

the top bungalow now stands. We had practices, but when real scares came, as 'Gerry' was looking for our copper factory, the whooping warning wail of the Works siren sent us flying into the shelter. Miss Warrington acted as 'spotter'. We had a hurricane lamp at each end and we all sat down each side on rafter seats while 'Pa' Brown took a lesson. I remember the excitement, the smell of earth and concrete, and the anticipation of what might happen next. I used to think Miss Warrington was ever so brave when she went outside to see if it was 'all clear'. When the continuous steady sound of the siren eventually came, I must confess that a feeling of anti-climax set in as we all trouped back into school!

War Weapons Week came in 1941 when the school raised £301.10.9, regarded as a wonderful record. Later in the year a collection for the Staffordshire Blind Association raised £1.8.7, with Savings Certificates amounting to £1,005.15.0. 'Splendid'. 'Pa' Brown encouraged thrift. 1942 brought Warship Week in which £618.0.0 was raised, more than double that of the previous year, while Empire Day brought in £2.17.0 for the Tobacco Fund. In October a Harvest Festival was held at which Mr.Brown emphasised how much we owed to God. £4.8.0 was raised from a sale of produce for the Merchant Navy War Fund. An annual collection for the Blind raised £2.10.0. Our school won the Salvage Shield for the area, with the average weight of paper per child being 46.7lbs. I remember salvage collecting as good fun. The secret was to salvage as many heavy books as possible, Dr Bearblock's was a good source for me as many old medical text books landed my way, so that all could be weighed before being thrown into an enormous salvage bag in the Boys' porch. Salvage bags had a smell of their own! Many iron railings were removed in the district for melting down for the War effort. An Evening School Social raised money so that 10/- could be sent to every former student who had joined His Majesty's Forces. At the Christmas party, each child received a half crown [2s 6d, or 12 $^{1}/_{2}$p] War Savings Stamp.

Throughout the War 'Dig for Victory' posters loomed large. In February 1943 'Pa' Brown

Olde English Fayre, April 27th 1940. This was the first morale booster of the War years, with 8 Olde stalls, many other attractions, a whist drive and a dance in the evening, which raised money towards the purchase of an Ambulance for the Forces. The ambulance was provided.

The Princess and the Enchanter, performed for the Open Day in 1945. The Enchanter was Peter Wilson, the beard was heavy, and the Princess was Emily Barks. We were surrounded by all our friends. It was magic! Leavers returned for a repeat performance in October. This is the only photo I have of my schooldays as few were taken during the War.

ordered 5 spades, 5 digging forks, 4 rakes and 4 hand trowels, to be quickly followed by a wheelbarrow. The garden in front of the school flourished. I used to enjoy gardening lessons, apart from the weeding. Wings for Victory followed with a huge sum raised, the amount not specified. In the autumn we were all measured for the forthcoming issue of Clothing Coupons. In a Book Drive we collected 6,505 books, coming second in the Salvage Drive. 1944 brought Salute the Soldier Week, during which £1,219 was raised. On November 27th that year, England's largest ever explosion, the Fauld Explosion, killed many people when 4,000 tons of bombs went up. Such was the shock wave that travelled some 20 miles that it broke a window next to where I was sitting in the school. At the end of the year W.L.Brown gave in his notice. 'Pa'Brown made a considerable impact on Oakamoor during his ten years at the school, particularly during the War years when his conscientious and outstanding teaching was not hindered by the many other duties that fell upon him. I learnt many things from Mr Brown as, besides the necessary basics, he stimulated the 'mind's eye' in music, poetry and good literature, with many stories about our national heritage. The cane whizzed on occasions, but all deserved it. Although it was wartime, I feel that he gave us a fine education. It was a privilege to represent Oakamoor at 'Pa' Brown's funeral in Tamworth in the early 1980s.

Mr W.L.Brown was followed by Mr David S.Pyatt in January, 1945. The War was still on and Sergeant Massey of Uttoxeter Police gave a lecture on 'Dangerous Objects to be found on the Ground'. We were shown many exhibits, including bombs and detonators, but I must confess that I had seen such ammunition before, dead blanks as used at the O.C.T.U. at Alton Towers and by our local Home Guard. £1.10.8 was collected for the British United Aid to China Fund. We had a day's holiday on May 8th to celebrate VE Day. I left Oakamoor School in the summer of 1945 with happy memories of school days, open days, plays, conker fights and whip and top in which I could whip my 'flyer' all the way home to Stonydale. Whoever plays whip and top today? Continuing in the school, it was not until October 1946 that the managers held their first meeting since March, 1939, with Mr F.A.Bolton in the chair. Shortly afterwards the air raid shelter was demolished. 1947 brought the worst winter ever, still unsurpassed for its severity and longevity. The school, still collecting salvage, came first in 1948. At the Open Day in 1949 it was claimed that Oakamoor could have a new school within five years, as dry rot had been discovered in the New Schools. The dry rot was eradicated and the school survived.

For the next 50 years of the story I will but dip into notable events, some of which include my family. Mr Frank Bolton died at Moor Court, bringing to an end the Bolton Family connection with the Oakamoor Schools first established by the founding of the Mills School in 1871. By the end of 1952 the Education Committee negotiated the purchase of the New Schools from Mr Frank's executors. To mark the Coronation of Queen Elizabeth II the Oakamoor Community Council purchased the Broadwood Grand Piano from the executors of F.A.B. for £20. This 'grand old lady' had been on the premises since the school was built, being used on many musical occasions and knocked about during Wartime dances. My father mended it on many occasions. By 1957, my father retired from the teaching of woodcarving and cabinet making at Oakamoor Evening Institute, after 30 year's service. I followed in his footsteps. When major structural alterations started in the school in 1960, the Oakamoor Choral Society's music, which had been stored in the Band Room for many years, was taken away by my uncle, Albert Wilson. The banners of the Oakamoor Branch of the Oddfellows were also removed, never to be seen again. Mr Pyatt retired in 1967. When I interviewed him 23 years later he reminisced. 'During the War years teachers were moved around to fill vacancies. When Oakamoor came vacant it was not advertised. I was approached by the Deputy Director of Education to see if I was interested in the Oakamoor post. At that time I was teaching Art and Gardening at the McKenzie School in Cheadle. I was told that Mr Frank Bolton was looking for somebody for the post who would also be secretary to the cricket team, play the organ at the Memorial Church on occasions and that sort of thing, all of which I was willing to do. As with all appointments during wartime, it was temporary, with the understanding that at the end of the War all teachers would re-apply for different jobs. I was never asked, nor was I given a permanent post. I must have been temporary for 22 years! At the end of each month, Mr Jack Alkins always came round and paid me in cash'.

In the summer of 1968 Miss Mary Warrington retired as Infants' Teacher after 42 years. Mary had attended the school as a pupil until 1919, she returned for a year as a student teacher, and after qualifying, came back as a member of staff. Miss Warrington taught me, she also taught my children during her long years of service. She once told me 'By the time I had finished blowing noses, wiping clean, drying up, I just managed to get in a bit of teaching where I could'! This was indeed a unique record. Many old pupils gladly donated towards her retirement gifts. In the 1970s Oakamoor School still kept up its musical traditions, encouraged, I have to say, by my musician wife Ruth who taught at the school. She had string and wind players who reached such high standards that the County Music Advisors made frequent visits to hear progress. John Taylor, County Inspector of Music, referred to Oakamoor as 'The Jewel in his Crown'. From this era, my daughter Rebecca, a violinist, who became a member of the National Youth Orchestra of Great Britain at the age of 15, went on to study music at the University of Birmingham, my second daughter Susanna, a 'cellist, went on to study with Florence Hooton at the Royal Academy of Music, and Sarah Whittingham, a violinist, went on via Chetham's to the Royal Northern College. While at Oakamoor, Susanna and Sarah each gained an Associated Board Gold Medal for gaining the highest marks in the country, a remarkable feat by two girls from the same village school. Together with my cousin Mary Dawson who studied at the Royal College in London after the War, and all the previous musical successes gained in the 20s and 30s, including old boy Christopher Dearnley who became organist at St Paul's Cathedral, London, I feel I can claim that Oakamoor has an outstanding musical heritage. I must add, however, that many old scholars have gone on to higher education with distinction in many other fields.

At present the Valley School has 46 children on the books. With Mrs Valerie Slater in charge, and ex-pupil Mrs Celia Bevan, née Hysel, on the staff, the whole team has just received an excellent OFSTED report. Every time I see the children, which is often, it is apparent that they are so happy in Oakamoor. Long Live the Village School.

The Retirement of Miss Mary Warrington in July 1968, after 42 years conscientious teaching in Oakamoor. Generations of children owed a lot to Miss Warrington who gave them a thorough start to their education. There was one senior school teacher who could pick out most of the Oakamoor children when a new class appeared before him. He said, 'Miss Warrington, you know, Miss Warrington'.

Mr Peter Fisher with the Class of 1972. Standing; Marie Warrington, Karen Dotzauer, Brian Brass, Mary Adamson, Nicola Burton, Mary Tipper, Ellen Mycock, Tracey Jackson, Rebecca Wilson, Gary Charlesworth, Stephen Payn, David Hollins, Norman Mycock, Anne Redfearn, Adrian Critchlow, Stephen Sutton. Kneeling; Stephen Critchlow, Douglas Charlesworth, David Arundel, Kevin Kent.

School, 1974. Staff: Berys Whittingham, Flo Barrow, Visiting teacher, Dorothy Ratcliffe, Peter Fisher, Ruth Wilson. My daughter Susanna has long blonde hair.

10

Cricket

Cricket has been played in Oakamoor for at least 140 years. On July 21st 1866, an established Oakamoor Cricket team entertained Leek on the ground by the river. The team in those days consisted of local gentry, clerics from Cotton College, but with most members coming from the village. Oakamoor lost this encounter, with Leek scoring 64 and 50 in their two innings, with our home team scoring 40 and 55 for nine. Oakamoor's Rev.C.Ward bowled very effectively, securing 13 wickets in the two innings, with Mr Bill of Farley Hall scoring 23. Some matches were actually played before breakfast, wickets being pitched as early as 6a.m! In the return match up the valley, Leek won in one innings. We made 20 and 53; Leek 76. In Oakamoor's score of 20, there were 8 wides! Ah well, Leek was a big place. In Jack Wilson's 'Reminiscences of Oakamoor Cricket', published in the Sentinel in September, 1935, he comments on the conditions of the sports field in the 1880s 'when it had a very rough outfield, rushes and swamps, and you could easily lose the ball yards off the pitch. Mr S.Mellor, sen., was then the landlord and we were only allowed to mow 40 x 40 yards. Cattle and sheep grazed on the rest of the field and various fences were erected without success and occasionally whites had to go through the wash tub before the next match. The team had to travel to the outlying villages in a grocer's trap, the horse of course had blinkers on; later when brakes were to be had travelling was much more comfortable. Although we had to push up bank and put the slipper on when going down, the journeys were always enjoyed as we were not particular about what time the return journey was made'. Over the decades Oakamoor travelled by the Churnet Valley Railway to play at such places as Leek and Ashcombe Park. The Jubilee Year of 1887 brought Oakamoor a victory over Ashcombe Park, when Oakamoor scored 83, James Walker 30, before getting the home team out for 64. 1890 saw the formation of the North Staffordshire League. On June 28th in the second round of the Junior Cup, Oakamoor, at Hednesford, beat West Cannock Colliery Team 170 for 4 to 55. J.Whitehurst was 85 not out and F.Bottom scored 70. The journey to Hednesford involved a 6a.m. start in Frank Tipper's three horse brake, with home cured ham sandwiches and beer. After a stop for fresh horses at Rugeley, the team arrived in time to record the victory. The team celebrated for so long that they did not arrive back in Oakamoor until 6am on the Sunday!

By 1897 the Churnet Valley League had been formed. That year the team travelled to Highfield at Leek to score 113, F.Buttress 37, with Highfield scoring 72 for 6. Oakamoor now had a second team which attempted to take on Rocester. The team down the valley scored 229 for 9, with Oakamoor being all out for 26. Nevertheless, they had made a start, and by 1899, the seconds were runners up in the Leek and District League. First team run scorers were emerging at this time, such as Sam Walker, Jack Wilson, W.F.James, G.E.Bennett, J.R.Goodwin and the Rabone Brothers. The 1906 season opened with no cricket in the district owing to snow, hail and rain, yet a few weeks later Leek II team 'received a severe slating' at Oakamoor when we scored 252 for 9, after which our star bowlers H.F.Rabone and G.E.Bennett dismissed them for 42, Rabone 6 for 17, Bennett 4 for 20. This year of 1906 saw the great Sydney Barnes play for Porthill in the North Staffs. League. In a match at Leek he scored 76 not out and took all 10 wickets. Barnes once gave a young boasting batsman a sealed envelope. On opening, the instructions said, "The first ball will be a leg break, the second an off break, the third will take your wicket." It happened!

In 1903 Oakamoor Cricket Club won the Churnet Valley League Cup. This was then their greatest achievement which was celebrated at the Annual Dinner in the New Schools on October 17th. A surviving programme from that day reveals a string of Toasts, from the Royal Toast; the President's Toast, Thomas Bolton, and ten Vice-presidents; and, after formal

Oakamoor Cricket Club, 1888. The earliest known photograph. Standing; Goodwin, Arthur Johnson, Harrison, Roland Mellor, Will Walker, Father Hamlin, Clem Tipper, Arthur Swinson. Sitting; Nean Tipper, Fred Bottom, Cain Mycock, Jack Wilson, Tom Buttress.

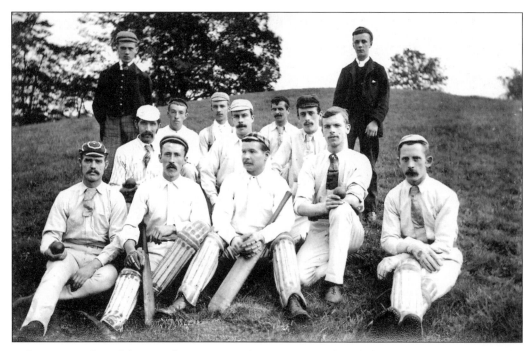

Oakamoor Cricket Club First Eleven, 1892. Their captain, Jack Wilson, is seated centre. The Club secretary, Jack Alkins, is standing on the right. This team played in the recently formed North Staffordshire League.

speeches, a Toast to the Chairman H.R.Brunt. Charlie Rabone won the batting prize, with his brother 'H.F' winning the bowling prize. Umpire Swinson was presented with a pipe, in recognition of his services, by Sam Walker. Churnet Valley League teams at that time were Ashcombe Park, Caverswall, Cheadle, Cheadle Albion, Cheddleton, Denstone, Leek 2nd, Leek Highfield 2nd, Rocester, Tean, Uttoxeter and Westwood, eight of which were approached by railway. From the 122 matches played against this opposition over the first seven years of the League's existence, Oakamoor won 67, lost 29, and drew 26. Some notes were kept on the 1903 season. 'The Club scored 2,211 runs, with the highest score being 178 for 9 against Leek 2nds. Rev.Fr.de Capitaine was the highest scorer with 77 not out. He also drove a ball across the Churnet, a splendid feat, only once before accomplished and that was over 20 years ago. C.H.Rabone and S.Walker hit the ball clean into the Churnet, remarkably good hits. Rabone against Westwood, bowled 2 men with 2 consecutive balls and the following ball hit the stumps without removing the bails. H.F.Rabone's best bowling performance was 7 for 8 runs against Leek Westwood. We had the advantage of being coached by J.Walker, who still holds the record of taking 8 wickets with 8 consecutive balls, 5 being clean bowled, 2 caught and 1 L.B.W. This happened when he played for Ashcombe Park against Tunstall in 1882.' These were wonderful days for Oakamoor Cricket Club, as a verse of a poem reveals: 'Here's a health to our eleven, Let us in their triumph share, They have brought the cup to Oakey, And they mean to keep it there'.

The end of the Edwardian Era brought three of the finest seasons that the Club has ever known. A major trophy, fought for at the time by all the best clubs in North Staffordshire, was the Sentinel Cup. The Oakamoor team, captained by Michael Bolton, entered this fiercely contested competition in 1910. Our team crept nearer and nearer towards their aim of reaching the Final. The Final was played at the old County ground in Stoke, which is no more. The scorecard from the 1910 Sentinel Cup Final reveals that Oakamoor got off to a disastrous start with their first five batsmen scoring but 23 runs between them. Sam Walker, fine batsman as

Oakamoor Cricket Club, Champions 1903 in the Churnet Valley League. Standing; Will Swinson, M.Brunt, Will James, Will Alkins, M.Swinson, Jack Alkins. Seated; George Lemm, Sam Walker, Jack Wilson, captain, H.F.Rabone, Jim Alcock. Front; Fred Buttress, Charlie Rabone. This team won the cup in 1901 and were runners up in 1902.

A Club photo of 1903. Standing; A.Swinson, Rev.Fr.De Capitaine, J.Salt, G.Lemm, Rev.Fr.Emery, H.F.Rabone, F.Buttress, J.Alkins. Front; W.James, S.Walker, J.Wilson, W.Emery, C.H.Rabone.

Churnet Valley League Champions yet again, c.1908. Seated centre with the cup is a young Michael Bolton recently down from Cambridge, where he had excelled in both cricket and hockey. Behind is the 'Knotty' railway carriage which served as a pavilion for many years. In the background can be seen goods wagons on the Churnet Valley line.

he was, scored only 5 runs in this final. Then Frank Walker, 23, G.Bennett, 25 and G.Swinson not out 31 were anchored down by century maker Tom Smith, before a tail end collapse drew the innings to a close at 250. Four members had scored virtually all the runs, apart from 38 attributed to 'extras'. The opponents Bignall End were a formidable team possessing many fine cricketers, including A.W.Ikin, father of Jack Ikin, the Staffordshire, Lancashire and England batsman. The Oakamoor bowlers W.Collier and F.Walker took most of the wickets, causing a complete rout of their opposition. Fast bowler Will Collier and very slow bowler Frank Walker picked out each batsman for what must have been one of Bignall End's worst scores; 66 all out. Only two batsmen reached double figures, A.W.Ikin, 11 and A Lockett 24. There were no extras. Well done Oakey! In 1911, after beating Tean and Cheadle, the team played Silverdale in the semi-final and won, Jack Johnson making 60. The Final, again, was against Bignall End. Oakamoor made 255, T.Smith 72, J.Johnson 52 and W.James 48 not out. Bignall End made 76, W.Collier taking 8 for 43. What of 1912? In the first round we beat Stoke at Oakamoor. In the second round we played Leek Highfield five times before a result was accomplished. Progressing further our village team yet again reached the Final in which their opponents were Audley. This couldn't have been much of a game as Audley batted first and scored only 68 runs 'in an innings of very slow and tedious batting'. J.J.Awty and J.R.Goodwin marched to the crease to knock off the runs very quickly without loss, Awty, 53 and John Robert, 15. This meant that Oakamoor had won the Sentinel Cup outright. Its resting place became the Coffee Tavern in Oakamoor, where many villagers viewed this fine 'Sixty Guinea Cup' over the years. In October, 1912, The *Weekly Sentinel* reported Oakamoor Cricket Club's 'Brilliant Season Commemorated at the Annual Supper'. The supper took place in the Infants' School at the end of the most successful season in the history of the Club, in which they had won both the League and the Sentinel Cup. 'Mrs Prince of the Lord Nelson Hotel provided an excellent menu'. The report went on to say that 'Mr T.Smith had had an invitation to play for the county, and in Mr Bolton they had in him a gentleman who was keen on the game, played it in a sporting way, and was the right man for the position. Mr Bolton, on rising to respond, met with a rousing reception'. After many Toasts and compliments the players were awarded gold medals by the Sentinel and also the Churnet Valley medals. 'The evening was spent convivially, songs being given by H.F.Rabone, R.Alcock, C.A.Nichols, S.Walker, W.H.Cope, and others'. Oakamoor's two teams lost only two matches out of 50 during that season of 1912. Jack Wilson reported that 'The Oakamoor ground is motor mown all over and the whole sports ground is quite attractive with its Bowling Green, Tennis Courts, Swimming and Clock Golf. For the above we have to thank Mr M.A.Bolton, also the firm of Messrs T.Bolton and Son'. Halcyon days indeed for the Oakamoor Cricket Club.

When we read of the 'long Edwardian summers' it is easy to realise why cricket was one of the most popular games. An Edwardian Pavilion was built at a cost of £97, and was declared open on August 1st 1910. Everyone seemed to play cricket in those days. One quite eccentric match was between Wootton Hall and Oakamoor Fishing Club. The Honourable Mrs Bourke lived at Wootton Hall and it was from there that a cricket team emerged, to score 48 against Oakamoor's Fishers, with E.Towers scoring 25. Then the Oakamoor men marched to the crease. The scoreline revealed the ignominy of that match. It read: W.Burton, 0, C.Goodwin, 0, C.Childs, 0, T.Mellor, captain, 1, J.Perrins, 0, G.Childs, 4, J.Collier, 1, F.Kerry, 1, A.Wilson, 0, J.Brett, 1, and P.Childs not out 2; total 10. What a performance! My uncle, Albert Wilson, was a fine musician, but he was hopeless at cricket. 'Theyst er bin better stickin ter thi cheller lad!' As for the village first team, they were champions of the Churnet Valley League several times, the last success being in 1914, but when cricket resumed again in 1920 the Churnet Valley League was defunct. A War veteran, Bernard Jordan, became groundsman for the sports field. He was still suffering physically in 1921, as a 'Grand Distribution of Prizes', a draw, took place 'In aid of B.Jordan who is still suffering from wounds received during the war'. I remember Bernard riding on a Dennis mowing machine, along with another injured veteran, Lawrence Hassall, in the 1940s. Oakamoor Cricket Club ran two teams right up to the

Group of cricket supporters gathered for the opening of the Edwardian Cricket Pavilion on August 1st 1910. Three generations of my family can be seen on this photograph. My father Richard is the boy in the cap peering from behind a taller boy at the front. One side is Marion Wilson, the other side is Albert Wilson. Directly behind his children is my grandfather Richard, wearing the hat with a wavy brim. At this time he was foreman wire drawer in the factory. Two places to the right, with the white beard, is my great grandfather Caleb who in his turn was foreman wire drawer.

Frank Walker and Jim Alcock descending the steps of the new pavilion to open the innings in a Sentinel cup match, c.1911.

The Sentinel Challenge Cup won by Oakamoor for the first time on September 19th 1910. Tom Smith of Whiston Eaves played a magnificent innings of 106 in this match. This 'Sixty Guinea Cup' in silver was won outright by Oakamoor in 1912, after being Champions for three consecutive years.

outbreak of World War II, participating in the Blythe Bridge League. After the War the Club emerged as Boltons, participating in the North Staffordshire League. I started playing in 1949, at the age of 15, at a time when many villagers were unable to get a game in what was by then the factory club. True, T.B.and S. maintained the ground to a high standard, with Bernard Pyatt and later Arthur Finney as groundsmen, but it was a great pity that more Oakamoor youths were unable to play at that time. A new man by the name of Mr Gilmore upset many of the old members by first removing the Stonydale footbridge over the Churnet, causing several cricketing families, one with a disabled son, to have to walk the long way round by the railway bridge to watch a match. The original Victorian bridge fell into decay, after which the new one had but a short life. This would never have happened in Mr Michael's day when village and firm were one. One old member from Stonydale was Jack Alkins who had been a member of the club since late Victorian times, eventually serving as secretary for decades. Jack was by this time the only surviving trustee of the Sentinel Cup which was resting in the clubroom at the Coffee Tavern, almost forgotten in those post war days. He took the decision to present our cup to the North Staffs. League, and it is now the League Championship Trophy. This extremely valuable cup is now 'alive', but above all it remains in the heart of Oakamoor's cricketers. National Service and college took me away from Oakamoor in the mid 50s, but on return I played for Boltons for a number of years. I often used to think of Sentinel Cup days when visiting such grounds as Audley and Bignall End which still had an Ikin playing for the club. At home, the firm erected a new pavilion, perhaps without realising that it was on the site of the old Victorian pavilion which was a 'Knotty' railway carriage. One of my team mates was Derek Barnett who brought along a young Kim Barnett to start his cricketing career at Oakamoor, before moving through Leek, Staffordshire, Derbyshire, where he became their youngest ever captain, to England.

The late John Davies recorded that 'In 1976 a determined band of young men and women from the village, based appropriately at the Cricketers Arms, started a cricket club. With no home ground and an unsuccessful application to use the spiritual home behind them, the club wrote to every landowner in the area asking for use of land for a ground'. They finished up in a field, opposite to Lightoaks, which had a small square laid many years earlier by Michael Bolton as a practice wicket. The ground was prepared, a pavilion erected and the club launched forth into league cricket. There were many keen members, but perhaps the keenest of all was John Davies who served as secretary for 23 years till his death in 1999. John was a credit to Oakamoor. In spite of being handicapped at birth with muscular dystrophy, he refused to let it hamper his life. He would be taken with his motorised wheelchair to watch both the village cricket and football teams in action, with perhaps cricket being his preferred interest. It is quite remarkable that John passed his exams to become a qualified umpire. John turned up on many occasions to watch Staffordshire and Derbyshire, with offers of visits to matches involving the national team accepted with alacrity. For 20 years the 'Club in Exile' ran parallel teams with the 'Club in the Valley'. At this time Richard Worthington spent many hours nurturing the valley ground, an activity which became a labour of love. It was a great day indeed when in 1996 our two local clubs 're-joined' to form the Boltons and Oakamoor Cricket Club, with none other than John Davies as secretary. Four teams now turned out on Saturdays; both grounds were maintained. John was delighted to announce that an Oakamoor man, pace bowler Ian Worthington, a former member of both clubs and an under-19 county player, had been engaged as professional. The Club now runs its Saturday teams, a Sunday team and a number of junior teams. In 2003 the Club purchased the sports ground by the river from the Firm, gaining back its heritage and confirming its line of succession from the mid-Victorian Founding Fathers right down to today. Oakamoor Cricket Club is to be congratulated indeed! The umpire's decision is 'Not Out'.

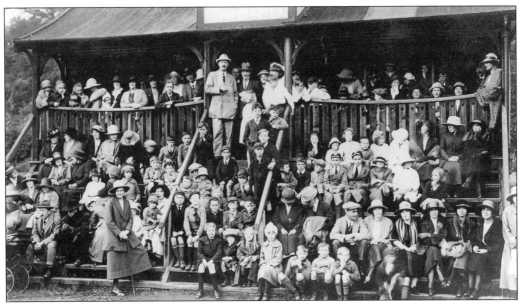

Supporters crowding the pavilion steps to watch Oakamoor Schoolboys win the Schools Championship in 1923. Dr McKenzie of Cheadle, Chairman of the League, stands at the top of the steps.

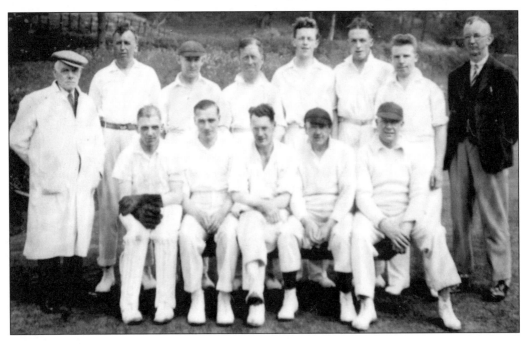

Oakamoor Cricket Club, c.1935. Standing; Umpire George Alkins, Jack Johnson, John Robert Goodwin, Wilf Swinson, Harry Shemilt, Ivan Finney, Jack Alkins, secretary. Seated; George Critchlow, Reg Moseley, Wilfred Walker, captain, Fred Shipley, Harold Webb. All these players lived into their late seventies and eighties, with the exception of Wilfred Walker. Wilfred was a qualified pilot when he joined the Royal Air Force at the start of the Second World War. Whilst piloting a Hampden bomber on a mission to bomb Eschwege aerodrome on July 19th 1940, Wilfred was mortally wounded by a single bullet that penetrated his head just behind the ear. His navigator and great friend David Romans miraculously brought the plane home, only to lose his life a short while later. Oakamoor had lost a most stylish batsman.

North Staffs. Cricket League dinner held in the works canteen at Oakamoor, c.1948, when the teams were called 'Boltons' and had just won the League Shield. 3rd from the left; Bill Rushton, wicket keeper, 5th Barry Hysel, Frank Walker, wearing glasses and still taking wickets with his slow bowling at over 60, Jack Alkins, Richard Wilson, Bert Whitehurst and Herbert Capewell sen., ex Staffordshire wicket keeper.

From 1978 Oakamoor ran a successful club 'on top of the hill', parallel to the Boltons' club in the valley where the village's true heritage lay. It was a great day when the clubs rejoined forces in the 1996 season. Re-named Boltons and Oakamoor Cricket Club, the honours to play the first home match fell to the Second team. Led by Terry Finney, the captain, the team comprised A.Clarke, J.Clowes, D.Stanton, D.Critchley, J.Emery, C.Jones, J.Edwards, J.Lowe, E.Barker and E.Tipper.

The fist home match of the re-united First team in the 1996 season brought fast bowler Ian Worthington back home as the Club professional and captain. Ian had played for both clubs, as had others. Back row; Darren Lowe, Steve Critchlow, Martin Cooke, Ian Worthington, captain, Jonathan Wood, Chris Collier. Front; Pete Matthews, Dennis Whitehurst, Robert Coxen, Kevin Whitehurst, wicket keeper, Ian Wenlock, with John Davies, secretary.

Mary Edwards, left, Oakamoor's scorer. Mary also ran the village post office.

The remarkable John Davies, qualified umpire and secretary of the Oakamoor Cricket Club for 23 years until his death in 1999, at the age of 50. At his death, John was secretary of the Boltons and Oakamoor Cricket Club, and also involved with the South Moorlands Junior Cricket League. Besides cricket, John was involved with football, serving as secretary to the Oakamoor Football Club for a number of years. As well as taking great interest in sport, he spent a lot of time helping to raise money for the charity Sequal which provided computer equipment for people with disabilities. In fact, John himself was skilled in the use of a 'voice activated' computer. Although the 'Great Umpire' raised his finger, John will never be forgotten for what he did for Oakamoor.

Oakamoor Cricket Club 1st Eleven, taken on April 24th 2004, on the ground that the Club now owns. This is the first season for over 60 years that the re-united Club has reverted to its historical name of 'Oakamoor Cricket Club'. Standing: John Edwards, Nigel Sergeant, Greg Stotesbury, Darren Lowe, Jonathan Wood, Ian Worthington and Alex Toft. Seated: Matthew Owen, Martin Critchlow, Sohail Rauf, professional, and Steven Critchlow. This first match of the season was won, with fast bowler Ian Worthington taking 5 wickets for 23.

The Oakamoor
Sports Field and Beyond

A while ago I came across a letter in *Memory Lines*, a magazine of nostalgia produced by Thomas Bolton and Sons in 1977, in which Arthur James, by then aged 93, gave an account of his sporting activities during the Edwardian era. Arthur wrote:

'I was interested in every kind of sport when I was younger and won prizes for football and cricket. I also played hockey for Staffordshire and, in fact, it's only very recently that I threw out my hockey sticks! I used to be a very keen pigeon fancier and in my time have won nearly every available prize for that, and I loved taking part in amateur dramatics, too. Talking of football reminds me of when I was a lad. I was going in to work one Saturday morning and saw a canvass shoe lying in the road. I called out to Jim Salt, who was a very good goal keeper, to save it but for once Jim missed and the shoe went flying through the Coffee Tavern window, knocked all the clay pipes off the shelf, and caused a terrible mess. I owned up to Miss Smith, the Manageress, and later Mr.Bolton summoned me to him. He said, "Arthur, I'll have to fine you 3/9d for the damage" but I said, "Well, Sir, I only get 3/6d a week." So I lost one week's wage and the extra 3d was stopped from the next week's pay. I would swim, too, from the pool just below the railway bridge at Oakamoor, to the weir and back again, and I used to change in Kent's boat house'.

Football

Glancing through the notes of the late J.R.Goodwin I found a reference to early activities on the football field. No doubt young men were kicking footballs around Oakamoor throughout Victoria's reign, but this account from around 1890 described how before the sports ground was developed, the side nearest the railway was a marsh with tufts of reeds down the whole length. This field formed part of the Alton Towers estate and was let to Sammy Mellor at an annual rental. Sammy Mellor kept the Cricketer's Arms ale house at the time. The local youth, being unable to obtain a field elsewhere, applied to Sammy who agreed to let them have it for one year for £1. The lads were delighted and by the end of the season the tufts had disappeared and they looked forward to a reasonable game of football in the following season. Meanwhile, they had not considered Sammy Mellor's business acumen! When they applied to Sammy he said, 'Yes, you can have it, but it will be £2 rent now, as it is a lot better field than it was last year.' Fifteen to twenty years later Mr M.A.Bolton arranged for ten tons of sea sand to be spread over this pitch annually.

In the years after the First World War, Oakamoor United played many games of football in the Moorland League. The Leek Cup was won in 1922 when Oakamoor beat Caverswall in the final played on a flooded field. In 1925 the team gathered for rather an unusual reason. Not only had they won the cup, again, but they had the distinction of winning a good conduct prize, probably the only one ever gained by an amateur side in North Staffordshire's long soccer history and, as the newspaper account went on to describe, probably the only award of its kind in the country. Sir Phillip Brocklehurst, Bt., JP, of Swythamley Hall, himself once a player for Wincle FC in the Moorland League, had a thirst for fair and square football and so keen was he, in fact, to see stamped out anything of an unworthy character in the grand game that he offered a prize of £10 to the club which, at the close of the 1924-1925 season, came out with the highest marks for good conduct. My father Richard, who was the Club secretary for about twelve years, was always proud of the team's achievement. Some of today's bad tempered international players wouldn't have stood a chance!

'Windy Bank Rovers', c.1905. Back; Harry Ryder,   Jack Whitehurst.
Middle;   Fred Bryan. Front; Arthur Gilbert,

Oakamoor Boy Scouts Football team, c.1915.

Oakamoor Football Club, champions of the Moorland League and winners of the Leek Cup in 1925, also the year in which they won the good conduct prize awarded by Sir Phillip Brocklehurst, Bt., JP Back; Jack Wilson, Richard Wilson, J.Swinson, R.Alcock, S.Brookes, E.Critchlow, C.Sutton, C,Bond, A.Swinson, J.Swinson and Percy Brookes, trainer. Middle; J.Whitehurst, Dr Peter Bearblock, W.Kidd, W.Collier, capt., R.Barker, J.Woolliscroft, Richard Wilson, Hon. Sec. Front; R.Carr, M.Wilson, E.Hatton, A.Elks, E.Barker.

Sometime in 1963 the *Evening Sentinel* carried the headline, 'Stanley's Famous Final boots go to Oakamoor'. The account told of how one of the biggest football 'captures' of the season was to bring a real museum piece of soccer history to the village club at Oakamoor, members of the Leek and Moorland League. The boots that Sir Stanley Matthews wore in that wonderful Matthews Cup Final of 1953, were to have a place of honour at the Oakamoor F.C. headquarters. How did this outstanding 'transfer' come about? Stanley, who had carefully preserved the boots as a reminder of his finest hour, accepted an invitation to open Cheadle Cricket Club's new pavilion, and had generously handed the boots to the club to be auctioned off during the evening to help their funds. They were bought for £11 by Percy Wright, then a lime company director and Vice-president of Oakamoor F.C., who then gave them to the Club. Percy went on to say that in his mind the boots were of some historical value to football and he thought they would be a great fillip to the Club. Asked if he thought £11 was too much for a pair of 10-year-old football boots, he replied, 'Not at all. In fact I have been told that if the boots were sold on the Continent, they would fetch up to £100'. My father, who was President of the Club at the time, made a glass fronted case for these prestigious boots. The case, with its valuable contents, is now screwed to a back window sill in the Lord Nelson for all who might be interested to see. The boots are well looked after.

As with cricket, the village team became separated from the Bolton's Factory team, playing first in a field near to the sand works, then in a field at Whiston, before reverting to the pitch on the Bolton's ground. At this time Arthur Davies, our village police officer and eventual postmaster, served as secretary, to be followed by his son John. Both gave loyal support to the Club. Over the years, Oakamoor Football Club has given hours of enjoyment to all who have been involved. This is its true value, so that when in 1987, not one, but two trophies were won, for the first time in many decades, they came as a glorious bonus. On that occasion, Ian Worthington became a hero after scoring the winning goal in the first of the two finals. Two days later Oakamoor beat the same team, Endon, in the final match for the Leek and Moorland League Cup. Player-official Mick Edwards was outstanding at this particular time in the Club's history. Mick tragically died in 1987, at the age of 40, when playing for his beloved village team.

To conclude this short account of our village football heritage I look back to another occasion when Oakamoor won the Leek Cup. The year was 1907. Try to imagine yourself as a villager living in Oakamoor when Edward VII was on the throne. There was no television, no wireless, hardly a motor car, with the journey out of the village either by train, a horse drawn vehicle or, for most of us, on foot. The entire social calendar was village generated. With this in mind it might be possible for you to enter into the spirit of the times. A contemporary account records:

'Surely such a time was never known in the history of the Happy Valley as that which took place last weekend'. The writer went on to state, 'In my notes a week ago I ventured to predict that the said trophy, the Leek Combination Cup, would find a resting place in the Happy Valley. At that time I was taking all our supporters to be a sober, steady going, stay at home sort, but that bit of plate has caused some restless times both for itself and them. What a time we have had. It was like this. Referee Holmes of Hanley was the adjudicator, and Leek Reserve, who had at least after three efforts proved their right to oppose us, won the toss and elected to kick uphill. A blind man could see that we had come for the cup by the way that our lads went in search of it.

Seven minutes from the start Prince raced away, and a capital centre from him found C.Brookes in the right place, and we were one up. Every man on both sides was playing up to form, first one team and then the others getting away, only to be pulled up by the defence. Our backs of course were in grand trim, they always are when we win, and the goal keeper was seldom troubled. Once again Brookes beat the goal keeper with a regular trimmer. On resuming, Leek pressed, and after our keeper had saved from a fast grounder, he was beaten by Wordsley, having slipped or methinks Leek would have come off empty handed. We were not to be denied, and the blood of the Plough Boys, as the Leek crowd somewhat facetiously called our lads, being warmed up, we craved for more. Goodwin missed one chance and Brookes almost knocked the cross bar to splinters with another, whilst just as E.James was about to put the finishing touch to a splendid effort the whistle sounded to cease firing, amidst great cheering, especially from the one hundred and sixty who had booked with us. This was a right good performance. We calculated to fetch the cup from Leek with a purely village team, but nothing to the lightening printers, who had everybody thunderstruck by placarding the village five minutes after the finish with bills, 'OAKAMOOR WINS THE CUP, Grand Tableau at the Pleasant W.E.Concert. Come and Cheer Them'. The Band met the team at the station, and the captain was carried shoulder high right up to the school. Here the team had a great reception. On Monday night we went one further with a procession through the village, headed of course by our loyal band. Mr.Whalley of Leek presented captain J.Goodwin, of ours, with a gold mounted stick in recognition of his team's performance, and Jack responded in a most suitable manner. During the week telegrams of congratulation have poured in from Ball Haye, Alton, Leek Olympic, and other quarters'. Returning almost a century to the present day, the torch passes on.

Hockey

When Michael Bolton came down from Cambridge in 1904, he brought with him a considerable talent and enthusiasm for the game of hockey. Within a very short time Michael had founded a hockey team in Oakamoor, inspiring talented village sportsmen in the skills of the game. During the years leading up to the First War other teams began to emerge, giving opposition to the Oakamoor team. Whenever an important match came on the horizon, Michael would root out his team mates from the factory where he was manager, quite often

The Bolton Family Hockey team, taken at Lightoaks, c.1905. Michael Bolton is seated centre, with his eventual wife, Gladys Mary Higgin, wearing the goal keeper's pads. Also included are several Cambridge University players. After pondering on this photograph of a classic Edwardian house party, the 'Fourth Thomas', Michael's son who died at Lightoaks in November 2002, said to me, "Nothing to do, nothing to do!"

The crack Oakamoor Hockey team of c.1912, with Michael Bolton, capt., seated centre.

A match in progress on the sports field, c.1920.

Oakamoor Hockey team, c.1935. Forster of Stallington, R.B., F.Shipley, goal, W.Swinson, L.B., E.Goodwin of Stallington, umpire, W.Collier, L.H., W.Cope, C.H., A.Whitehurst, R.H. Forwards: R.Moseley, R.O., E.Swinson, R.I., I.Finney, C.F., M.A.Bolton, L.I., capt., H.Perrins, L.O.

The Oakamoor Ladies' Hockey team, winners of the Count de Sieyes' Cup for Leek and District, 1934-35. From left; ? Dulson, Murial Alkins, Margaret Moseley, Annie Wannan, Ethel Wannan, Nancy Barker, Freda Walker, Hilda Walker, Mary Moseley, Dorothy Barker, Mary Warrington.

Oakamoor Ladies' Hockey team taken by Mr.Rabone of Leek on May 1st 1937, at Farley, before the final of the Leek Cup competition which they won 7-0. In the 1936-7 season they played 21, won 16, drew 3 and lost 2. Goals for: 126, against: 26. Standing; M.Milward, R.I., F.Walker, L.I., M.Perrins, R.O., A.Wannan, R.H., N.Barker, C.F., H.Walker, L.O. Kneeling; H.Edwards, G., D.Barker, L.B., E.Wannan, L.H., M.Alkins, C.H., W.Marsdon, R.B.

Above: The Boltons Oakamoor team, taken in October, 1964. Back row: John Walker, Stoke Tech., Mike Rogers, who became Chief Inspector of Schools for Staffordshire, Arthur Gilbert, Ted Small and Herbert Capewell of T.B.&S., Peter Wilson, St.Joseph's College and the City of Stoke-on-Trent Sixth Form College, and Ken Mascurine, our star Indian player and T.B.&S. Front row: Barrie Williams, vicar, who was tragically killed in a car crash when young, Robin Wood, Earls Cement, Chris Elks, Teacher of Physical Education, Mike Pointon, Primary School Head, and Alan Thorley of T.B.&S. and lecturer at Stoke Tech. During this period we had Monsignor Tom Gavin, Irish International rugby player and headmaster of Cotton R.C. College, a very regular Staff member Terry Owen, two Methodist Ministers, an outstanding player from C.S.O.S. at Woodhead, and several local teachers in the team.

Left: The captain in retirement. Michael Alfred Bolton at Lightoaks in July, 1937, wearing his Cambridge blazer with the Staffordshire Knot in sticks.

at short notice, for an impromptu training session on the sports field. Skills were honed to such a high standard that the team never lost at home for 17 years, during which period Michael gained county status. In the opening game of 1910, Michael scored 7 goals. In October 1912 a depleted team travelled to Alstonfield, as three were playing for Staffordshire. Although the home team were worthy winners by 3-2, a 'capital tea' was enjoyed, followed by dancing and songs till late in the evening.

Michael encouraged silence on the field of play, a quite remarkable attribute. Most of the home games were played in front of the pavilion, with occasional use of the second team pitch situated beyond the cricket square and by the river. Quite often, as in my playing days, thick fog would very quickly develop over the far pitch. During one such encounter the fog closed in to such a density that it was impossible to see beyond a few yards. The umpire abandoned the game and led both teams back to the pavilion. After a short while somebody said, 'Where's Charlie'? On re-piercing the fog, Charlie Nicholls, the goal keeper, was found still in position in the goal mouth. When told the game had ended he said, 'I thought it had gone quiet; I thought we were pressing'! Shortly after the Second War I remember watching a match played out on a sleet covered pitch when Barry Hysel was captain. I think the opposition was North Staffs. By the time the orange segments were sucked, Oakamoor were losing 5-0. After the turn around, a remarkable thing happened. Barry was a very hard player who was absolutely in his element at centre half. Goodness knows what he said to his team at the interval, but the ball hit the back board behind the goal mouth on no less than seven occasions! Our team won 7-5, with all twelve goals scored at the Alton end.

I started playing hockey in 1949 at the age of 15, gaining experience with the Boltons Oakamoor second team. During my final year at Leek High School I was fortunate to be selected for the county under 19 team, before being called up into the Royal Air Force in 1952 for my two years National Service. Five years later, after playing for Loughborough College for a further three years, I returned to the club, playing at centre half for a good many years. We had a pretty good team in those days with Cannock, Leek, Congleton, Stafford, Stone, Macclesfield and several others providing stiff opposition. On one occasion at Oakamoor, when we were leading Derwent 1-0, I picked up an injury from a particularly aggressive confrontation with the Derbyshire centre forward, putting me out of the team for several weeks. Thankfully, this was the only 'nuisance' injury I had, all the rest being 'irritants' that were never felt until the day after! Of all the teams we came against, no player could hit the ball as hard as our centre forward, Herbert Capewell. It was music to our ears when Herbert struck the back board with his powerful and accurate shots. Arthur Gilbert was a clever player who had a career longer than most, as he was still umpiring around the county well into his seventies.

Perhaps the cleverest stick player of all was our Indian full back Ken Mascurine. Ken was barely five feet tall, lulling opposition forwards into thinking he was an easy match, until his penetrating stick removed the ball from their feet on so many occasions. Thank you Ken for teaching me how to flick. Ken also introduced us to the Indian stick which had a smaller and tighter curve than the English counterpart. We all moved over to the smaller hook, with the exception of Robin Wood who regarded it as 'nothing but a crocheting hook'!

Our umpire was Tom Boden of Denstone, ex Nottingham University player and by then the Vice-president of the N.F.U. In the mid 60s a new rule came out giving the umpire the authority to send a player off the field into the 'sin bin' for, say, ten minutes. Tom was eager to try this out. My friend Arthur must have been egging him on, as when I made the mild comment of "Oh no Tom?" when he allowed a goal against us that I felt was off side, Tom said, "Off the field Peter!" I was annoyed at missing ten minutes of play, my father awoke in the night concerned that I had blotted my copy book, and my team mates to a man thought it a great joke that this new rule had been tried upon me. Without being sanctimonious, I was far from being the most garrulous member of the team! Any nominations chaps? What fun we had on the hockey field. What fun they had in Mr Michael's halcyon days. Hockey was played in Oakamoor for some 75 years. Shortly after I retired from the fray in my early forties, interest waned until the remaining good players went off to Leek for a quality game. Throughout the years Thomas Bolton and Sons kept the sports field in immaculate condition, a fact appreciated by all teams. The clashing of sticks has not been heard in the valley for 25 years. We have perhaps the most delightful ground in the county. Surely, some people might be interested in re-starting our hockey club? Hockey's tradition, at the end of every game, is to call for three cheers for the opposition. "Hip Hip," but I hear nothing. Come on. It is our heritage.

Bowls

Another feature on the sports field of Edwardian days was a round bowling green. I have no reference of a club being in existence at that time, but bowls was played by workmen and villagers, sometimes in the dinner break. Just after World War I my father challenged one of the best bowlers to one such dinner break encounter, for fun I must add. One of the quirks of the old round green was a feature nick named 'the camel's hump'. My father had worked out some strategy that if he could land the jack on top of this bump, he would stand a better chance of beating a far better player, as 'heavies' would roll away for random distances. This he did, with success. By 1919 it was decided to build a bowling hut, and as my father was a keen bowler at that time he spent many hours with friends constructing the new bowling hut in timber. Once the new bowling hut was in use, attention turned to the round green. It was quickly decided to create a square green, with the first clod cut on August 30th 1921, by my great uncle Jack Wilson who was a keen bowler.

Bowling on the round green in 1919. The foundation blocks for the new bowling hut can be seen in the background.

Oakamoor Bowling Club, c.1924. Back; J.Alkins, W.Collier, M.A.Bolton, R.Wilson, S.Walker, G.Alkins, H.Lucas. Middle; Waltho, J.Buttress, C.Lucas, Measham, A.Collier, W.Kidd, J.Heath, T.Wilson, E.Moseley, T.Mellor, T.Healey. Front; G.Bennett, T.Harrison, J.Woolliscroft, J.Wilson, T.Scott, C.Wannan, G.Chadwick, F.Kerry, B.Jordan, E.Bottom.

Happy Bowlers, Easter Saturday, 1930. M.A.Bolton of Lightoaks re-opening the much improved bowling green at Oakamoor. From left; J.Alkins, J.Wilson, Sec., J.Woolliscroft, part hidden, T.Wilson, E.Moseley, T.Scott, Capt., with wood in hand, T.Mellor, G.Harrison, W.Alkins, part hidden, F.Barker, C.Wannan, J.Heath, G.Chadwick and Miss Freda Bolton.

The following year the game of bowls was put on a more permanent footing when the Oakamoor Bowling Green Club was established, with Jack Wilson elected as its first secretary. By 1927 the Churnet Valley Bowling League was formed. With League status, further improvements were made. On Easter Saturday, 1930, Michael Bolton re-opened the much improved bowling green by playing the first ball. Sam Walker's membership card for the 1939 season reveals that Michael Bolton was President and Life Member of the club. There were ten vice-presidents, with the Hon. Secretary and Treasurer being Colin Cope. Jack Heath was the captain, with Will Alkins as vice-captain. There was a committee of 12 and a selection committee of six. Bamfords, L.M.and S.Railway, Cheadle, Kingsley, Leek and Fenton were among the opposing teams.

The Bowling Green club was now a serious affair, as some of the rules reveal. All the usual management rules were listed, with the annual subscription set at 5/-. Rule 5 stated that 'The Season shall commence at any time fixed by the committee'. All woods had to be safely lodged in the place appointed, dried and oiled. Members were requested not to occupy the green too long when other members were waiting. Neither trespassers nor dogs were allowed on the ground. Then rule 15 stated that 'Betting shall not be permitted, nor will improper language be allowed'. The funny thing was that the only sponsored advert for a village trade to appear on the membership card was for 'C.Weston, Commission Agent, of Spring Hill, Oakamoor'! After the War the bowling club continued and today a keen nucleus of members are restoring the bowling green and its surrounds as an excellent village amenity. As for the bowling hut, the venue for bowls and cricket teas, and also the venue for the wedding reception for Sam Walker and Phyllis Dulson in 1938, it still continues after 85 years of use. Sadly, a collection of old photographs were removed by a philistine official some time after the War. Surely, the ash bottomed urinal should be preserved for ever! It is good that the sharp click of wood on jack can still be heard in Oakamoor.

Tennis

Tennis was played in Oakamoor as far back as the 1880s, when the court was situated by the riverside on the site now occupied by the houses of 'Tennis Corner'. The game continued to be played on this site until new courts were constructed on the sports field. On May 10th 1915, the Oakamoor Tennis Club was opened, with Miss Mabel Mills as secretary and Miss Edith Walker the treasurer. The Misses Mills and Pryor played the opening match. Miss Mills was the daughter of the works accountant Mr Mills, and granddaughter of Rev.John Mills, the first chaplain to the works. Miss Pryor was the daughter of Mr Joseph Pryor of Barley Croft, who was the works manager. The years following the First War brought halcyon days for the game, with the cry of, "Anyone for tennis?" echoing round the clubs and country houses throughout the land. Oakamoor was no exception. There was a grass court tucked away in the left hand corner near to the entrance to the sports field, and in April, 1925, two new hard courts were

Oakamoor Tennis Courts, opened in the summer of 1888, photographed in 1893. The end of the newly built Riverside can be seen on the left, with the New Schools of 1892 on the right. The houses of Tennis Corner now stand on this site.

Tennis party on the sports field, c.1944. Back; Joseph Walker, Bill Cope, Barry Hysel, Seated; Norah Edge, Hilda Walker,

opened. They proved very popular with the tennis set, until washed away in a flood in the early 1960s. Freda and Hilda Walker, Phyllis Dulson, Mary Lemm, Norah Edge, George Harvey and many others had such fun on these courts, with the laughter clearly heard in far Stonydale. Although the hard courts were set to grass, interest for tennis quickly evaporated. At this time, Tom Bolton upgraded his court at Lightoaks. Wilf Cope said that he could still hear Hilda's laughter in Stonydale, this time floating down the valley from Tom's home. Perhaps the tennis story faded away with the Stonydale set? Will anyone restore the sports field tennis courts and re-start the village club? At this moment there is no game, no set and no match. Is there no one for tennis?

Swimming

In Victorian times Oakamoor youths went swimming in the River Churnet in the nude, usually upstream from the weir as down stream was polluted by the factory. No better facilities were available until Frank Bolton had a small swimming pool built for the villagers. This project took a long time to materialise, as it was first put forward as an idea to commemorate the coronation of HM King George V and Queen Mary in 1911. F.A.Bolton offered 'to erect such Baths at his own expense', for the use of the parish, providing a fund could be raised to cover working expenses. A fund was started, with everything kept on hold during the War, before the project could be completed. Situated in a sunny spot in the highest corner of the sports field, near to the railway line, the pool was first filled with water in June, 1919. It was 3'6" deep at one end and over 6' at the other, with a small diving board at the deep end. A high wooden lap fence kept out the wind. The opening ceremony formed part of the peace celebrations of that summer. As a boy I often found my way down to this pool on hot summer days, always to find the water extremely cold. On occasions, War veterans like Lawrence Hassall would enter the water, displaying war injuries that normally were not seen. Shortly after the Second War this little swimming bath fell into disrepair and became dangerous. Its final days were spent as a coke bunker, supplying the fuel for the groundsman's stove, before it was eventually filled in.

Swimming Bath built for the use of the parishioners by F.A.Bolton of Moor Court in June, 1919. George Tipper about to dive in.

Fun in the swimming bath, c.1935.

Athletic Sports

On September 4th 1901, the Second Amateur Athletic Sports took place on the sports field. Under the presidency of Thomas Bolton, the starter was W.H.Kerry and the judges E.Jackson and W.H.Leake. Events included a 120 yards flat race, a quarter mile flat race handicap, a veterans' race for men over 40, an obstacle race and a one mile bicycle race. Field events were throwing the cricket ball, putting the shot, and high jump. Jack Wilson, cricket captain, entered the cricket ball, T.H.Barrow, village policeman, the shot, and village tailor O.Beardmore, entered the high jump, presumably before he had a leg amputated after an accident. No ladies

121

took part at all as it was not the fashion. Fashion began to change slightly in 1902, however, when part of the Coronation Festivities for King Edward VII in June of that year included the following events for ladies: an egg and spoon race, an obstacle race and a cricket match, the ladies with bats and the gentlemen with broom sticks. Was this an early example of women's lib? There were a number of races for the schoolchildren.

Many more athletic events took place over the decades. The ones I remember in particular were war time meets of the 1940s when young men from the Officer Cadet Training Unit at Alton Towers would compete against local opposition such as the young men from the Air Ministry at Woodhead Hall. These events were always well organised, with Corporal Taylor's Public Address System supplying the information. The Churnet Valley Sports for local schoolchildren took place annually during the 70s and 80s, when crowds of children and many parents enjoyed the facilities of the sports field.

Other Clubs

There were a number of activities which, by their nature, took place beyond the sports field. Golf was once played on the Ranger, but there was a delightful nine hole course laid out by Mr Frank Bolton at his home at Moor Court. Villagers with an interest in the game became members of the club, gaining much help from the club professional who in the 1940s was Alf Cockfield. My friend Roy Davies started out on this course, taking me round with him on occasions, before being called up into the RAF Roy became an outstanding golfer over the years. There was boating, ice skating in the winter, fishing, a gun club, a holiday club, a boot club, a photographic society, a homing society, a poultry society and, wait for it, an anti-swearing club! The Oakamoor Mills Anti-Swearing Club of the 1890s had Thomas Bolton as its president, F.Bolton and T.Mills as vice-presidents, H.Jordan as secretary and C.Wilson as treasurer. This club was formed 'to put down swearing, and to raise the general tone of conversation to a higher moral standing. A man of high moral standing would rather treat an offence with contempt than show his indignation by an oath.' Words such as 'vulgar', 'indecent', 'contemptible' and 'wicked' were used in the aims of the club, with rule one stating that 'Each member shall contribute one penny per week, and shall be fined one penny for each offence'. Any member leaving the works could withdraw his subscriptions, but not his fines! How much might there be in the kitty today?

The five Walker brothers on the nine hole Ranger golf course, c.1905. My father could remember the positions of all the tees and greens long after the fields returned to farmland. Left to right; Fred Walker, Froghall Works Manager, 1890 – 1924, William Walker, Widnes Works, T.Walker, Widnes Works, Sam Walker, Oakamoor and Froghall, and John Walker, Oakamoor and Froghall Works. These brothers had a total of 250 years service with T.B.&S.

Left: Keen local golfers were always welcomed as members on this private course. Bill Cope is seen, centre, watching, I think, Sam Walker putting out. Alf Cockfield was the last professional golfer employed by F.A.B. at Moor Court in the 1940s.

Above: Boating on the Churnet, c.1898. You could hire a boat from Mr T.Kent. Alan and Harry Ford take Mr.Coates for a row. The end of the canal cottage, the Lord Nelson and The Square can be seen.

Bank Farm duck pond, often used by skaters in the winter. I remember David Bolton having a bad fall on the ice in 1944, knocking himself out and, with blood pouring from his head, being helped off the 'bending ice' by Joe Robinson who then took him home to Barley Croft. The Doctor's pond at Stonydale, where I learnt to skate, was a popular venue, yet accidents did occur. I can remember both Barry Hysel and Jeffrey Perrins coming croppers. Once the freezing weather took hold, with three hard frosts needed before the ponds were safe, we all ventured onto the ice, keeping well clear of inlets and outlets where there was moving water. Ice that would bend was unsafe. There was always a procession of skaters down the Red Road when the cream of all venues, the Smelting Mill pond, became safe. On these and many more occasions my guardian angel must have worked overtime!

The Oakamoor Rifle club, c.1887. Point 303 bore rifles were used. Tom Wilson, third from the left on the back row, is wearing a 'boiler end'.

Oakamoor Photographic Society, 1907. Youths standing; Albert Wilson, George Child, Richard Wilson, my father. Seated; Richard Wilson, my grandfather, Caleb Wilson, my great grandfather, William Swinson, Elijah Jackson, Arthur Swinson, Fred James, Sam Harvey and Enoch Berrisford. I still have Caleb Wilson's camera and beautifully made tripod stand in ash. The society enjoyed many meetings when visiting experts came to speak. In July, 1909, Mr Edgar R.Bull, F.P.S., the well known architectural photographer, lectured to about 30 members and friends on 'A Plea for Record Work'. I still have a number of his slides which contain examples of outstanding skill with the camera. Mr Frank Bolton, too, was an outstanding photographer, being admitted to the Fellowship of the P.S. in 1899, after submitting examples of his work, with one, 'A Spring Pasture', gaining a silver medal in 1896. His work became well known in London exhibitions around this time when he was secretary to the Photographic Society's Postal Club.

Village Entertainment

The antidote to hard work, misfortune, illness and sometimes tragedy was found in village entertainment. Work in the factory was hard; music, acting, singing and dancing brought such pleasure to the people of Oakamoor and district. Our ancestors could associate with the two faces of the theatre, tragedy and comedy, as they had experienced both. The Mills Brass Band was leading processions in the 1850s. The first account I have found of indoor entertainment was in the *Staffordshire Advertiser* of January 7th 1871, which reports 'An amateur concert was held on Tuesday in aid of the cricket club. The entertainment gave great satisfaction, but owing to the severe weather the audience was not so large as its merits deserved'. There were about 12 'principal performers' which suggests that this was a variety concert of verse and song. The last quarter of the nineteenth century brought a great upsurge of entertainment in Oakamoor. Thomas Bolton formed an Orchestral Society and an account of their third annual concert in February, 1888, in the Mills Schoolroom, reads 'Mr.Thomas Bolton, the president of the society, acted as conductor of the band with much ability. The instrumentalists were: 1st violins F.Bolton, W.Coates and J.Walker; 2nd violins C.Bolton, C.Wilson, E.Wilson, M.Brooks, J.Pattinson, J.Wilson and H.Leak; contra bass D.Jackson; violoncello T.Powell; piccolo F.Walker; clarionet R.Wilson; 1st cornet H.Shipley; 2nd cornet, W.Lovatt; euphonium T.Kent; tenor horn W.Walker. The performances of the band were marked with much precision and purity of tone, and showed a great improvement in minor details upon their previous performances. The selections consisted of "March from Christ and his Soldiers," J.Farmer, "Gavotte," J.S.Bach, and the overture for "Box and Cox," Sullivan. The glees were sung by members of the choral class, the most deserving of commendation being a setting of Tennyson's "Break, break on the cold grey stones, O Sea," with a determined recall being especially made for Mr.Thomas Bolton's happy rendering of "Come into the garden, Maud," Balfe. The concert was an exceedingly popular and successful one. The proceeds were devoted to the funds for the proposed coffee house'. Pure Victoriana! A.S.Bolton's 'GleeBook' turned up a few years ago and is in the safe keeping of my friend Michael Redfearn.

All manner of public performances took place. The *Cheadle Herald* of June, 1881, reported a Choral Festival at the Free Christian Church, the performers being members of the choir and friends, organ and string band. Sacred songs were rendered, with 'looseness in the bass lead of the chorus in "For His is the Sea."' Sacred Concerts became fashionable. The Mills Chapel Choir moved to the Mills Schoolroom to sing compositions by Mozart, Gounod and popular Victorian composers, many of the latter being in the 'tear jerking' mode. Again, proceeds went to the coffee house and Working Men's Institute fund for the village. The children were not left out. Their 'Band of Hope' society gave two performances of a juvenile play entitled *A Happy Family* to large and enthusiastic audiences. Lectures were delivered. Professor Carpenter of London spoke on "The Falls of Niagara," 'exhibiting photographs by means of the magic lantern. The Rev.Father Ullathorne, of Alton, kindly lent his lantern'. A.S.Bolton proposed the vote of thanks. Mr Charles Bill of Farley Hall delivered a lecture on New Zealand. Mr Bill considered the subject of the over population of our country a very serious one, and spoke of the blessing of having an outlet and a refuge for our surplus people such as New Zealand afforded. He gave an interesting account of his last visit to his estate in the North Island and a general description of the country. In his vote of thanks, Alfred Bolton 'hoped it would not be necessary for the people of Oakamoor to seek fresh fields and pastures new as an outlet for their labour'. Alfred was proud of his workforce. About this time, c.1888, there was a dramatic performance of a light comedy *My Wife's Second Floor*, with parts played by Tom and Frank Bolton and a village cast. *The Blind Beggars*, a musical play, rounded off the

125

Oakamoor Mills Brass Band, pre 1880. The earliest reference to this marching band was in the summer of 1854 when newly weds Alfred and Rebecca Bolton returned to Oakamoor.

Right: The Mills Brass Band resplendent in their new uniform in 1889. Band-master Shipley, reputed to be the finest cornet player in the district, is at the front.

The Band playing in the park at Moor Court in 1908, on the occasion of an Oddfellows' rally.

On the march through Oakamoor, leading a procession of the Oddfellows in a grand parade of 1910.

Bandmaster Harry Collier, c.1913. A fine musician, Harry became bandmaster after the death of Bandmaster Shipley in 1895.

My grandfather Richard Wilson who played the double bass in the Oakamoor Orchestra, c.1925. Two of his sisters played the violin, as did his brother Jack. Their father, Caleb, was a cellist.

Marion Wilson, a pianist, with Albert Wilson, c.1914. Although my aunt Marion graduated, she told me that it was hard work yet everything was so easy for uncle Albert. He was a natural.

My father Richard Wilson playing the violin he made in 1928. Richard was a craftsman in wood who taught cabinet making and woodcarving in Oakamoor for over 30 years. He was employed by the firm for most of his working life, heading the transport department for his final ten years. Photo. 1956.

evening. The Mills School was 'brilliantly lighted by the electric light, which has recently been introduced into the school'. In the spring of 1889 there were concerts given by the Choral Society, the Choral Class and the Orchestral Society's Band. In December, 1892, the Choral Society opened their season with a concert in the New Schools. The choir 'upwards of 60' were accompanied on the piano by Miss Brown, with the president, Thomas Bolton, the conductor. *The Messiah* was about to come! Hardly a week passed without some form of entertainment. There was a buzz in the place.

More forms of entertainment were to join this heady mix when, in 1893, the Amateur Dramatic Club staged *The Babes in the Wood*. As always, Tom and Frank Bolton led the cast, which included Frances and Margaret Robinson, daughters of Dr Robinson, the village doctor, who lived at Wood Bank. The *Staffordshire Advertiser* of January 28th 1893, said that 'Miss Frances Robinson charmed all spectators. Miss Robinson, as Lady Macassar, must be especially complimented on her night walking scene, a la Lady Macbeth, in which a tragic reverie breaks without abruptness into a dance to the tune of "Hokey-Pokey."' This production raged for four evenings. The first 'Oakamoor Pantomime' had been born, establishing a tradition that was to last for almost 35 years. *Blue Beard* followed a year later. In April, 1894, an important dramatic production took place in the New Schools, before a large and distinguished audience. The *Staffs Weekly Post* recorded that 'the distinguished audience included Mr Charles Bill, MP, Mr and Mrs Blagg, Mr and Mrs Masefield, Mr and Mrs A.S.Bolton and party, Dr and

Mrs Robinson, Mr and Mrs Cull, Mr Brett and Revs.A.H.Boucher, W.C.Green and W.Tomline'. Why was there such an auspicious gathering? They were invited to see the New Schools 'fitted up with a splendid stage, with all the necessary accessories of a modern theatre, and the room is lighted throughout with the electric light'. The farcical comedy, *The Private Secretary*, was produced. 'The efforts of the artistes were hailed with considerable applause'. A few weeks later the New Schools was the venue for a meeting of the Temperance Society. The Good Templars met under the presidency of Rev.George Ryves of Tean. The Rev.Pebendary Grier gave 'a most eloquent, clear, exhaustive address, advocating the entire disuse of alcoholic drinks as the only remedy for prevailing drunkenness'. Binge drinking was a curse, even in Oakamoor! The entertainment mix continued. In January, 1897, a concert of music and song took place, 'the object of which was to add to the funds of Miss Constance Bolton's Oakamoor Boys' Home, an institution originally opened at Oakamoor but since removed to Colwyn Bay for providing for orphan children. There was a large audience'. Constance Bolton, A.S.B's daughter, always tried to identify with the common man in a humble abode. It is said that she used to practise 'black leading' grates. In 1890 she built the Oakamoor orphanage, now turned into cottages, beyond the Mills School. Constance eventually married and went to live in Leek, where she joined the Salvation Army. 1899 saw Nigger Entertainment in the village. The Oakamoor Minstrels became very popular, raising money in aid of Wives and Families of Reservists from Oakamoor Mills. 'Soldiers of the Queen,' 'Razors in de air' and 'The Storming of Dargai' were typical songs presented by the troupe.

Throughout this period the Mills Brass Band was very popular. In a love letter written on December 27th 1889, by my grandfather Richard Wilson to his fiancée Emma Lee, he wrote of Christmas Day; 'I did not receive mine', Christmas card, 'till night for we started banding early and did not get back till seven at night so I had no Christmas dinner, only bread and cheese and beer, it was a splendid day for us to turn out in our new dress'. The Band had spent all day playing in parts of the village and at the big houses on the hillsides. They would be called upon to lead processions for coronations and jubilees, also processions for the Oddfellows, one example being the grand parade of May 1910 when 97 adults and 43 juniors carried their two new banners. Another new uniform was provided in August, 1909, when the Band went to Whiston Flower Show. The Band saved up for their holidays, as in July, 1914, £305.19.10 was paid out to members. When a War hero, Joe Brett, came home on short leave in January, 1916, the Band went to meet him at the railway station. Rehearsals were held in the Mills School, and on one evening when they were off form, Sam Harvey said, "Thi arner fit be ite er dowers." The Mills Band had two bandmasters who were outstanding. Tragedy hit one in 1895. On commenting on the death of bandmaster Shipley, aged 44, the paper records that 'he was considered one of the finest cornet players in the district, and had held the position of leader for about twelve years. He leaves a widow and large family. The procession moved from Churnet Terrace, headed by a band of players from Oakamoor, Kingsley and Cheadle, about 36, who played the "Dead March." Messrs. Bolton and Sons allowed the suspension of work during the service, their workmen numbering upwards of 500. The band played "The Vital Spark" at the graveside. Mr J.Beardmore, a fellow musician, had the music arrangements in hand. The deceased's silver cornet was placed upon the coffin in the procession, and the wreaths were numerous'. Mr Shipley was also a member of the Earl of Shrewsbury's Band at Alton Towers. The other leader was Mr Harry Collier. At a Smoking Concert in the New Schools in July, 1913, a presentation was made to Harry Collier who had been in the band for 25 years, 16 of which he had been bandmaster. Harry's father had been the Earl's organist at the Towers for 16 years before becoming bandmaster of the old Cheadle Rifle Band, also the old Alton Band. The band played, Mr M.A.Bolton made the presentation of 'a splendid English Lever Watch and Silver Chain', with the evening concluding with 'other selections'.

As with village sport, Edwardian days were halcyon days for village entertainment. Concerts were always 'in aid of' some cause, as with the building of the Coffee Tavern. Earlier, in 1890, the householders, numbering 108, voted for a scheme of street lighting with 12 candle power

The Green Valley Dance Band, founded by Peterkin Bearblock in 1920. Back; Albert Wilson, Frank Woolliscroft, Bert Brough, Albert Collier, Sydney Alkins. Front; A professional musician, Bert Beardmore, Kenneth Beardmore, Sam Walker, Peterkin Bearblock, Walter Forrester, Fred Bryan.

Oakamoor Rhythm Boys, c.1930. Albert Wilson, ? John Pattinson, drums, ? Sydney Alkins, Sax., Albert Wibberley, piano. The Oakamoor Rhythm Boys were directed by Albert Wibberley and were open for all engagements for four, five or six players. 'For terms, phone Oakamoor 37, or write Hawthorn Villas'.

lamps, with the power coming from the works dynamo or batteries. The cost was 2d. per household per week. Nothing came of it until 1906, but the fund raising by this time was phenomenal as the village had a cause. A public body under the name of 'Pleasant Winter Evenings' set about raising money to help Oakamoor become the first village in England to have street lighting by electricity. Dipping into the activities of the 'Pleasant Winter Evening Society' reveals many efforts. A 1906 concert comprised sketches, monologues, recitations, violin solos by Miss Phyllis Higgin and gramophone interludes. The 1907 season contained a programme of music which started with a piano duet by Misses Denman and Parsons; Rev.Charles Denman's daughter and the Infants' mistress. The programme ended with a vocal duet in which J.Waller and R.Ewin sang, "Our ands ave met but not our earts." The P.W.E. raged on, with 'The Scarlet Dominoes' making their first bow to the public in 1908. This production was set to the music of "The Captain's Song" from *Pinafore*. A critic of the time recorded 'the wonderful finish and versatility of the Troupe. The bone soloists, G.Critchlow and E.Jackson, were accorded quite an ovation. J.Jackson's stump speech was excellent'. 'The General' was also the drummer in the Mills Band. I also note that my relation 'Little Miss Nellie Wilson won golden opinions in the part she played in the Swing Song, her dainty appearance, together with the natural and graceful way in which she sang and acted, irresistibly appealing to all'. The Oakamoor Handbell Ringers were around at this time, emanating from the parish church. 'Grand Social Evenings' were billed in 1909, featuring the Orchestra, cornet solos, recitations and dancing from 10.15, or thereabouts, to 11.30. The MC was the village butcher, John Davies. In February, 1912, "The Skylarks" ascended to the scene, destined to give a few public performances before the onset of war. Troupe members were J.Jackson, F.Child, G.Alkins, C.Goodwin, J.J.Awty, G.Harrison, G.Perrins, G.Woodward, J.Alkins, J.Wilson, A.Pattinson, E.Berrisford, F.Walker, H.Lucas and R.W.Bottom. The accompanist was Miss Brookes. After the opening chorus, the first song was 'Who were you with last night,' followed by monologues, humorous duets, a Lecturette on 'Cricket,' with the first part ending with the Troupe. As was becoming the fashion, Part II was a sketch 'Wanted, a Confidential Clerk.' Entertainment was modified during the first War, producing the Oakamoor Concertina Band in October, 1916. The Orchestra continued, with J.Wilson, J.P.Wilson, A.Wilson and R.Wilson as members. A year later the Works Canteen was opened, the occasion marked with a dance. It wasn't long before the Canteen Orchestra was formed, playing for many social functions. The Oakamoor Ladies' Hockey Club held a dance in the Canteen in 1920, with the music on this occasion provided by Mr P.E.Bearblock's newly formed 'Green Valley Dance Band.'

The 1920s brought a series of pantomimes which drew large 'houses' in the New Schools. *Aladdin* was produced in 1921, followed by *Dick Whittington* a year later. The libretto for this 1922 production was written by Commander H.C.Anstey R.N., a T.B.&S. manager. Mr G.Perrins was the stage manager, with Mr M.A.Bolton the musical director. The cast comprised members of the Bolton family, many villagers as always, and Rev.A.E.Dudley, vicar. The village orchestra was in the pit. Special trains plied the Churnet Valley for a week, transporting nightly audiences. The pantomimes raged, year after year, *Pom-Pom, Babes in the Wood*, many more, until fate ended the run in 1934. In January that year, *Aladdin* was produced. Then one April evening my father was at rehearsal with the village orchestra, when its conductor and musical director, Michael Bolton, was suddenly called from the school to be told that his second daughter, Beatrice, had lost her life in a double fatality, a few days after celebrating her 21st birthday at her home at Lightoaks. Her best friend, Elisabeth Kearns, died with her. 'They were both killed instantaneously when Beatrice's "baby" car was involved in a collision with a five-ton motor lorry'. This sad tale has still to be told, but for now, this tragedy brought to an end a long run of pantomime productions in our village.

The stitches were eventually picked up. Whist drives, which had been popular for decades, still thrived, raising money for many charities. The second War came, with the New Schools being a popular venue for entertainment. Officer Cadets from the O.C.T.U. at Alton Towers were only to pleased to support the many dances that took place in Oakamoor during these years. Local girls had a whale of a time! Will anybody tell? The Dramatic Society, under Hugh Anstey, was active.

I remember attending a production of Priestley's *Eden End*. Captain Cyril Payn, the works electrician, was always in charge of the electrics on the stage. At this time of wartime 'blackout', much fun was had in front of, and behind, the scenery! The Mills Brass Band had become defunct in the 1930s. Rosemary Cope told me of how her parents at Stonydale Farm, Mr and Mrs Jack Heath, used to prepare breakfast for the band before it set off on its Christmas journeys. One year, bandmaster Collier said, "Right chaps, we will finish with 'O Come...'" A voice from the band said, "But I've just played that one!" The band may have led the Coronation procession in 1937, but the final word goes to my uncle, bandsman Albert Wilson, who finished up playing to an empty barn at Cotton. "Well lad!" As for the brass instruments, the last time one was seen in the village was at a fancy dress social in 1961, when my dear friend Peter Redfearn carried a euphonium whilst wearing a placard that said, 'Wife and Eleven Children to Support.' Echoes of the pantomimes could be heard during wartime, when the 'Dame', Harry Lucas, used to give impromptu performances when waiting to be served in Norman Weston's shop. The Choral and Orchestral Society tiptoed out of the War, to be conducted by Albert Wilson. I remember a performance of *Olivet to Calvary* being given under the oil lamps in Cauldon Church, with Miss Collier playing the piano, also the last performance by the village orchestra and choral society in the School in 1949. A few dramatic performances, such as *The Late Mrs Early*, have taken place in the school, but we now leave it to the children to carry on with the stage tradition. In 1990 a recital was held in Lightoaks in aid of the RNLI Performers were Rebecca Wilson, violin; Susanna Wilson, cello; Peter Jones, piano; and David Neil-Smith, verse. Susanna played a cello sonata which was written in Lightoaks by Gilbert Benson Bolton, and dedicated to cellist Albert Wilson, before 'Gibby' fell in the first World War. The recital came to an end with "The Lost Chord." Susanna's professional trio came to

Harry Lucas, the pantomime
Dame, c.1920.

Princess Chrysanthemum, c.1912.

the other 'big house', Moor Court, in April 1996, by invitation of the new owner, Peter Thornley. The violinist was Nicholas Evans-Pughe, the pianist Jonathan Rutherford. The performance ended with the Mendelssohn Trio in D minor, opus 49. Entertainment from the 1850s to the Second World War filled a tremendous psychological need for the village as it was then, a village with an unbreakable link with the copper industry and the Bolton family in particular. We had 'the best of times, the worst of times', the two faces of the theatre. Oakamoor is now a delightful village, but so, so different from the industrial days of the past.

"Beseech you, Sir, be merry; you have cause,
   So have we all."   Shakespeare.

The Oakamoor pantomime, *Babes in the Wood*, which played to a week of full houses in 1924.
Back row; Elsie Elkes, ? P.Kerry, ? G.Perrins, T.Barker. Centre; Freda Burton, David Bolton, Babs Kerry, Edna Ash, F.Haywood, ? Dorothy Webb, ? ? E.Alkins, ? Front; ? Tim Healey, C.Tipper, Laurie Pryor, B.Simpson, H.Lucas, W.James, Cmdr Amstey, Mrs G.M.Bolton. The rabbits; Freda Walker and Murial Alkins. A critic wrote 'Many a professional company would be proud to boast of such a contingent of competent and talented actors and actresses, and it is no wonder that each performance this week has been so well patronised'. Michael Bolton was the conductor, with the Oakamoor orchestra in the pit.

Photo taken on the lawns at Lightoaks, on July 21st 1990, on the occasion of a recital of music and verse to raise money for the Royal National Lifeboat Institution. Rebecca Wilson, violin, Peter Jones, piano, Susanna Wilson 'cello and David Neil-Smith, verse.

133

For Men, For Women, and the Country

In a register of Friendly Societies in Staffordshire of 1874, Oakamoor is listed as a Male Friendly Society holding funds amounting to £689. On April 26th 1875, the Churnet Valley Lodge of the Grand United Order of Oddfellows was founded, with the aim of supporting workmen and their families in time of need. Accident, illness, misfortune and bereavement could hit any family or bread-winner at any time. The Oddfellows would contribute and raise funds to be kept in trust, so that when a Brother was unable to work, welfare grants could be provided for his family. Even today, when workmen are away ill, they are said to be 'On the Club.' Then, the NHS was still 70 years away!

The Churnet Valley Lodge, No.126, set about raising funds for the G.U.O.O.F. In September, 1878, they held a Grand Gala on the occasion of Oakamoor Wakes. The admission to this fun day was three pence (3d). My grandfather Richard Wilson joined the Oddfellows in February, 1885, a few days off his 18th birthday. He had joined a Society which was to help him in later life. For the first 15 years of the Lodge's existence they held processions, services and annual dinners, besides their fund raising efforts such as the popular whist drives. Then, the ceremonial side of their activities must have gone quiet, until a newspaper report of 1908 revealed a revival. 'Whit Monday was truly a red letter day for the Churnet Valley Lodge, for, after a lapse of 18 years, the members decided to celebrate their anniversary by a procession, service and dinner.

There was a large muster of members for the parade to church, which was headed by the Oakamoor Mills Band'. After the service, the procession, which included 30 members of the Juvenile Lodge, next stopped at Moor Court. This was followed by a return to the New Schools 'where an excellent dinner was prepared and well served by Mrs Prince of the Lord Nelson Hotel'. Rev.A.W.Greeves, vicar, and Rev.C.Denman were always involved. The Lodge increased its numbers over the years, from their 1875 start with 16 members, to the 1910 figures of 135, with a Juvenile membership of 43. It was Rev.Denman's turn to preach that year. He referred to Cain after he had killed his brother; he ended with a plea to 'stretch out a hand on either side to help a brother'. Mr Pirrie was the organist and Dr Bearblock read the lesson. After the usual parade and dinner, Brother C.Wilson, who was a Primitive Methodist, proposed the loyal toast to 'The Bishops, Clergy, and Ministers of all denominations.'

The Oddfellows marched on into the First World War. The G.U.O.O.F. monthly magazine, mid 1916, announced the death of Brother Major Cecil Wedgwood, DSO, who was killed in action on July 3rd of that year. The eulogy describes his distinguished life, leaving the last word to a *Sentinel* writer who recorded that, 'I have never met any man who had a higher sense of public and private duty, who was more devoted to his country, his neighbourhood, and his family'. Major Wedgwood's memorial plaque rests in the Memorial Free Church. September brought an 'Armlet Parade' for young members. The parade mustered at the railway station ready to process to the New Schools. Newspaper photos show the parade passing over the railway crossing by the gate house, approaching the river bridge by the splendid Georgian railings in pre-canteen days, thankfully the rails still grace the other side of the road, and following the band into the heart of the village. Bandmaster Collier can be seen 'marking time' with his beloved band outside the Wesleyan Chapel, then used by the Infants' School, with 'Stonewall Jackson' banging the big drum. Two banners are held aloft near to the original bridge over the brook, with Star Wood Terrace beyond.

In a powerful wartime sermon, Rev.Charles Denman complimented the juveniles who were prepared to wear armlets, and the workers for the war effort, as "Thrice strong is he that hath his quarrel just." The proceeds went to providing comforts for local soldiers and sailors. In

Above: Officers of the Grand United Order of Oddfellows gathered at the end of the New Schools on Whit Monday, 1908. They had celebrated their anniversary with a procession, service and dinner.
Standing; John Davies, E.Moseley, Richard Wilson, grandfather. Seated; Charlie Bond, J.B.Collier, W.Coates, John Moseley, A.Swinson, W.Burton. Ground; C.Brookes, Jack Wilson, Jack Swinson.

Right: The Oddfellows' procession led by the Mills Brass Band passing through the Square on Whit Monday, 1908.

Left: The Juvenile Banner showing the portrait of Alfred Bolton. John Davies and Richard Wilson have changed places.

December, 1919, the Lodge held a memorial service in their lodge room, the New Schools, when a society roll of honour was unveiled. Out of 38 serving in the Great War, three members and honorary member Major Cecil Wedgwood had been lost. Major Wedgwood, DSO, was mortally wounded at La Boiselle in France; Pte G.S.Allen died a prisoner of war in camp hospital 11, Munster; Pte Harold Cartledge was killed in action near Ypres, and Pte Bernard Prince was killed in action near Bullecourt, on August 23rd 1918. The names of the fallen were inscribed within a laurel leaf, 'a credit to Mr.Pirrie's penmanship'. Dr Bearblock made an earnest speech in which he pleaded 'for consideration for the parents, the widows, and the fatherless of the common soldier, the backbone of our army'. The Oakamoor Churnet Valley Lodge gave support.

To mark the 50th anniversary of the founding of the Lodge, the G.U.O.O.F. held a banquet in the newly built bowling green pavilion. The catering was in the hands of Bro.J.Wilson with a willing band of lady helpers. By now, the lodge had a membership of 208. J.B.Collier proposed "The Grand Master of the Order." From 1925 onwards, membership began to fall. After the second War, with the advent of the National Health Service, interest waned. The Oakamoor Lodge was eventually administered by Bro.Jim Bracking of Cheadle, who in good time, was elected to the highest office in the Oddfellows movement, that of "Grand Master." The Grand United Order of Oddfellows never forgot the families of its members. I had small grants from them on the death of my parents. They are to be admired for the support that percolated through to many families in Oakamoor for many years, due entirely to the efforts of the 'Men of the Mills' in the Churnet Valley Lodge of this worthy society.

The Oakamoor Women's Institute was founded in 1921, with Mrs Frank Bolton of Moor Court serving as president. They met in the afternoon, once a month, in the old Wesleyan Chapel which came to be known as the WI room. With a membership of over 40 housewives, they were originally introduced to many topics which would improve their domestic skills. Hygiene, food preparation, first aid, cooking, baking, knitting, sewing, and, of course, jam making, were typical. Was flower arranging around in those days? Every meeting would include a competition for members, such as the best home made sponge cake. On one such occasion the judge criticised some members for not having equal quantities of ingredients in each layer. Tell this to a harassed mother with seven children! I served on the county speakers' list for quite a few years, and I was always asked to judge the competitions which were always good fun. In 1936, the members entered a county wide competition for making a counterpane. They won the cup. Well done. During wartime, a number of electric cookers were delivered to the WI room. My mother was a member of the jam making team who, in season, had jam making sessions for the war effort. They really had to work at it to finish on time.

Group meetings were always good fun. Oakamoor was host to one such gathering in the New Schools in the late sixties. At the beginning of proceedings, my wife, Ruth, sat at the Broadwood grand piano, new in the school in 1892 and still in use, to accompany a spirited rendering of 'Jerusalem.' Miss McWilliam, the governor of Moor Court prison, was the president. The main entertainment was a play, 'World Without Men,' which was well received. WI meetings were still popular in the 60s, taking place in the Mills School which by then was the village hall. The average age of the housewife member had now almost reached pension age. One character, Jessie Moseley, was still thrusting her brass ear trumpet at all those who were talking to her, but sadly the finer points of making up were lost. When the lipstick went onto the model, Jessie said, in her loud whisper, "That's what they used to do to mummies in Egypt!" A dinner was held in 1971 to mark 50 years of the Oakamoor WI By then, the membership was getting less as seniors passed on. Due to changing social patterns when young wives started to gain employment, interest waned until the membership collapsed within a few years. A few keen members transferred to Whiston. Does anyone think a revival might be viable? 'And did those feet......?'

In 1940 there was a real threat of invasion, prompting Churchill to form the Local Defence Volunteers. Oakamoor men 'got fell in'. They had no weapons; their uniform was an arm band.

Oakamoor Women's Institute of 1921, photographed in front of the Wesleyan Methodist Chapel which was to become their WI room. Back row; Mrs Haywood, Miss G.McKnight, Misses D. and C.Fowler, Mrs Peake, Miss T.Ratcliffe, Miss N.McKnight, Mrs C.Beardmore, Mrs R.Ratcliffe, Mrs A.Brough and Mrs Powell. Second row. Mrs Plant, Mrs Plant, unknown, Mrs Wannan, Mrs Bradbury, Mrs Combes, Mrs Plant, Mrs Barker, Miss Martin, Mrs Martin, Mrs Ratcliffe, Mrs G.Alkins, Mrs Coates, Mrs Mees, Mrs Burbridge, Mrs Elks and Mrs J.Heath. Third row; Mrs W.Woodward, Mrs Murray, Miss T.Howlett, Mrs Swinson, Miss Turnock, Mrs McKnight, Miss F.Bolton, Mrs Goodwin, Mrs R.Cope, Mrs Waring, Mrs Ainsworth and Mrs Tipper. Front row; Mrs M.A.Bolton, Miss C.James and Miss E.Snow.

The 1936 WI with the County Cup won for making the best counterpane. Back; Mrs Enid Goodwin, Mrs Ethel Davies, Front row; Mrs O.Morgans, Miss Freda Bolton, Mrs Frank Bolton, Mrs L.Brown Mrs Rosemary Cope.

A few of the office holders and husbands celebrating the 50th Anniversary of the Oakamoor WI at the Isaac Walton Hotel, Dovedale on June 10th 1971. Standing; Mary Burton, Sam Burton, Rosemary Cope, Bob Cope, Mrs Edge. Front; Flo Gibson, treasurer, Barbara Warrington, president, Miss M.Jones, vice-president and Mrs Rose Moseley. A piece of Anniversary Cake was sent to all surviving members, one being their past president, Mrs Frank Bolton, who still lived in the south of England.

Their duty was to watch for enemy parachutists from their Lookout Post, a small wooden hut on Lightoaks Park. The fact that Alton Towers was an officer cadet training unit gave confidence to our men, as Mr Michael in Lightoaks gave the order: "If any Gerry comes, knock me up and I will phone Alton Towers!" Vincent Ryder remembers being on Lightoaks Park when George Critchlow gave the classic Dad's Army command, "When I shout 'Scatter', follow me!" On the formation of the Home Guard, Oakamoor Platoon had their headquarters in a wooden building in Mill Road in what had been the Transport Office, an office I knew well as my father used to work there. All were volunteers in this first line of home defence. After putting in a full day's work at their jobs, from 6a.m. to 5p.m., they met every evening, Sundays included, for two to three hours training. Strategy was discussed in either the Nelson or the Cricketers! Captain Cyril Payn, the works electrician, was their 'Mainwaring'. The Home Guard eventually had uniforms with the first issue of arms being American P60 rifles. These were followed by Browning sub-machine guns, Sten guns, hand grenades and Anti-tank weapons. One night, following an emergency call out when it was thought that parachutists had dropped, one member accidentally discharged a bullet at the stone work of Oakamoor bridge. It ploughed a furrow which is still there. At another demonstration of the Thompson sub-machine gun given by a Regular Army Sergeant Major, he too accidentally pulled the trigger. The live round went downwards through the table, through the papers in the drawer, hit the floor, ricocheted around the walls and the ceiling and miraculously came to rest without hurting anyone.

As a boy I used to see many of the training sessions and manoeuvres of the Oakamoor Home Guard. Perhaps what made it easier was that my best friend was Geoff Payn, Captain Payn's son, and so we were often close by the scenes of 'action'. Geoff's dad used to keep his revolver in the sideboard drawer, and when this came out we knew that there was something afoot. Much of the training took place on the sports field. There would be combat training, use of weapons and manoeuvres. One particular dramatic training session which also involved the O.C.T.U. men from Alton Towers took place at the bottom of Stonydale, where a platoon was ambushed with blank fire coming from Jack Heath's hayrick. This was most exhilarating for two small boys. Then we somehow found out that tanks were coming to Oakamoor Station. A goods train loaded with tanks could not off-load its cargo at Alton station as it was in a deep cutting., so it came to Oakamoor siding where the tanks drove off in a straight line over the many links and the final buffers, before travelling to the Towers.

They would cross Oakamoor bridge on this journey, passing between the enormous concrete road blocks at the corner on the bridge. Perhaps a week later we would here rifle shots coming from the quarry above Stonydale which was used as a shooting range. It didn't take us long to approach a nearby thicket from where we could spy on the activities on the range. Afterwards, we would prize out shrapnel from the quarry face. On more formal occasions, Oakamoor Platoon would march, sometimes in Oakamoor, sometimes in Cheadle where Colonel Blizzard took the salute. After the War their memories marched on, remembering the orders barked out by their Commander. "OAKAMOOR PLATOON, QUIIICK M'RCH, ULFT, ULFT, ULFT YITE ULFT." They were to march on until the Supreme Commander called them home one by one.

As with all towns and villages in the land, Oakamoor gave a hearty welcome to 'Returned Warriors' from the Great War. Returning sailors, soldiers and airmen who belonged to the parish received souvenirs, with mementos given to the families of the fallen. The *Uttoxeter Advertiser* of August, 1919, reveals 'these souvenirs took the form of handsome bronze shields, framed in fumed oak. In the afternoon, a procession of all children in the parish, headed by the Oakamoor Brass Band, was formed in the middle of the village and marched to the cricket field'. There were sports, games and a tea party for the children. 'At seven o'clock the adult residents in the parish sat down to supper in the New Schools, together with returned sailors, soldiers and airmen, and friends of those who had fallen on active service'. The gathering was presided over by Dr Bearblock, with the chief guest Brigadier-General Sir Hill Child, Bart.,CB,MP The centre table on the platform had the words "God Bless our Boys" running

Above: Oakamoor Home Guard taken in front of The Beehive, next to the Canal House in Churnet View Road, in 1941. Standing; ? ? ? Ted Gunning, ? ? ? Cpt Philips, Wilf Swinson, Cpt Cyril Payn, ? Percy Grinrod, ? Stanley Blythe, ? Front; Massey, ? Harold Woolliscroft, Fred Bryan, Bill Cope, Doug Swinson, Malcolm Ratcliffe.

Above left: Flying Officer Wilfred Walker who paid the ultimate sacrifice. In the summer of 1940 a Hampden bomber took off from its base to bomb Eschwege aerodrome. Wilfred Walker was the pilot, with his great friend, Canadian David Romans, as navigator. On the return journey Wilfred was mortally wounded, shot in the head, and David Romans extricated his body from the cockpit in order to save his falling plane from the sea. The wireless operator thought they were taking evasive action. For this act of gallantry, David Romans was awarded the DFC, before he, too, was killed. Wilfred Walker was laid to rest at the Memorial Church, in one of two graves registered by the War Graves Commission.

Above right: April 1st 1922. The opening ceremony of the Oakamoor War Memorial. The Mills School of 1876 and the Wesleyan Chapel of 1860 can be seen in the background.

Left: Armistice Day service in 1937 when the Act of Remembrance took place at the Eleventh Hour of the Eleventh Day of the Eleventh Month, and not on the nearest Sunday as today. My mother stands third from the left with me in the push chair!

Right: Rev.Brian Dingwall, B.Th., leading the Service of Remembrance in the year 2000.

Left: A wartime photo of P C Cooper with his Special Constables in front of the Bowling Pavilion. Standing; Bob Cope, George Swinson. Seated; Frank Cox, PC Cooper, Bill Elks.

right down the middle, each letter composed of masses of pink rambler roses. There was a Roll of Honour surrounded by a heavy laurel wreath. 'The loyal toast was drunk with enthusiasm, the canteen orchestra played the National Anthem, the Vicar of Oakamoor, Rev.A.E.Dudley, gave a very sympathetic address in memory of those fallen, The Very Rev.Canon Hymers proposed "The Army and the Navy," the orchestra played "Rule Britannia," after which General Sir Hill Child presented the souvenirs and gave very interesting reminiscences on the many occasions on which he had been in action with the men of North Staffordshire'. The local press stated 'August 23ʳᵈ will for a long time stand as a red-letter day in the history of Oakamoor'. Indeed it was.

The British Legion was founded shortly after the First World War. Oakamoor had an active branch which met in the Mills School, until the room was referred to as 'The British Legion Room', a title it kept until it became our village hall. Combining with Cheadle, the Legion held a 'Drumhead Service' at High Shutt on Sunday, July 25ᵗʰ 1937. The drums, as on the battle field, became the Altar for this service which was conducted by Rev.W.E.Drinkwater, M.A., the Rector of Checkley. 'O Valiant Hearts' was one of the hymns, Rev.Drinkwater gave the Address, prayers were said and 'The Last Post' sounded. 'Reveille' and the 'National Anthem' brought the service to an end. In January, 1922, 'Pattinson's men commenced work on the memorial in the Square'. They progressed well, enabling the opening ceremony to take place on April 1ˢᵗ of that year. Remembrance services were maintained throughout the Second War, but inevitably the passing years saw fewer old servicemen at each anniversary. The Legion still gave children's parties at Christmas. At a branch dinner in April, 1973, presentations were made to Arthur Davies and Gib Heath for their 25 years' service. In time, the branch had to close. Even so, Oakamoor still remembers the Fallen, with the annual Remembrance Service attracting large congregations.

The Fallen

First World War

George Samuel Allen
William Amos
Reginald Birks
Gilbert Benson Bolton
Joseph William Brett
Harold Cartlidge
Thomas Fearns
Arthur Wellesley
Greeves
John Wellesley
Greeves
Edward David
McKnight
Bernard Prince
Bertram Salt

Second World War

Wilfred John Allen
David Malcolm Bolton
Ronald Edward Cooper
Edwin Pant
Wilfred Walker

They shall grow not old, as we that are left grow old;
Age shall not weary them nor the years condemn.
At the going down of the sun and in the morning
We will remember them.

We will remember them.

Oakamoor was once described as 'the idyllic and the practical, side by side'. Amidst this the Oakamoor Floral and Horticultural Society was formed, holding their First Annual Show on the 'middle meadow', in front of the bridge, in 1874. This field was not taken over for factory extensions until the 1890s. The annual show became very popular, as by the Thirteenth Show of 1887, the society boasted a list of 90 subscribers, made up of villagers and local landed gentry. A.S.Bolton and Mrs.Bolton were the main patrons, Tom Bolton was the president, with the keenest of gardeners forming the committee of 17. The 1886 balance sheet revealed that subscriptions amounted to £14.3.6, with cash taken at the gate £18.8.3. Payments included Punch and Judy, Fireworks and Tub Race, £5.15.0, the Band, £3.0.0, Judge fees and refreshments, £1.5.0 and the cost of the tent, £1.11.6. Prize money amounted to £7.0.1 and a half penny! As time went on, competition between gardeners began to hot up as the annual show approached. A newspaper report of May 14th 1892, states 'Instruction in Cottage Gardening'. This was given by the County Instructor for Gardening, who, 'in company of a party of villagers, walked through a number of their gardens, giving a practical lesson of nearly two hours, taking as text the fruit trees, flowers and vegetables which he found under cultivation. An adjournment was made to the schoolroom, where Mr Cock, under the presidency of Mr A.S.Bolton, delivered an instructive lecture and answered a large number of questions'. Mr Bolton, in his thanks, 'earnestly recommended increased attention to the culture of fruit and vegetables as valuable items of the daily diet, bearing in mind the information Mr Cock had given. He considered home made jam a most wholesome and nutritious article of food for children'. Perhaps those who eschew a healthy diet today should accept this century old advice? Our gardeners did, as two years later in March, 1894, Robert Cock returned to give a lecture on 'Garden Work and Beekeeping'. 'Mr.Cock described the various operations of garden work necessary at this season, the time and manner of planting, sowing of seeds, the value of manures to crops, and the fertilization of plants. A number of lantern-slides were used to illustrate the various stages of bee-life, hives, and other appliances'.

The century turned. The gardeners sharpened their dibbers. The shows grew in size, by which time they were held on the sports field. The 'flyer' advertising the 1906 show lists the president as F.A.Bolton, his brother Tom Bolton had left the village by then, eight vice-presidents and a committee of 16 headed by Dr Bearblock. Richard Wilson was a committee member, his brother Jack the secretary. Included is a delightful photograph of the approach to Oakamoor bridge. The shows raged on, year after year, until in February, 1917, Jack Wilson wrote in his diary 'Commenced ploughing in Beardmore's field for allotments'. For 25 years, Oakamoor's diggers had been looking for allotments, and at long last they had been granted a field in the corner of the Moor Court estate high up the Star road. My grandfather Richard marched forth from Stonydale, where he already had a substantial garden, to dig his patch on this new venture. After much hard work, it was pointed out to him that he had dug somebody else's patch, so in disgust he tramped home and lost interest! Show mania continued. In November, 1919, the Oakamoor Poultry and Pigeon Society held their first annual show. Held in the New Schools, and opened by Mr Frank Bolton, this new venture attracted a large gathering from a wide field. The account states 'The Society is bent upon stimulating local interest in the scientific breeding of pigeons, poultry and rabbits'. In the poultry section there were nine classes attracting 112 entries, for which Mr J.F.Entwistle of Wakefield was the judge. The winner in one class was Dick Prince of Oakamoor, whose entry was described by the judge as 'probably the best hen in the county'. It was a spotless white Wyandotte which had won numerous prizes and honours. My grandfather kept white Wyandottes for years and I well

Paying a visit to Oakamoor Fête and Fancy Fayre on the sports field in 1907 was the Cheadle Volunteer Fire Brigade, with their captain, J.R.B.Masefield. His daughter Mrs Margaret Blizzard told me that the Fire Brigade was her father's pride and joy. On hearing of a fire, of course, it was 'first catch the horses'! J.R.B. always wore his fireman's helmet when climbing up to inspect an owl's nest in a tree in his garden at Rose Hill, Cheadle, as the 'old hooter' used to scratch him.

Part of the 1907 procession posing with their 'Fancy bicycles'. 'Knotty' goods wagons can be seen on the Churnet Valley line.

Oakamoor Floral and Horticultural Society's Committee of September, 1912. From the left: Richard Prince, ? William Swinson, Frank Kerry, Finney Elks, Dr Peter Bearblock, chairman, Ernest Moseley, Mrs Pryor, ? Mr Joseph Pryor, Oakamoor Works Manager, Sam Harvey, Jack Whitehurst, Jack Wilson, Frank Cox, Henry Woodwood.

The Oakamoor Show Committee of 1925. Back: Mr Tipper, Frank Walker, Frank Cox, Mr Scott, Jack Whitehurst, ? ? ? Tom Wilson, Mr Collier, Albert Wilson, ? Mr Wannan, Bill Elks. Front: Charlie Brookes, Miss Collier, Mrs Gwen Wilson, Jack Wilson, ? Dr Peter Bearblock, Mrs Babs Smith, ? Mr McKnight, Mrs McKnight. In the 1920s the village shows had become enormous affairs, attended by large crowds. In addition, there were several side shows, a programme of sports, bowling matches, with the Oakamoor Mills Band playing selections and for dancing on the cricket field. Later a dance was held in the New Schools, at which nearly 300 were present, the music being supplied by J.B.Collier's Band, with T.Scott and H.Lucas officiating as MCs.

remember his ten foot tall wire netting run which didn't always keep these 'game-like flyers' inside! Poultry farming was encouraged after the first war in an attempt to increase the food supply of the country. Oakamoor families did their bit. There were six classes for pigeons, with 151 entries. A bird entered by Mr G.Armishaw of Bridgtown, which was awarded first prize, 'was an ideal type of racing pigeon'. The 'working homers' class was won by Mr A.Warrington of Alton. As for the two classes for rabbits, the best example was a black Dutch, entered by Mr E.Plant of Oakamoor. In 1924, the membership fee for the poultry society was five shillings.

The 1920 show for the Floral and Horticultural Society was a record one as 'the quality of the exhibits had never reached such a high degree of general excellence'. There were many classes of vegetables, fruit, and 34 classes of flowers. Mr J.Wilson 'won 12 prizes out of 14 exhibits, his successes being chiefly in the flower classes'. The judges were W.H.Upton of Heybridge and T.Avery of Denstone College. Dr Bearblock introduced the opener, Mrs Osborne, who, as the daughter of Rev.Charles Denman, had been brought up in Oakamoor. In 1930, 'no sooner had Sir Joseph Lamb, the member of parliament for this division, opened the proceedings and crowned the Queen, Miss Elsie Bradbury, than down came the rain'. The following year was worse, as 'continuous rain having flooded the cricket field, the annual exhibition had to be abandoned'. At a hastily arranged ceremony in the New Schools in the evening, Dr and Mrs Simpson crowned the Rose Queen, Miss Joan Cope. 'After the crowning, several of the day school girls gave a neat display of country dancing, Miss Collier, who had trained them, deserving every praise'. Oakamoor's gardeners were undaunted. They dug even harder until, in September, 1933, 'Mr.C.Brookes, of Oakamoor, has succeeded in producing two crops of potatoes, from the same ground, on his allotment this year. Sharpes Express were sown the first time and Great Scott the second. Great interest had been shown in the attempt by his fellow allotment-holders and by Mr Stoney, F.R.H.S., the well known expert, and he had been heartily congratulated on the result'! Some years, the judges' decisions didn't go down very well with our gardeners. Apparently, oft time winners Jack Swinson and Will Alcock, always thought they ought to have won on the occasions that they came second! Over the years, the gardeners were invited to Moor Court for their prize winning ceremonies. During the Second War our gardeners excelled when they 'Dug for Victory'.

The War was a watershed in the gardeners' story, as it was in all walks of life. The show was over. The motor car took over, and by the millennium, hardly anybody cultivated vegetables. The remaining few, such as George Bevans, John Redfearn, and Peter and John with their plot on Church hill, still continue this tradition. Many gardens, however, have been landscaped with shrubs and flowers, presenting a new well kept feel to the village. Well done to the Oakamoor Action Group whose members strive hard to encourage us to make Oakamoor a better place. In this one time industrial village, it was indeed a great achievement to be adjudged 'Best Kept Village' in 2002. 'All things bright and beautiful....The Lord God made them all.'

But Michelangelo said, "God could not make a Stradivarius Violin without Antonio."

Pirate Ship at the Oakamoor Show, held at the sports field in 1925. Willy Cope, P.Bearblock with sword, B.Tipper with striped shirt, J.Shipley with white coat, C.Goodwin in dark jersey, H.Bond at the wheel.

Above: Oakamoor Show Committee, 1932. Back: Jack Wilson, Mr Scott, Jack Heath, Bill Cope. Front: Dr P.Bearblock, Miss J.Collier, ? Mr Wannan. Taken in front of the Bowling pavilion.

Right: The Best Kept Village emblem placed by the war memorial in the centre of the village in 2002. This was the first occasion that Oakamoor had won this coveted trophy, showing how public spirited the inhabitants are in making our village beautiful. The conscientious chairman of our parish council, Garth Ratcliffe, can be seen making the acceptance speech. Watch out Garth, the Staffordshire Knot could hang three at one go!

Oakamoor Gardeners at Moor Court, c.1932. Every year between the wars, the gardeners were entertained at Moor Court, with the main ceremony being the presentation of the cup for the best allotment. Mr Frank Bolton is to the right, Mrs Frank behind, with their family at the end, Penelope, Bridget, Alison and Martin. F.A.B. was High Sheriff of the County of Stafford, an honour bestowed on Martin some thirty years later.

'Be Prepared'

The Boer War hero, Sir Robert Baden-Powell, founded the Boy Scout movement in 1908. 'The Scouts' became very popular throughout the land, and it was only a matter of time, therefore, that the 'First Oakamoor Company' was formed. My father, who was born in 1897, became a member at a very early age. He was quite indignant when somebody drew a picture of him on the school blackboard and referred to him as a 'Boy Sprout!' The troupe was established under the command of an ex-regular soldier, with one side drum, two bugles and several rifles for 'rifle drill'. Uniforms became available, topped off with the familiar 'Mafeking ' scout hat with a large brim and pointed crown. The girls were not left out as the 'First Oakamoor Company' of the 'Baden-Powell Girl Guides' was soon established. Baden-Powell realised that if one could get hold of the nation's youth at a time when their minds were capable of being moulded, one could teach them almost anything in the way of good conduct and useful action. In Oakamoor we had Cubs, Scouts and Rovers for the boys, with Brownies, Guides and Rangers for the girls. All learnt the promise and the law before being admitted to the companies. Part of the promise was, "I promise to do my best, to do my duty to God and the King, to help other people at all times, and to obey the scout law".

Oakamoor Scouts and Guides became very active in the village. The Guides were first off the mark with entertainment as, c. 1911, they put on a concert in the New Schools. Admission was 2/-, 1/-, and 6d. Doors opened at 2.15 and 7.15 one April day. The first part of the programme included action songs, solos, and piano items by Lieuts. Reeve and Walker, with a pianoforte solo by Miss Muriel Denman who was their captain. The second part comprised *The Sleeping*

The 1st Oakamoor Company of the Boy Scouts, c.1910. The Scout leader is probably an ex-army veteran. This photo is taken above the bend on Carr Bank, hardly the right place for a forward march as this hill has a gradient of 1 in 4! The chimneys of the Square and factory can be seen in the background.

Beauty, with twenty five performers. A year later, *Rumpelstiltzkin* and *Cinderella* were performed. Then in April, 1913, The *Staffordshire Weekly Sentinel*, in describing a 'Picturesque Wedding at Oakamoor', states: 'There was a pretty incident at the church door, a number of Baden-Powell Girl Guides, under Miss Reeve, Lieutenant, were assembled on each side of the entrance, strewing the path of the happy pair with varicoloured blossoms'. The wedding was that of their captain, Miss Muriel Denman. As for the boys, they took up the practice of woodcraft and nature lore, the open air life of the camp and the route march, all ideal in Oakamoor. It was generally agreed that boys who had trained as scouts became better and more self-reliant than boys who had never undergone such training. David Lloyd George remarked on the scouts 'being prepared' when it came to military training which had to follow.

After the first war, Oakamoor Scout Company thrived. Jack Dawson came from the trenches, where he had two brothers killed either side of him, to live in the village after he married my aunt, Marion Wilson. Jack had been Drum Major in the Green Howards, the Yorkshire Regiment, during the war. He rapidly set about training our scouts in the ways of the scout movement, earning much acclaim for the high standards achieved in those days. The First Oakamoor Scout Band became the best in the county, being asked to lead county processions on many occasions. Jack could also lead with the mace which he would toss in the air and always catch as it fell, a skill learnt in his Green Howard days. He slipped up once, however, as in one important procession, the Union Jack was flown at 'distress'. Scouts should understand what this means! On they marched into the 1930s, enjoying many camp fires in the wood behind Oakamoor Lodge, the home of Dr and Mrs Bearblock, where their son Peterkin was a keen scout. They enjoyed many camps, too, aptly summed up by Vincent Ryder when he said, "We'd had breakfast, dinner and tea by nine o'clock in the morning!" Happy days. The Guides had a happy time between the wars. Their large Company was led, in turn, by Beatrice

The 1ˢᵗ Oakamoor Scout Band at Oakamoor Lodge in 1923. This Band was regarded as the smartest in the county. Back; Bill Cope, Nigel Bowen, Jack Murray, Jack Swinson, Ted Bradbury, Richard Mycock, Cyril Cartledge, Cecil Goodwin. Sitting; Sydney Alkins, Harry Shipley, Charlie Nicholls, Jack Dawson, Scout Captain and drum major, Mrs Beatrice Bearblock, Dr Peter Bearblock, Harry Lucas, Bernard Salt, George Tipper and, standing, Ernest Swinson. Ground; Peterkin Bearblock, A.Charlesworth, Bert Tipper and George Lowell.

1st Oakamoor Scouts in camp at Colwyn Bay, 1924.

Bolton, tragically killed in 1934, and Norah Bolton, both of Lightoaks, and Penelope Bolton of Moor Court. The Guides met, either at Lightoaks, or in the works canteen where, in March, 1935, they held an 'Apron Social'. A poem was written, 'Get Out Your Tape Measure'. It read,

'This neat little apron is sent to you
And this is what we wish you'd do,
The little pocket you'll plainly see
For a special purpose is meant to be,
Just measure your waist line inch by inch
And see that the measure does not pinch,
For each four inches that you measure round
Into the pocket please put one penny sound.
The game is fair you will admit,
You 'waist' your money, we 'pocket' it'.
The Guides enticed an audience to a programme of entertainment.

Perhaps one of the greatest achievements by the Oakamoor Scouts was the successful appeal to purchase an ambulance for the war effort of 1940. £500 was its cost; £500 had to be raised, a formidable total in those wartime days. How on earth did they manage it? Under the leadership of their captain, Peterkin Bearblock, scouts and 'old-scouts' set to work. A small committee of 'old-scouts' guided the efforts. The statement of accounts tells the story. Jack Dawson's house-to-house collection at Christmas, 1939, raised £53.15.5; Donations from various organisations and well-wishers came to £145.17.10; Entertainments under Ted Jackson made £78.7.2; a Cinema show by Bob Cope, £1.10.0; Miscellaneous, under Jack Swinson, £61.18.6; Whist drives organised by Cecil Goodwin, £10.1.9; Sports under Clem Ratcliffe, £13.8.3; Bazaar organised by Gib Heath, £168.11.8; and Bank interest £4.9.11. As a result of this monumental effort, a cheque for £504.9.11 was paid to the Under-Secretary of State for War. One Sunday afternoon in December, 1940, a large crowd gathered in Jimmy's Yard where the ambulance was parked ready for the handing over ceremony. It bore the inscription 'Purchased from a fund organised in the postal district by the Old Scouts and Scouts, supported by a wide circle of friends.'

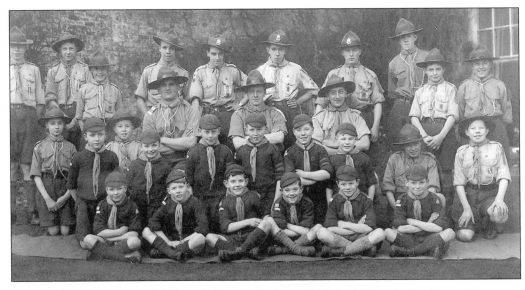

The 1ˢᵗ Oakamoor Scouts and Cubs at Oakamoor Lodge, c.1930. Back; Jesse Leake, George Forrester, ? ? Lawrence Shipley, ? Douglas Salt, Gilbert Heath, Gerald Chritchlow, Vincent Ryder. Officers; Harold Bond, Peterkin Bearblock, Cecil Goodwin. Kneeling; Robert Baisley, David Leake, Malcolm Goodwin, Clive Inskip, Michael Warrington, David Byatt, Basil Ryder, Colin Bond, ? Kenneth Fearns. Front; Roy Wright, Frank Barker, Laurence Jordan, Brian Ryder, John Roberts, ?

The 1ˢᵗ Oakamoor Rangers and Guides, 1932. Back; Norah Bond, Monica James, Ethel Wannan, Phyllis Swinson, Tess Bradbury, Joyce Murray, Beatrice Harvey, Norah Swinson, Dorothy Lemm, Joan Cope, Hilda Swinson, Norah Edge, Dorothy Carr. Middle; Betty Alkins, Muriel Alkins, Beatrice Bolton, Violet Bolton? Front; Kathleen Moseley, Mary Alcock, Joy Jackson, Mary Harrison, Dorothy Bryan, Eva Wright, Eileen Kent, Betty Cope, Grace Plant, Margery Perrins, Nancy Berrisford.

The 1ˢᵗ Oakamoor Guides at Lightoaks, c.1935. Back; Josie Perrins, Betty Alkins, Eva Berrisford, Betty Cope, Nelly Plant, Mary Dawson, Joan Walker, Eva Wright. Kneeling; Joan Cope, Norah Edge, Muriel Alkins, Norah Bolton, Joy Jackson, Hilda Swinson. Sitting; Beryl Brookes, June Bolton, Barbara Woolliscroft, Peggy Byatt, Iris Broomhall, Peggy Ryder, Ena Leake.

The newspaper reported: 'The children of the Oakamoor Council School were present under Mr Brown, Headmaster, and Miss Warrington; the 1st Oakamoor Rangers, under Mrs J.W.Burton; the Oakamoor Girl Guides, under Miss Penelope Bolton; Boy Scouts, under Mr P.E.Bearblock; Home Guard, under Mr Payn; First-Aid Volunteers, under Mrs Baird; and members of the A.F.C. under Mr Baird'. Before making the presentation to the War Office representatives, Dr Bearblock thanked all who had taken part in raising the money to purchase the ambulance, reminding them that during this time the Oakamoor Rangers had raised an extra £150 for hospital purposes. There was still a surplus of £27.13.3 which was handed over to the Cheadle Rural District Spitfire Fund. Col Durbar acknowledged the gift on behalf of the War Department. Col Dudgeon, who was in charge of the allocation of these vehicles, said that only the day before he had received an urgent call by telephone for more ambulances. He was able to say that he had got another, but not enough. In congratulating the Scouts he said that he himself had been a Scout. A verse of the National Anthem concluded the proceedings before the ambulance was inspected. It was finally driven away by the officials. Well done 'The First Oakamoor.'

At the age of eight I joined the Cubs. Cub meetings took place at Oakamoor Lodge, under the leadership of Margaret Perrins. Summertime meetings took place under a huge oak tree in the field below Barley Croft, the home of Mr David Bolton. To get to this oak tree on Cub nights I would climb over the wood fence at my home in Stonydale, cross Jack Heath's mowing meadow, keeping to the edges just before the harvest lest a roar of "Get Out" came from the farm, before climbing through another wood to the tree. We were taught all sorts of things about the countryside, passing 'badges' one by one. Margaret was a wonderful cub leader as the meetings were always so exciting. The height of excitement came when we were asked to join a wartime procession of service personnel which was to start in Jimmy's Yard for a march to the sports field.

On the day in question, tanks were lined up to head the procession, but where would the Cubs be? We started to walk past the gathering contingents of the armed forces, the Home Guard, Churnet View, Riverside, Woodside, until the cinder track of the Bungalows had been reached. I passed the Guides, the Brownies, the Scouts until, you've guessed it, the tail end was reached. The final let down came when, as the smallest cub, I finished up last in the whole procession. Even the Brownies were in front of me! I had no idea of what was going on at the important head of the procession which was round two bends and a long way off until, as with a huge dinosaur, the message started to filter to the tail end and we moved off. It was a matter of annoyance and humiliation to an eight-year-old cub that when I eventually got as far as Riverside, I could see the tanks crossing the bridge. I was so envious of the leaders of that procession, that the fact that I was last bore even more heavily upon me. It taught me a good lesson, however, when I realised that I had actually taken part.

The time came when I could eventually move up to the Scouts. My 'tenderfoot days' had begun. Peterkin Bearblock had a back room at the Doctor's Lodge, which he called the 'Scout Room'. Oakamoor Lodge, built by the Ironmaster George Kendall in 1761, was a fine example of Georgian architecture, but I did not realise this at the time. To me, the Lodge was a mysterious old house, with dark corners, shadows and strange people going to and fro. After climbing the steps to the main entrance and ringing the bell, Peterkin would open the glass paned door to let us in. The Cubs would then be taken down a wide passage, with the dining room and drawing room either side, which led to the back of the house. There we turned right into a huge kitchen. Beatrice Bearblock sat there, often surrounded by her many cats. Beatrice was Sarah Beatrice Bolton, the fifth child of seven, born to Alfred and Rebecca Bolton in 1861 and destined to marry Dr Peter Bearblock. The old doctor would be about the house, sometimes going out on calls as he was still in practice during the war. Several odd looking servants would be around. There was Joe, who happened to be passing a tree up the Farley road when it was struck by lightening! There was Charlie who paid daily visits to the Lodge kitchen garden at Stonydale. There were cats, everywhere, over 20 of them, that

At the instigation of the Scouts, over £500 was raised by the people of Oakamoor to purchase this ambulance which was sent to the front in December, 1940.

Oakamoor and Alton Scouts in camp at Kibblestone, in 1955, on the occasion of the visit of the Chief Scout, Lord McLean. David Robins, Michael Redfearn, Edwin Brindley, ? ? Melvin Robins, ?

Mrs Bearblock adored. Occasionally she would lose one, but rumour had it that the old Doc's needle did the necessary to relieve an old cat of its misery on more than one occasion. Above all, there was the all pervading smell associated with these animals! I often wondered why the Bearblocks kept such strange servants, yet it was not until many years later that I found out that Dr Peter Bearblock started his medical career on the staff of Cheddleton Lunatic Asylum, as it was then called, before being married to Beatrice Bolton and taking up the position of T.B.& S. work's doctor in January, 1909. These servants came from Cheddleton where they were trained to work in a good home.

At the other end of the kitchen was the Scout room with a large internal window from the days when the room was probably used for the preparation of game, meat and the like. There was one central pendent light with a conical shade that was installed in the 1890s and powered by the works 100 volt system. Under this dim light we were taught the principles of scouting, often being tested for different badges. There was the Observation badge, in which we were given two minutes to memorise about 30 different artefacts on a tray before it was whipped away and we started to write. No scout ever got them all, but there was a pass level. Then we had to attempt the Knots and Lashings badge in which six practical rope knots had to be learnt, otherwise a tent might blow down. There were other badges. Once I had gained my 'tenderfoot', the uniform was acquired. Khaki shorts and a shirt with '1st. Oakamoor' on the shoulder, tabbed garters on the long socks, a neckerchief held by a woggle and, bliss, O rapture, the 'Mafeking' hat. Ash staff in hand I marched off as a proud member of the 'Peacock Patrol'.

Outdoor activities followed. There were many campfires, lit by a maximum of two matches or you failed, after which you had to rub two sticks together in a certain way in an attempt to ignite dry grass by friction. On another occasion we all cut clean sticks, stuck a lump of dough on the end, before attempting to bake it by twirling the stick over the open fire. Black, half cooked dough had a wonderful taste! We followed paper trails through the woods, a different colour for each patrol, with the most energetic run being to cover a mile within 12 minutes. This took some doing in Oakamoor as we started at the mile post up the Star road, this was short of the Star Inn, ran down to the village, crossed the bridge, with the final haul up the Church hill to the mile post half way up. Stop watches had been synchronised and the first started at a given time, followed by a scout at one minute intervals.

On this occasion, Margaret Perrins started last and made the grade. She was a brick. There was not a car in sight to spoil the fun. For a county Jamboree at Cotton College, each patrol had to map their route from Oakamoor, and after the Jamboree, follow a different patrol's map to get back again. I somehow found myself returning by Farley Cliffs, while another patrol came down the Car Bank drumble. Camping was restricted during the war years, but this did not stop us borrowing the scout bell-tent which was modelled on the style of the Boer War affairs. The idea was to sleep with feet to the middle, but where we pitched in a wood at Stonydale, on a considerable slope, this was not possible. What with grease pits, gadgets, smoke and a garnish of fir pins and dust on our fried eggs, we managed. In fact, the experience was magical. Our captain, Peterkin Bearblock, was such a sport. We had such fun, within a framework of discipline, of course. Anyone who failed to conform was sent home. Fair enough.

Beatrice Bearblock died in 1948 at the age of 87. Three years later Dr Peter Bearblock died, age 81, after serving Oakamoor and its factory for most of his professional life. Their son, Peterkin, after a short illness, moved away from the village when he married. He had two daughters. As for Oakamoor Lodge, nobody was interested in taking it on. It is a matter of great sadness that this, too, had to go, razed to the ground in 1953.

The Scouts continued after the War, led by Harry Evans, with his wife in charge of the Guides. In the years 1950 to 1952, 'Revues' were presented in the school, using the same stage and scenery that had been used over the decades by various village societies. Well done Scouts and Guides for providing such good entertainment for others, and themselves, showing spirit in those days of post war recovery. The Scouts carried on for a while longer, eventually merging with the Alton Company, holding their meetings in Alton. The Oakamoor Scouts had disbanded by the early 1960s.

Interest in the Guides had waned after the War, but a few years later Doreen Johnson started them up again, holding most meetings in the School. Help and advice was given by Guide Leader Anne Makeig-Jones of Cheadle, a leader of great experience, who used to take the Guides into the woods for some meetings. Sadly, the Company disbanded in 1966. As for the Scouting movement of today, I still think that it is an outstanding activity for young people. It is a desperate shame, however, that recently a perfectly honourable local Scout leader, when leaving a meeting, had to experience the cry of 'paedophile'. Come on; this is sick. The dissenters must not be the deciders. Rise up, honourable Scout leaders, for the sake of today's youth.

Oakamoor and Alton Scouts in the large hall of Oakamoor school, in 1956, before alterations swept away much of its character. David Swinson, Lindon Hall, Louis Dotzauer, a visiting Queen's Scout from London, Donald Heath, in front, Melvin Robins, Denis McNicoll, David Robins, Michael Redfearn.

Captain Doreen Johnson leading the 1st Oakamoor Guides in the St George's Day procession along Cheadle High Street in 1966. The Scout leader standing to the right of the butter cross is Stanley Akers. From left; Janice Allan, Julia Bowen, Sheila Pattinson, Susan Hawley, Celia Hysel, Helen Cope, standard bearer, Susanne Goodwin. This turned out to be the last march of the Oakamoor Company before it disbanded.

It was not all Copper

Although Oakamoor's business was mainly copper, there was more than a score of other occupations in the village and its surrounding area. *Kelly's Directory of Staffordshire, 1924*, reveals commercial activities. There was a doctor, a nurse, two ministers of religion, garage owners, brick makers, farmers, haulage contractors, a blacksmith, tailors and drapers, a butcher, a bank, half a dozen shops, two public houses, an insurance agent, gardeners, joiners, builders, boot makers, a post office, the railway, and more. Take Edgar Goodwin, who was born in Oakamoor in 1878. He started work in 1890 as a page-boy at Moor Court. In 1961, he recalled that one afternoon Mr A.S.Bolton sent for him, and asked him if he would accompany a certain gentleman to Oakamoor station, and carry his bag. The bag was both large and heavy, and all the way down station fields the gentleman seemed to be in a terrible rage, and struck at the wayside bushes with his walking stick as he walked along. On reaching the station he said: "I suppose you found the bag heavy; here you are, take this penny."

Feeling rather upset at the smallness of his reward, the page-boy returned to Moor Court, to be met by Mr Bolton, who asked, "Did the gentleman give you a handsome tip?" When told about the penny, he patted Edgar on the shoulder, gave him a shilling, and continued: "Never mind, Edgar, I'll tell you now who the gentleman was. His name is Callender, and he has been here to discuss with me the advisability of linking his firm with mine. It was my refusal to fall in with his suggestions which made him so cross." Four decades later it was the fate of Thomas Bolton & Sons Ltd. to be taken over, in 1932, by British Insulated Callender's Cables. Edgar Goodwin stayed in his first job for 18 months, before going to work for Arthur Davies who kept a butcher's shop at the Carr Bank end of the Lord Nelson. The landlord at the time was Bloor.

Builder and contractor, carpenter, joiner, undertaker and wheelwright, John Pattinson, sent out a funeral account in September, 1893, for William Mosley of Oakamoor. It read '1 Oak Coffin, polished compleet £2.18.0, Pall 5-6, Extry 2.6; total £3.6.0. His spelling was how he spoke. Even so, the family had to have three goes at paying it off! John Pattinson had a serious accident in July, 1915, when one of his own cows turned on him quite suddenly, knocked him down and then gored him severely before help was available. His cries for help were fortunately heard by his son. The injuries were serious and he had to be taken to the North Staffs. Infirmary to recover.

Dr Bearblock had a chauffer named Peter Kerry. When Peter died, in 1929, at an early age, the Doctor wrote: 'I am stating an absolute fact when I say Oakamoor loved him. Everyone was glad to see him. He has driven me many hundreds of miles in my car and in his own Crossley. He was always willing, always cheerful, yet always yearning for his own village, and his own people and so glad to get home'. Universal sympathy was shown at the funeral for this remarkable man.

There was Frank Kerry who, when he started work as our postman in 1893, was reputed to be the smallest postman in uniform. He proved that size was no handicap and, apart from a break for army service in the Great War, served the village for 45 years. For this he was awarded the Imperial Service Medal. I remember Frank driving round in his Morgan three-wheeler. In December, 1960, Mr and Mrs Tom Mellor celebrated their 70th wedding anniversary. Aged 90 and 92 respectively, they were the oldest married couple in the district. Tom used to be gamekeeper on the Lightoaks estate and by the time of their anniversary they lived with their grandson, Norman Weston, at the grocery shop on Carr Bank. Old Mrs Mellor served in the shop right up to the day she died. In a squeaky voice she would say to me: "Yes, why Peter"? when taking my order.

Oakamoor has been full of characters for years. Sam Harvey was a fine amateur botanist who

Old Briggs Mellor, 1884. He would have been born in the early years of the century.

Mrs Briggs Mellor, 1884. It would appear that she had probably lost most of her teeth by then

Samuel Mellor and his daughter Agnes c.1890. Note his beard in long ringlets. Sammy kept the Cricketers' Arms beer house where he brewed his own beer. Agnes married a pottery artist, Abrahams, who lived and worked in Stoke. They had a family of handsome daughters.

Arthur Gibson, the Lightoaks Estate woodman, felling a tree on the estate, c.1910. He would have a partner, as the next stage in felling a tree would be by the cross-cut saw which had a handle at each end. Then the trunk would be taken to the saw pit for dividing into planks, or to Pattinsons' Saw Mills where they had a large circular saw. Other specimens of oak or chestnut would be cleft into lengths for post and rail fences, some sections of which are still around after nearly a century.

was nick-named 'The Vicar'. Sometimes young men would poke fun at his botanical knowledge, and one day an enquirer pointed to a great drape of golden bloom near the river, asking "What's that stuff, Sam"? Sam solemnly retorted: "Abyssom [Allyssum] Saxatile, sometimes called gold dust, related to the cabbage family, and that's an end on't." Sam was also a master of the North Staffordshire dialect. When asked if he was going to a party, Sam replied, "Ar ramner!" This leads on to Charlie Thorley who, when mowing the grounds at the Memorial Church, said, "Arve nivver adser many men under may afower!" During the war I remember being frightened by George Stubbs, 'Tush', who had an enormous growth which hung on the end of his nose. Eventually he had it removed. When Rev.Leonard Fountain used to visit the old chauffer Fred Plant, at his home at Bank Farm on the Farley Road, Fred boiled his water in a handle-less saucepan placed on the open fire, and removed it when boiling with a pair of pliers.

His water came from a nearby well, yet Dr Webster said he was always so healthy. Many of Dr Gerald Webster's patients lived in Oakamoor after the war, and so he would leave his surgery in Alton to hold a regular surgery in the front room of a house in the Square, the one nearest to Jimmy's Yard. After vaulting the wall, he would pass his patients in the waiting room, which was outside, before calling them in. During the 1960s, many of the old retainers were passing on. There were so many of them in Stonydale at that time that the old Doctor referred to it as 'The Valley of Death'! Characters come and go; some are still with us, but I am sure there are fewer of them today as any eccentricities and physical defects have been ironed out during early life. Thankfully we still have our memories.

Oakamoor village tailors, c,1899. With beard, Mr Peddie, a Scotsman, Oswald Beardmore, Harry Askey. All worked for George Chadwick who had his shop at the end of Churnet View. Tailor George moved into the Beehive when it was built as a shop for him by F.A.Bolton in 1909.

Oswald Beardmore, village tailor who lived in Star Wood Terrace, c.1910.

Oswald Beardmore in retirement, c.1950. Oswald is seen here returning from the 'Old Post Office' in Mill Road which by this time was a paper shop. The works canteen can be seen on the left.

The Coffee Tavern, c.1890, shortly after it was opened with a reading room upstairs. Mrs Tipper with her son Clement are at the door. Above them swings the original Admiral Jervis sign which swung in front of the old pub for decades before. The Admiral Jervis lost its licence in 1871, regaining it in 1971.

The Admiral Jervis sign still swings above the Coffee Tavern door at the turn of the century.

Oakamoor Post Office in 1904. In 1892, Mrs Eliza Tipper was the post mistress. Letters arrived through Stoke-on-Trent at 7.15a.m. and dispatched at 6.25p.m., with a Sunday dispatch at 11.30a.m. Good old Knotty! Annuity Insurance could be purchased here.

Lime on top of Oakamoor lime kiln, ready to be fed down into the kiln, c.1902. The chimney to the left of the dog is that to the Oakamoor Toll House of 1777. Lowell's shop is across the road, the Square above. Clockwise from the Cricketers' Arms, you can see the canal keeper's house, Churnet View, the New Schools, the Memorial Church, the Lord Nelson, Car Bank dwellings above and below the Ebenezer Primitive Methodist Chapel of 1859, the Mills School of 1876, the Oakamoor Orphanage of 1890 and Star Wood Terrace.

Lime came from Cauldon Lowe by the tramways down to Froghall Basin, from where it was dispatched to Oakamoor by the Uttoxeter canal. Some would have come by rail after 1849, also loads may well have come direct by horse and cart. Winding drums would lower the loaded trucks down one section at a time, using the weight to pull the empty ones back up again. Sometimes, housewives and their shopping came up in the empties! A modern day health and safety officer would have loved it! A question. How did the empties pass the loaded trucks at the half way point?

The Ribden engine house in a state of decay, c. 1920. On 28th January, 1859, A.S.Bolton wrote 'Rode past Ribden, saw they were getting on fast with engine house'.

Oakamoor lime kilns in 2003. Lime burning 're-commenced' in one kiln in January, 1921, but did not continue for long. Billy Lowell, who owned the shop across the road at this time, owned and worked the lime kiln. He then built Myrle View, but sold it to Frank Cox in 1930. His daughter Edna told me recently that Frank was a keen gardener who set to work to make the top of the lime kilns into a garden. He found a very heavy clay soil which had been covered with a layer of ashes which had been the foundation for a dance hall of earlier times. The kiln holes were open and very dangerous, and his next job was to fill them in with ashes to make his garden safe. Congratulations to Lionel Richardson and our Parish Council for getting these lime kilns listed. They are part of the Oakamoor story which must not be lost.

Left: Jimmy and Hannah Critchlow from Boundary who used to visit Oakamoor with their greengrocery cart. Hannah was aunt to my father-in-law Bramwell Shaw. One wonders if Jimmy ever bought anything. He would look over a wall and say, "Yeown got som good rhubob theer." "Tack som" was the reply. Or, "Ast got er sup er milk, last nayts ull deow," and so on. He lived to 100.

Below: The scissor grinder visits Stonydale c.1904. My father is one of the children.

Pattinson's men in their timber yard, c. first world war. Oakamoor Toll house is in the background, with factory chimneys beyond.

The blade from an enormous circular saw at Pattinson's Saw mills, taken on 15.2.1919. I like the 'classic' roof line in the background!

October, 1923. Sammy Mellor's old shop was about to be taken down. Lowells moved into the new shop. Then Mr Southam ran this shop, along with a solitary petrol pump across the road by the lime kilns. The shop is now a dwelling.

Greendale Farm, c.1905. It was probably built in the 1830s as Thomas Patten's nearby Greendale Row of 1838 had similar characteristics, particularly the windows. This smallholding is typical of many of the farms in the Oakamoor area. Many farmers would work in the factory by day and pursue their farming activities in the evenings and at weekends. Jack Wilson recorded, on September 15th, 1912, 'Hugh Charlesworth carrying hay on Sunday'!

Jim Upton, the present owner of Greendale Farm, seen posing for a gun licence application photograph, taken by Norman Edwards. Jim told me, "Ay clapped may aginst er weow, but it wudner deow. Ar adt 'ave er nuther un." Regulation size it had to be, which meant a trip all the way to Cheadle!

Jim Edwards seated and Jim Upton driving his mowing machine at Greendale Farm in 1963. This invention was the only one in the land. It was made up of parts from an Austin 7 and various motor bikes, with a tree trunk chassis. The National Farmers' Union became so intrigued by this contraption that a cine film was taken of it in action, to subsequently entertain many farmers at branch dinners.

Luke Edwards with his steam roller in June, 2002. When Luke 'got up steam' he was always a crowd puller. Luke moved on to a traction engine, before acquiring an antique car. In some ways I was happy to see Luke sell his steam roller, as in October, 1955, Albert Dalton, a 59-year-old road worker for over 30 years, was killed when his 13 ton steam roller plunged into the Car Bank Drumble. What's next, Luke?

Dr Gerald Webster, seen in retirement. Dr Webster served the communities of Alton, Oakamoor and district as our doctor for over 30 years from the end of the Second World War. He would meet many of his patients on social occasions, particularly those who played Whist as, he too, was a keen Whist player. His son, Dr Vincent Webster took over the practice when his father retired.

Norman and Audrey Weston outside their grocery shop which had been in Norman's family for over 80 years. Photo June, 1997, shortly before they retired. The shop had to close eventually, through lack of support.

Inside Norman's Emporium. Do you remember Norman's old bacon slicer with its chipped blade? Once the handle was turned furiously, Norman would take a sudden lunge, propelling the side of bacon at the spinning blade with great force, before he lost momentum!

The Oakamoor Sand Works at Moneystone, two years after it opened in 1959. This became the largest sand purification works in Europe, with high grade silica sand being transported by rail and road to the glass industry at St Helens. Some of the sand has returned to Oakamoor in the form of milk bottles. Whilst quarries are an eyesore, this mineral is extracted 'in the national interest'. The present owners have plans to landscape the area once the quarry closes. They have made a start by re-locating a 17th century house.

Frank Bolton owned a series of Daimlers during pioneering days. He is seen here with his first Daimler, a ten HP two cylinder solid wheeled car of 1901, with chauffeur Fred Plant by his side. The law requiring number plates was still a little way off.

Of River, Road and Rail

The River Churnet rises somewhere near to the Royal Cottage which is situated on the Buxton road beyond Leek. After a journey of about 20 miles from high in the Staffordshire moors it joins with the River Dove at Rocester. Its two main tributaries in the Oakamoor area are Cotton Brook, which flows through Cotton Dell, and the stream in Dimmingsdale which rises in Lambskindale above Greendale. The water power of the Churnet has been harnessed for centuries, as at the Brindley Mill at Leek, the Cheddleton Flint Mill and several others, with centuries of water dependent industrial activity crowded into the valley at Oakamoor.

The famous canal engineer, James Brindley, used the volume of water in the Churnet to feed his newly constructed Caldon Canal which was opened to Froghall in 1777. Twenty years later another famous canal engineer, John Rennie, was engaged to extend this canal down through Oakamoor as far as Uttoxeter. An Act of Parliament of 1797 authorised the building of this Froghall – Uttoxeter canal, to provide transport for the copper and brass at Oakamoor and Alton, to provide an outlet for the Cheadle and Kingsley Moor coal in the Uttoxeter area, and to carry lime for agriculture. The Oakamoor stretch of the new 'cut' was constructed in 1808, with the finished canal opened to Uttoxeter in 1811. About this time, the Gibridding tramway

Oakamoor Weir a century ago. One row of The Square can be seen, with the Lord Nelson on the left and the end of Starwood Terrace on the right.

system was constructed, passing through 'Donkey Lane' in Cheadle, with its mule drawn coal trucks hauled to the head of Gibridding Wood, where the trucks were then let down an inclined plane by winding drum, before finally being mule drawn over the river bridge to join the new canal at a wharf by Jackson's Wood.

Just south of this wharf is a lock with the masonry almost intact, referred to on Bradshaw's map of 1831 as Morris's lock. The local name is California lock, probably renamed after the Gold Rush of 1849, even though by then the canal had been closed for three years. A few yards along the tow path can be found the remains of a canal bridge, now without parapets, walled up and overgrown. A little further still can be found a cast iron mile post, placed there in 1822, perhaps the only remaining one that has not been stolen from this canal by souvenir hunters. Nothing remains of the canal from where it entered Oakamoor. It had been systematically filled in with ashes from the factory furnaces, to reclaim land over which the houses and gardens of Churnet View, Riverside and Woodside were established. Jimmy's Yard and land beyond the canal house, now the Cricketers' Arms, became Oakamoor wharf. There used to be another mile post there. The canal continued its journey along the contour line, passing Oakamoor station site, to the pound beyond the sports field where isolated stretches are still visible, before snaking its way to Uttoxeter. John Rennie's canal had a short useful life of but 35 years, before the railway came. In the days before Oakamoor became an ecclesiastical parish in 1864, my great-grandfather Caleb Wilson walked up the canal tow path with his bride-to-be to get married in Kingsley parish church. Another couple making the journey had a row, and the bride-to-be threw the engagement ring into the 'cut', before running off! I often wonder who they were? In my schooldays in the 1940s, we often used to play 'up the cut side', even though the canal had been filled in for over 60 years.

The *Daily Dispatch* of November 13th 1929, pronounced 'Widespread Damage in the path of the Storm'. The photograph showed the Churnet in spate, racing behind the stranded Island. The power of the River Churnet was one thing; the swelling of the river was another. The fourteenth century Croxden Chronicles describe 'the 'Churnid' flooding, taking away crops of hay and corn. In 1372 a heavy flood destroyed all the grass growing near the water, and all the bridges across the river were totally destroyed'. In 1593, the wooden bridge over the Churnet at Oakamoor was 'carried down with the flood'. A few months after Alfred Bolton came to Oakamoor in 1852, the floods struck with a vengeance. Every generation remembers its 'worst flood'. In Edwardian days, my father used to carve 'notches' in the wooden railway fence near to the station, recording his worst floods. I hoped to continue, but one particular high flood swept away the fence itself, together with its notches, which put an end to our study of the river! Floods were lethal at times. In March, 1911, the Stationmaster's son, Harry Barker, fell into the Churnet and was lost. There were others. Although flood control in Oakamoor has improved of late, I think there is still room for improvement.

For centuries, Oakamoor has been a nodal point for many paths, pack horse tracks and cart tracks, either converging on the industrial site, or crossing the river by the wooden forge bridge or the ford. Wooden bridges were ever in need of repair, as the Stafford Quarter Sessions of 1708 heard. 'There is a decayed bridge at a place called Oakamore and a passage or foard there over the River Churnett very dangerous and dreadful for persons to pass over and is a very great road and that several persons, horses and cattle have been there drowned'. The Court decided that a 'stone cart bridge be built at the charge of the county, the said inhabitants to carry three hundred tuns weight of stone to the place aforesaid'. The bridge was built in 1709/10. When the turnpike system was established, an Act of Parliament in 1762 created the Blythe Marsh to Thorpe Turnpike road, linking the Derby-Newcastle road with that from Ashbourne to Buxton. The Oakamoor Turnpike Trust was established as this road was to cross the valley by Oakamoor's stone cart bridge.

At a meeting of the trustees in the 'White Lion' at Oakamoor, possibly now the Lord Nelson, in 1762, the order was given to erect a toll gate 'on the north end of Oakamoor bridge, and a side gate to take in the road to Whiston. A collector of toll would be appointed'. They also

The swollen River Churnet battering the old bridge in the flood of 1927. Much of the factory beyond the bridge was under water.

The 1927 flood racing through the ancient industrial site, with a row of cottages and the Island stranded. The Gate House, beyond, was above the flood, but was usually in the path of water that raced through the tunnel.

Jack Heath on horseback rescuing the Finney family from the 1927 flood. The row of cottages behind, backing on to the factory, stood at a right angle to the Island. They were the first workers' cottages to be built by Alfred Bolton in 1856. Wash houses were added in 1860.

The Victorian wooden foot bridge, linking Stonydale with the sports field, holding fast in the 1927 flood. This bridge lasted until the end of the second War. Its heyday would be in Edwardian times.

The 'wing line' suffering in the 1927 flood. In the exact centre of the photo is a stone gatepost marking the rail entrance to the factory, one of a pair that stand today. In the distance can be seen the end of the toll house and Southam's shop. It appears that the electric shunter is stranded.

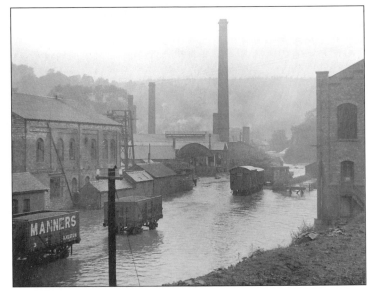

Doug Salt on Oakamoor bridge at the time of the 'millennium' flood.

Jimmy's Yard, beyond the river, where the canal entered Oakamoor Wharf. The canal keeper's cottage with its stabling for canal horses can be seen on wash day! In this photo of 1890, the cottage by now had been renamed Railway Cottage and the stables used for railway horses. The houses and gardens of Churnet View, 1887, are built over the bed of the canal.

The flooded bed of the old canal at Oakamoor wharf, c.1905. Part of Bottoms' brick works can be seen beyond the bridge.

Work begins on walling up the old canal bridge, c.1920. I find it very sad that this graceful Rennie bridge was filled in. The Star brook runs under the railway lines in the foreground.

The approach to Oakamoor bridge, c.1890. One set of Georgian railings still survive in front of Sunnyside.

On the bridge in 1923, following the route of the former Blythe Marsh to Thorpe Turnpike road. This is now the B 5417.

Ruth Wilson with her class of 1972 from the Valley School in Oakamoor following the Hawksmoor nature trail. They are by the cast iron canal mile post south of California Lock. It reads 'Etruria 19, Uttoxeter 11'. A few years earlier, thieves dug up this one remaining mile post on Rennie's canal, but while they went for a lorry, locals were alerted and Geoffrey Burton from East Wall farm came with a load of bricks and set the mile post in concrete. Well done Geoff. Why should thieves remove this bit of canal heritage from its original site? Anyway, a bird was nesting in the hollow top!

ordered 'that a house for the collector of the toll be built....to stand near both gates'. The first collector of tolls in 1765 was an ancestor of mine, John Wilson. The stone cart bridge began to take the strain of increased traffic. Public carriage roads were 30 feet wide, but turnpike roads needed to be 40 feet wide, and so the bridge had to be widened upstream in 1778. A further Act in 1831 was 'to divert a steep and dangerous road and make a new road' from Cheadle Grange to Oakamoor. The 'steep and dangerous road' was Church Bank. A map was drawn up in 1830 for the Trustees by George E.Hamilton, Civil Engineer.

This old map reveals that the road was to leave the turnpike road near to Cheadle Grange, cross farm land and Lockwood Lane, before following Hawksmoor, south of East Wall, on a meandering journey through the woods to re-join the turnpike by Sunnyside. This road was never built. Subsequently, Church Bank continued to be a hazard for carts, bicycles, motor bikes, cars, buses, lorries and even a fire engine! One pile up in 1942 saw damage done to the work's canteen, with one vehicle suspended over a nearby green vitriol tank. Then in July, 1949, an out-of-control lorry hit the church wall, narrowly missing a P.M.T. bus going up. Just two examples. Today, the onslaught of vehicles heading for the Alton Towers 'honey-pot' assaults Oakamoor bridge. Our dear old bridge, now listed Grade II, never flinches, tribute indeed to its design and our ancestors who built it nearly 300 years ago.

An Act of Parliament in 1846 authorised the North Staffordshire Railway Company to build a branch line through the Churnet Valley. By 1847 the N.S.R. had bought out the Caldon, Leek and Uttoxeter Canal Companies, enabling them to control their main competitors and to use the flat land where the canal was built for laying railway tracks. Surveying a route for a railway through the Churnet Valley must have been a challenge, due to the rocky nature and sharp river bends in stretches north and south of Oakamoor. The surveyor's map of 1844 shows that it was impossible to build a railway line through the village as many houses and the copper and brass works were astride a fierce right angle bend. The only way was to cut off the corner by driving a tunnel through the snout of high land beneath Church Bank that carried many natural springs, before emerging from a geological fault. The section drawing shows three boreholes, one at either end of the proposed tunnel and a very deep one sunk a few yards north of Woodbank. All three pierced red sandstone, with many layers of shale and marl. At 462 yards, Oakamoor tunnel became the longest, and wettest, in the valley, creating endless maintenance problems throughout its use.

The Churnet Valley line was opened on June 13th 1849, establishing an immediate connection with the homes and industries between Leek and Uttoxeter and, importantly, a connection with the outer world of trade and commerce. Regular trains brought copper workers to Oakamoor over a period of 110 years; from late Victorian times, many workers and their families left Oakamoor on special holiday trains to Rudyard Lake, Rhyl and other destinations. Although many trip trains passed through Oakamoor to Alton, where passengers would alight for Alton Towers, this most popular of destinations was approached on foot by the inhabitants of Oakamoor.

Shortly after the railway was opened, a branch line was laid from the station at Oakamoor into the factory and the village. Named the 'Wing Line', it is shown on the 1851 map advertising the sale of Oakamoor Works. Placed along the bed of the old canal it eventually reached Jimmy's Yard by passing under the canal bridge by the Cricketers' Arms. The canal keeper's house in Jimmy's Yard, where the canal horses were stabled, became 'Railway Cottage' where enormous shire horses were kept for hauling copper products around the factory. Generations of shire horses were used to pull the Atlantic wire and subsequent products to the wing line for nearly a century and were still active up to World War II. I well remember watching these giant horses being led through Oakamoor. Horse power was supplemented in 1917 by a unique battery electric locomotive that saw service in the copper works at Oakamoor for its entire working life until 1963. Built at the North Staffordshire Railway's locomotive works in Stoke, when it started to work in 1917, it replaced three shire horses. The locomotive's main duties were inside the works, but from time to time it would

Oakamoor Toll house, bottom left, built in 1764. The first collector of tolls in 1765 was John Wilson.

The High Shutt Toll house situated at Hawksmoor, photo 1900. By this time the house was owned by W.E.Bowers of Caverswall Castle, who finally decided to build a new property as the Toll house was in poor condition for the large family within. Note the Victorian letter box at the far end of the house.

Hawksmoor Cottage, built in 1906. The letter box was moved to Greendale where it is still in use.

Cotton Toll house, c.1935. Sadly, this house has now gone.

A pile up by the works canteen at the bottom of Church Bank in 1942.

shunt wagons across the main line into a siding at Oakamoor station, into the bay where tanks were off-loaded for the Army during the War. Every evening, and sometimes twice a day, the accumulators would be charged up by 'Big Nora' in the power house along the 'Crud'. This steam engine supplied the works and much of the village with electricity.

The loco had but two drivers throughout its service; the first was Arthur Adams and, from 1928, Bill Prime. As a boy, I had occasional rides on the footplate of steam giants as they shunted up the wing line, bringing me close to the electric engine as goods wagons were re-coupled to complete their journey into the factory. This unique engine is now preserved as part of the National Collection of Historic Locomotives in the National Railway Museum in York, where I have seen it, but I have also seen it on loan to the Churnet Valley Railway Society at Cheddleton Station.

The 'Knotty' story is as long as the line. Much has been written about it. There have been accidents, mishaps and tragedies, yet happy memories are legion. I remember many short journeys to Alton when, on rare occasions as a small boy I was permitted to spend a penny, not for what you think but in a Fry's Chocolate slot machine. The thin bar that came out was nectar! I spent many happy hours with friends in the signal box with Roger Lightfoot, just watching what went on, with bells sounding, levers in action and the full rush of so-close trains causing the box to shudder on every occasion. Roger used to sell papers from the 'Old Post Office' in Mill Road, and we would sit by his stove when the frost outside was far harder than we ever experience these days, reading *The Beano*. It was bliss. After leaving the box, we boys would open the crossing gates before running home. For seven years I travelled to Leek to attend Leek High School.

After leaving my home in Stonydale, I would break into a run on hearing the whistle at the Lord's Bridge telling me that my timing was perfect! After leaving the station the train would gather speed as it emerged from the northern end of Oakamoor tunnel by the Bungalows, before passing the old wooden bridge that carried the Gibridding plateway over the river at East Wall, and then Ross Cottages. The bungalows, bridge and cottages are now gone. I became fascinated with Oakamoor tunnel, with its curve and gradient, looking through goggles to try to estimate how soon daylight could be seen at the other end! It was possible to 'puff' to Manchester in those days. Three generations of my family were present when the last passenger trains crossed at Oakamoor Station close to midday on January 5th 1965, a sad benediction after 116 years of loyal service to the Churnet Valley. The last freight train left on October 3rd of that year. Thank you very much, Dr Beeching!! Many of the engines used to travel backwards on the Churnet Valley line, as they did on the 'Loop-Line' in the Potteries, as turning round was not always possible. For this, the N.S.R. earned the nick-name of the 'Arse-first Railway'! I leave the last word, however, to a railway man from Crewe who said, "God made all creeping things, and He made the Knotty as well"!

Oakamoor Station, c.1880. Very early days on the 'Knotty'. The original signal box is behind the Station Master in the centre. The Gate house can be seen at the tunnel entrance. Oakamoor Lodge is on the left.

Shunting goods wagons across the main line, c.1890. The houses of the Island, built for railway workers, stand beyond the 'wing line'.

Left: Looking out of the Oakamoor tunnel, past the Gate house and on to the station, 1902.

Above: In splendid retirement. This unique 0-4-0 electric battery driven engine of 120 horsepower, built by the North Staffs. Railway Company in 1917, spent its entire life shunting goods wagons between the main line and parts of the T.B.&S. factory in Oakamoor. It remained in service up to 1963. Rumour has it that it had a poke at the B.I.S. siding, but I am not counting that!

Below: A splendid view from above the tunnel, showing the Gate house, the Island, the wing line and the station in 1902.

Above: Collapse of the old wooden bridge over the Churnet at the north end of Oakamoor tunnel in March, 1929. It was replaced by a steel bridge.

Right: The last passenger train from Leek to Uttoxeter approaching Oakamoor Station at about midday on January 5th, 1965. I photographed my father Richard and daughter Rebecca on this sad occasion.

After the last train south departed, the Uttoxeter to Leek train appeared. They must have passed somewhere near to the Lord's bridge. The engine paused for a while for platform activity, but once this train moved from the station it went out of sight in a cloud of smoke and steam before it even reached the tunnel. It was perhaps as well I could not see it. There came a blast from the whistle before the tunnel swallowed up the music of this last passenger train ever to serve the people of Oakamoor. The station fell silent. A sense of gloom hit me. Over the years since that day this last train has become a 'ghost train' in my memories, for I was truly a 'railway child'.

I am still searching for information as to what went on in Oakamoor for the Silver Jubilee of the reign of Queen Victoria. Perhaps there was nothing as Prince Albert had just died. The nearest I have got is that A.S.Bolton held a dinner in the works for the workers and their families to celebrate the marriage of the Prince of Wales and Alexandra of Denmark in March, 1863. The Queen's Golden Jubilee was celebrated on June 21st 1887. Frank Bolton's diary recorded 'Jubilee Day'. The *Staffordshire Sentinel* stated 'The villagers threw themselves heartily into the work of decorating…An elaborate archway was erected over the centre of the bridge on which was placed the portrait of her Majesty Queen Victoria. Smaller arches were erected at each end of the bridge. Divine service was held at the Church, and at the Mills Chapel, Stainer's anthem, "Let every soul be subject," written for the Jubilee, being rendered at the latter. At 2.30, the children of the Mills School were marshalled by Mr Elam and the teachers through the village to Oakamoor Lodge, where they were joined by Mr and Mrs A.S.Bolton and Mr and Mrs T.Bolton, after which a return journey was made through the village. A halt was called near the centre, when the planting of a Jubilee oak was undertaken'. This duty was carried out by Tom's four-year-old son, Michael. This tree has now gone. The people then walked to Moor Court where the National Anthem was sung. Three cheers were called for Mr and Mrs Bolton, after which Mr Bolton said 'a few suitable and most loyal words'. Games followed, with entertainments. 'An entertainment was provided in the way of conjuring and Indian juggling, for which purposes Professors Harcourt and Monlahux had been engaged. Fire balloons were frequently let off, races were engaged in by the children; medals were distributed to all the children. Refreshments were provided for all, the adults having tickets, entitling them to tea, coffee, lemonade, or other temperance drink, together with pie, sandwich, bread and butter, on three separate occasions, while the children were equally provided for en masse. At 9.30 the people proceeded to Below Hill, where a beacon fire had been prepared and from which salutes of cannon had been given throughout the day, beginning at 5.30 a.m. A final salute was made at 10 p.m., when a light was placed to the beacon. Showers of rockets were let off at intervals during the next hour, and towards eleven o'clock a torchlight procession was formed from Below Hill to the village, where the Chinese lanterns were all alight, and candles were seen burning in each window….The celebration was such as to live for ever in the memory of every Oakamoorite'.

Ten years went by till the Diamond Jubilee of Queen Victoria's reign was celebrated on June 22nd 1897. Frank Bolton recorded 'The Great Jubilee Day, cannons firing at 6 a.m. at Below, 800 people at Moor Court, all parish invited for afternoon. Steam merry-go-round and swing boats, brought by Alex Beech of Potteries, Refreshments, cricket, dancing. 9-30, bonfire and rockets on Below Hill, then torchlight procession all the way round the road by Farley to O'moor, where Bridge decorated and illuminated by electric lights in the form of VR on arch'.

Spirits in Oakamoor were lifted so high on June 26th 1902, for this was the Coronation Day of His Majesty King Edward VII. Three weeks earlier, news had reached Oakamoor that Peace had at length been declared in South Africa. The Boer War had ended. Amid the general rejoicing the children were given a day's holiday. They met on the bridge at 12.15 where dinner tickets were distributed by the teachers. Then the Mills Band lined up to head the procession of children which marched off at 12.20 in the direction of the school. The first dinner, for children and mothers, had been fixed for 12.30. A second dinner for adults began at 2 o'clock. All had tickets, with a few available for a number of visitors staying in the parish at that time. The crockery, knives and forks that were used at the dinner were offered for sale at the Office, Oakamoor Mills, a few days later. Souvenir hunters could pay 6d for a large plate, 2/9 the half dozen, and 5/- for the dozen. Small plates were 5d each, 2/4 the half dozen, and 4/6 the dozen. Pie dishes were 1/6 each, large pudding dishes 1/6, and small pudding dishes 1/-. Tumblers and teaspoons were offered, with knives and forks at 3/6 per dozen pairs. I wonder if any of these still exist in the village? At 3 p.m. a procession headed by the Band meandered its way from the school to the sports field. On arrival, the National Anthem was sung, followed by a rendering of the Coronation Song by the children. At 3.30 the Sports commenced. All entries were free. There was an obstacle race for competitors under the age of 18, a sack race for men, a three-legged race for boys, an egg-and-spoon race for women, a sack race for boys, a veterans race for those over 50, an obstacle race for men, a bun-eating competition, an obstacle race for women and, finally, a wheelbarrow race. Prizes were previously on view at John Davies' Butcher's Shop. Entertainment raged! A cricket match took place during the afternoon, Ladies with bats and Gentlemen with broom sticks. The Nigger Troupe gave a Variety Show, after which there was Maypole Dancing, an exhibition of Drill, and a number of races by the school children. Refreshments were on sale at 'reasonable prices'. At the end of this wild afternoon, all the children were presented with a Coronation Mug. Then at 5.30 tea was served for the children only at the school. The grown-ups still hadn't finished on the sports field, however, as from 6.30 onwards the Band played for dancing until 8 o'clock. Maybe some villagers were exhausted by this time, but they still had more to go. At 10 p.m. a Bonfire was lighted on Below Hill. At 10.30 the National Anthem was sung, after which a torchlight procession wound its way back to the village. Yet again, what a day for the community of Oakamoor.

A public meeting was held in the New Schools in May, 1911, to consider how to celebrate the Coronation of King George V. Some 30 parishioners were present. Several ideas were put forward, including that of adding money to the existing Diamond Jubilee Dole Fund, the income of which was distributed at Christmas to deserving widows in the parish. No decision was reached and so the meeting was adjourned for one week to appeal for more support. The chairman Frank Bolton opened the adjourned meeting with 140 parishioners present. Plans were then agreed. *The Cheadle and Tean Times* carried an account of Coronation activities on

Charles Pirrie processing with the school to Moor Court for a children's Treat on the occasion of the Coronation of George V and Queen Mary, June 22nd, 1911. This procession was headed by the Oakamoor Mills brass band.

June 30th 1911. 'Through the kindness of Mr.F.A.Bolton of Moor Court, the whole of the inhabitants of the parish were invited to tea of which about 800 accepted. A procession to Moor Court was formed at the New Schools about 2 p.m., headed by the Oakamoor Mills brass band. Immediately in front of the band was a decorated brake drawn by 3 horses in which were the old people of the village. Following the band were the Juvenile Scouts, the Oakamoor Wood Pigeons, the Oakamoor Boys' Corps, the Juvenile and Adult Oddfellows, School Children, Parish Council and Inhabitants of the Parish'. Mr Frank and Mrs A.S.Bolton met them at Moor Court where sports went on until late in the evening. There were swings, see-saws, cocoa nut shies and daylight fireworks. At 4 o'clock the National Anthem was sung, led by the band. The children received Coronation mugs and new pennies, after which teas were served in a large tent. At 10 p.m. the usual Below Bonfire was lit, followed by a procession through Farley and Moor Court to Oakamoor. Mrs Prince of the Lord Nelson catered.

The Silver Jubilee of the Reign of George V was celebrated on Jubilee Day, May 6th 1935. Frank Bolton recorded 'Heard broadcast of the Jubilee procession and service at St.Paul's, and in the evening heard the King broadcasting. We went down to the schools at 4.30 to see the children's Jubilee tea and the presentation of mugs and new 6ds to the children. We all went to see Torchlight procession thro' O'moor at 9.30 and then to Below to see bonfires all round, then along top road and afterwards up to the O'moor Fire which was at top of Lightoaks Park. Out till 11.30 with all the children'.

On May 4th, 1935, for the Silver Jubilee of the Reign of George V, the Oakamoor Playing Field was declared open. Frank Bolton wrote, 'Beautiful day, v. fine and bright and warmer. Busy in the morning with final arrangements for opening of the new Children's Playing Field. At 3 o'clock went there for the opening ceremony. I spoke and then called on Col. Hunter to open the Field. Afterwards, Col. Cowan planted Jubilee Oak tree in top corner of the Field. Tried the swings, sea-saw, etc. There were a lot of people present, and we had a number of the principle subscribers here for tea afterwards'. The Jubilee Oak still stands on this land donated by F.A.Bolton but, sadly, the children do not play there any more. With the onslaught of road traffic the Field has become too remote and potentially unsafe. Another area is being planned.

After the saga of the 'Uncrowned King', Edward VIII, and the reluctant accession to the throne of George VI, Coronation Day was finally fixed for May 12th 1937. The Oakamoor Coronation Committee had met since 1936 to plan a programme. Frank Bolton described the day itself. 'We listened in to the Coronation till about 11.30 when the King had entered the Abbey, then Martin and I and Alison played golf till lunch time. All went down to the Playing field at 2.30, where the Coronation Queen was crowned by Gladys, Lightoaks, and we planted 5 sycamore trees, the Queen planted one, and I planted one as chairman of the Coronation Committee, the Vice-chairman, Secretary and Treasurer also planted each a tree. Came home for tea and Martin and I went out with rifle afterwards. Heard wireless programme including the King's speech at 8. Went in car at 9.40 to see bonfire in Bull's meadow and torchlight procession, and up to Three Lowes to see other fires'. Although the people of Oakamoor enjoyed Coronation Day, it was not the rumbustious affair that our Victorian and Edwardian forefathers had experienced. Since 1911, the Titanic had sunk, the First War had happened, there had been lean times for T.B.&S. and many families were poor. Nevertheless, the spirit was there. I remember seeing the bonfire in the field next to the playing field, even though I was barely three years old at the time. There were car tyres burning ferociously in the centre of the blaze.

May 12th, 1937. Coronation Day of George VI. Procession passing the Oakamoor Post Office which had been decorated by my uncle Jack Dawson, the village postmaster. They were heading for the Oakamoor Playing Field where Betty Cope was to be crowned Queen. This was probably the last time that the Oddfellows' banner depicting A.S.Bolton was carried in public. Did the Mills brass band head this procession?

183

Queen Elizabeth II's accession to the throne was in February, 1952, on the death of her father. The Coronation was celebrated in June, 1953. For the first time ever the Coronation Service was broadcast live to the Nation, not only a first for radio, but for television as well. It appeared that everybody wanted to be there, either in London where Ruth just happened to be at college, or in spirit by way of the media. As a result, I have been unable to find what, if anything, happened in Oakamoor. The Parish Council marked the occasion by placing Coronation seats at walking distances along the roads out of Oakamoor. Most have now gone. As for me, I was serving in the Royal Air Force in Aden at the time, and the nearest I came to the Coronation was to purchase a tin of 'Coronation' talcum powder from the NAAFI, which was a great improvement on the RAF issue of regulation foot powder of the time. Aden is one of the hottest places on earth and I do remember that at midnight on Coronation Day, the temperature had fallen to 90 degrees Fahrenheit! Ah well, at least I saw the film when it reached us in October. By the time the Silver Jubilee was reached in 1977, Oakamoor, Cotton and Farley had got their act together. A committee was formed, under the chairmanship of Mrs D.Walden, in an attempt to bring new interest to the life of the community. There were close on 50 fund raising events, with all children receiving a Jubilee Beaker and a special book marker from the Mothers' Union. The Silver Jubilee Festival was on June 7th 1977, presided over by the Queen, Mary Edwards, who had her sister Judy and friend Norma Cooper as princesses. The crown and cloak for the Queen were provided by Mrs Betty Knight who was the Oakamoor Queen for the Coronation of George VI in 1937. A procession left Cotton College at 10.30 a.m. comprising 16 decorated floats including the one carrying the Jubilee Queen with her attendants. They halted at Cotton, Farley and Moor Court before arriving at Oakamoor where a large marquee had been erected on the picnic site by the bridge. After a Thanksgiving Service there was music by the Burslem Police Band, hot air balloons were prepared and ten teams competed in 'It's a Knock-Out'. There was a display of 'Health and Beauty', majorettes marched, clay pigeons were shot, trophies were presented, and the day of celebrations ended with a dance in the marquee. The Golden Jubilee for Queen Elizabeth II,

The procession entering the picnic area in Oakamoor on the Silver Jubilee Day in the Reign of Queen Elizabeth II, June 7th 1977. The picnic area covers the centuries old industrial site.

marked in June, 2002, was a much more modest affair. Events took place around the Village Hall, the Cricketers' Arms, the Lord Nelson and the grounds of the Memorial Free Church. To cap it all, the rain came down. At least the children enjoyed some games, pony rides and a tea party before everybody was driven indoors. A year later, on June 20th 2003, over 100 children from the Valley School in Oakamoor and the Faber RC School at Cotton gathered outside the Oakamoor Village Hall where they gave a musical welcome to Lord Lichfield before he unveiled a plaque commemorating the Golden Jubilee of his relation, the Queen. In his speech Lord Lichfield referred to Oakamoor's involvement with the Atlantic cables of the mid-ninetennth Century. Above the plaque, high on the gable end of the Village Hall, the Golden Jubilee Clock began to 'pass the time'.

June, 2002. Songs of Praise in Jimmy's Yard commemorating the Golden Jubilee of Queen Elizabeth II. Oakamoor Primitive Methodists held Camp Meetings on the same spot a century earlier.

June 20th 2003. Lord Lichfield, with Frank Meadows, unveiling the Golden Jubilee plaque on the end of the Village Hall. The Jubilee Clock is high on the gable end above.

Lord Lichfield having received a collage of paintings of Oakamoor scenes by local artist Lois Scragg. The presentation was made by Flo Barrow who is seen with Mr Bill Cash MP.

Lord Lichfield and Mr Bill Cash MP with the children of the Valley School on the occasion of the commemoration of the Golden Jubilee Clock on the Village Hall, June 20th 2003. The children are standing on the site of the old Wesleyan Methodist Chapel, 1860, and next to the Mills School of 1876, which is now the Village Hall.

Pupils and Staff of the Faber RC School, Cotton, with Lord Lichfield and Mr Bill Cash MP at the Golden Jubilee Clock ceremony, June 20th 2003.

Conclusion

This story of Oakamoor has been told through my eyes and has revealed my family's involvement in the evolution of Oakamoor for many, many years. I have included photographic evidence of seven generations. Quite often I have merely scratched the surface, leaving many nuggets for possible exploration in the future. Do help me with this by letting me see any further accounts of historical interest, any old photographs, or any tales from the past that you might have, otherwise some, or all, might be lost for ever. I often say, "If only, if only I had asked my great-uncle Tom!" You know what I mean. Our immediate forefathers could have told us such a lot about times gone by in Oakamoor.

Oakamoor has a remarkable heritage. Much has been revealed, yet there is more to be unearthed. Our newly established 'Oakamoor Heritage Trail' tells some of the story. The intention of this book has been to reveal much more. I hope I have been successful.

The spirit of our ancestors abounds in this place. We are thankful for their foresight and contribution to the Oakamoor story. In February, 1675, Newton wrote to Hooke, 'For all that we know and can do, we are, so to speak, standing on the shoulders of our ancestors.....on the shoulders of giants.' Surely, this is the 'Spirit of Oakamoor.'

The Wilson Family gathered together for the Golden Wedding celebrations of Caleb and Margaret Wilson, September 7th 1909. Caleb worked on Atlantic wire, becoming foreman on the death of his father Richard. My grandfather, Richard, who by this time had become foreman wire-drawer, stands behind his mother, with my father Richard on the ground, directly in front. Photo taken at 'The Croft'. Alton, which Caleb built in 1901. Two of Caleb's unmarried daughters lived on in The Croft until 1930, afterwards sailing for Canada to join their sister. The Croft was sold on July 17th 1930, for £920.

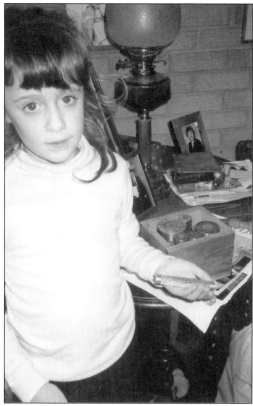

Richard Wilson, the son of Thomas Wilson, born in Oakamoor in 1807. Richard was foreman wire-drawer under the Pattens. Hounded out of the village by religious persecution, he went to live in Holywell in North Wales, until Alfred Bolton brought him back again to Oakamoor, as Richard was the man with the wire-drawing skills needed for re-starting the factory. The wire for the Atlantic cables and many more passed through his hands. He died in 1869, aged 62. His wife Mary died in 1862, aged 48.

My granddaughter, Maria, seven generations and 150 years away from Richard Wilson of Atlantic wire days, holding a section of that very first cable. At the heart of this cable is the seven stranded Oakamoor high conductivity copper which made Alfred Bolton and Oakamoor famous. In the box behind can be seen examples of subsequent submarine cables, still with the gutta-percha insulation intact.

The Opening of the Oakamoor Heritage Trail on April 2nd 2004. In the centre is June Bolton, great-granddaughter of Alfred Sohier Bolton of Thomas Bolton & Sons, Oakamoor. From left; Peter Wilson, Opener; Garth Ratcliffe, Chairman of Oakamoor Parish Council; Lionel Richardson, Planning Cabinet member and Ron Locker, Chairman of the Moorlands Partnership of the Staffordshire Moorlands Council.

References and Acknowledgements

References

The Iron Valley. Herbert A.Chester. 1979.

Channel 4 Time Team Dig at Old Furnace Cottage, and East Wall Farm, National Trust. July, 2003.

Thomas Bolton & Sons Limited. John Morton. 1983.

Notes on Atlantic Wire, *1857 to 1866*. Richard Wilson.

Information on Submarine Cables, 1857 onwards. Reginald P.Shaw, Works Manager, retired.

Richard Wilson's Notes, 1905.

Early Journals of Alfred Sohier Bolton, 1844 to 1851. Volumes 1, 2 and 3.

Transcriptions of later Journals of A.S.Bolton. Lindsey Porter.

The Diaries of Francis Alfred Bolton, 1902 to 1951.

Transcriptions of early Diaries of F.A.Bolton. Lindsey Porter.

Transcriptions of Beatrice Bearblock's Common-Place Book, c.1900 to c.1940. Dr W.E.Alkins.

Thomas Bolton's Life Book, 1914 to c.1945. June Bolton, Michael Brookes.

News Cuttings of A.S.Bolton and F.A.Bolton.

Visits and Interviews, 1960. Dr W.E.Alkins.

Historical Extractions, 1960s. Dr W.E.Alkins.

Memory Lines. T.B.&S. Magazines, 1977.

The Works Chaplaincy and the Memorial Free Church Records, 1868 to 2003. Peter L.Wilson.

Primitive Methodism and the Ramsor Circuit, 1994. Rebecca M.Wilson, The Salvation Army.

Historical Notes on Holy Trinity Church, K.J.Collier.

The National Society.

A Short History of the National Society, by H.J.Burgess and P.A.Welsby, 1961.

Interviews with Senior Villagers, 1989 to 2003.

The Mills School Admissions Register, 1871 to 1893.

The Log Books of the Mills School, 1871 to 1932, transcribed by Peter L.Wilson, 1989 to 1991.

The Log Books of the New Schools, 1892 to c.1970, transcribed by Peter L.Wilson, 1989 to 1991.

The Hawksmoor Archives, National Trust, collated by Peter L. Wilson.

Hawksmoor Nature Trail Booklet, Peter L. Wilson, 1967. 8 editions.

The History of Cheadle, 1881, Robert Plant.

John Wilson's Diaries, 1893 to 1942.

Kelly's Directories of Staffordshire.

The Cheadle and Tean Times, The Cheadle Post and Times, and *Sentinel* Newspapers.

Historical Records, glass Magic Lantern slides and Family Archives, Peter L Wilson.

Historical Collection of small slides on Oakamoor, Robert Cartwright.

The Lightoaks Branch of the Bolton Family. Thomas Bolton and June Bolton.

Historical Maps, Fred Johnson, Turnpike, and Basil Jeuda, North Staffordshire Railway.

Exploration of the 'Moor Court Room' in Croxden Abbey, Martin Alfred Butts Bolton and Peter L. Wilson.

Many other sources.

Acknowledgements

I wish to thank all those who contributed to this book, including:

Martin and Hazel Bolton, Thomas Bolton, June Bolton, Michael Smith, Robert Cartwright, Dorothy Bowen, Wilfred Cope, David Neil-Smith, Michael Pointon, Arthur Gilbert, Michael Brookes, Joan Williams, Michael Beardmore, Rebecca Wilson, Sadie Pattinson, Norian Hammersley, Lois Scragg, Betty Davies, Dot Chadwick, Betty Knight, Norman Edwards, Luke Edwards, James Upton, Robert and Angela Chapman, George Short, Geoffrey and Margaret Burton, Lindsey Porter, Dilys Baker, Maggie Wheeler, Edna Whitting, Mary Robertson, Michael Redfearn, Geraldine Webster, Vincent Webster, John Redfearn, Edward Green, Robert Blythe and others.

The *Cheadle and Tean Times, The Cheadle Post and Times, Staffordshire Sentinel* Newspapers, The Oakamoor Village Hall Committee, The Hawksmoor Committee of the National Trust, The Valley School in Oakamoor.

Some sources are unknown.

MORE LOCAL HISTORY BOOKS

If you are keen to know more about the history of the Churnet Valley
these fascinating books are a must for your collection

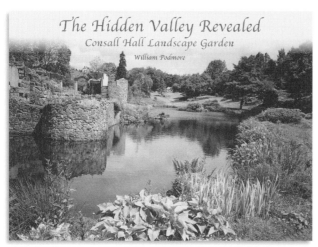

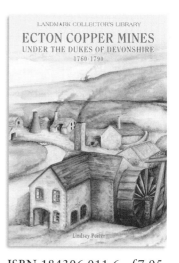

ISBN 184306 141 4   £14.95
170 x 245mm (landscape),   80pp
This is a lovely full colour book on the development of
one of the finest gardens in the region. It extends to
nearly 80 acres and has been 45 years in the making.
Many photographs show how a former industrial
landscape has been converted into a haven of beauty. It
has been designed like a living picture from each of the
many carefully chosen vantage points. In Victorian times
2,000 people worked in the adjacent mines and one
colliery was even within the current garden. Nearly
500.000 tons of spoil had to be removed as part of the
development.

ISBN 184306 011 6   £7.95
A5,   112pp
Details the 16th century iron
works at Oakamoor and
Consall Forge, plus the
Victorian 'iron rush' of the
Consall Forge–Froghall area.

ISBN 184306 125 2   £19.95
246 x 174mm,   240pp
A new study; includes a substantial section on the
Whiston copper smelter; Kingsley and Foxt Wood
Collieries; roads and transportation around the Churnet
Valley; social conditions etc, using many Devonshire
Collection records for the first time. Also includes details
of many small businesses and other collieries etc in the
area which were at work in that period.

Available from good bookshops or direct from the publishers
Landmark Publishing Ltd
Ashbourne Hall, Cokayne Ave, Ashbourne, Derbyshire DE6 1EJ England
Tel: (01335) 347349 Fax: (01335) 347303
e-mail: landmark@clara.net   website: www.landmarkpublishing.co.uk